THE SENSE OF GOD

THE
SENSE OF
GOD

SOCIOLOGICAL, ANTHROPOLOGICAL
AND PSYCHOLOGICAL APPROACHES
TO THE ORIGIN OF
THE SENSE OF GOD

BY

JOHN BOWKER

FELLOW OF CORPUS CHRISTI COLLEGE, CAMBRIDGE

CLARENDON PRESS · OXFORD

1973

*Oxford University Press, Ely House, London W.*1

GLASGOW NEW YORK TORONTO MELBOURNE WELLINGTON
CAPE TOWN IBADAN NAIROBI DAR ES SALAAM LUSAKA ADDIS ABABA
DELHI BOMBAY CALCUTTA MADRAS KARACHI LAHORE DACCA
KUALA LUMPUR SINGAPORE HONG KONG TOKYO

CASEBOUND ISBN 0 19 826632 4
PAPERBACK ISBN 0 19 826633 2

© OXFORD UNIVERSITY PRESS 1973

PRINTED IN GREAT BRITAIN
BY BUTLER AND TANNER, LTD.
FROME AND LONDON

FOR MARGARET

ἐν σοὶ πᾶσ᾽ ἔγωγε σῴζομαι·
... ἀνζρί τοι χρεὼν
μνήμην προσεῖναι, τερπνὸν εἴ τί που παᾶθοι.
χάρις χάριν γάρ ἐστιν ἡ τίκτουσ᾽ ἀεί.

PREFACE

THIS book is based on the Wilde Lectures, given in Oxford in 1972. The subject matter of the lectures is defined in these terms:

For the purposes of this lectureship the term Natural Religion shall be taken to mean man's conscious recognition of purposive intelligence and adaptability in the universe of things on which he is dependent for his continued existence and well-being and with which he endeavours to live in harmonious relations. Comparative Religion shall be taken to mean the modes of causation, rites, observances, and other concepts involved in the higher historical religions.

In choosing the title, 'The Sense of God', I have tried to keep as close to the intention of Wilde's bequest as possible. I have not attempted to make a survey of the different kinds of belief which human beings have held about God. There are many such surveys available, ranging from the twelve volumes of Schmidt[1] to the more modest enterprise of a previous Wilde lecturer, who made a survey of this kind under the title *The Concept of Deity*.[2] I have concentrated, instead, on these central questions: how does a sense of God arise in human consciousness? How do human beings arrive at their sense, or senses, of God? Can those senses of God 'make sense', or are they ultimately nonsensical? What happens when existing senses of God come under strain, when, for example, they become implausible? Why is it that they do not necessarily disintegrate in those circumstances, but can become reconstructed beyond the ruins?

The Wilde Lectures are given over three years. In the first year, represented in this book, I have attempted to examine the account which the so-called behavioural sciences give of the origins of the sense of God. In the following two years, I intend to look at the other side of the picture, at the theistic traditions themselves, in relation to the same questions. The present book is, therefore, completely self-contained, but it will eventually be complemented by a study of the theistic traditions as such. In this way it will be possible to see to what extent the behavioural and theistic accounts relate to each other.

---

[1] *Der Ursprung der Gottesidee.* (Full details of references in the notes will be found in the bibliography.)   [2] See bibliography under James.

In the present work, I have first sketched very briefly some issues in the background of attempts to explain human behaviour, with particular reference to the kinds of explanation which seemed possible when Wilde was alive. I then ask whether a full sociological explanation of the origin of the human sense of God is as possible as it seemed to Durkheim. This, I argue, seems doubtful, principally because the failure of so exclusive an explanation suggests that there must be a more adequate anthropological component—a conclusion not unlike that of Talmon (in a more specific context), who suggested that the adequate understanding of Melanesian cargo cults appears to demand 'a veritable rapprochement between history, sociology and anthropology'.[3] I therefore go on to propose a new framework, or context, of explanation within which an anthropological understanding of religion can occur. This then raises the question whether religions can be understood as route-finding activities, routes by which men and women are able to trace a path from birth to death (and through death). This, in turn, makes necessary an examination of the extent to which these 'routes' are structurally composed, so that they become entire and extensive 'universes of meaning', and of whether structural accounts of religious phenomena are viable. One structural account which I will suggest is not viable as it stands is that of Lévi-Strauss, because the way in which he defines what is procedurally proper in the case of myth makes it almost impossible for adequate weight to be given to the contribution of individual or innovatory sense, externally derived. But if that is so, it then becomes imperative to look both at psychoanalytic and at experimentally based understandings of how psychologically individuals arrive at their sense of God (including claims to an experience of God under the influence of hallucinogenic drugs, such as LSD), and of how a sense of God appears in consciousness. That programme, the attempt to understand how things 'appear in consciousness', is also fundamental to phenomenology. For this reason a brief account is given of the way in which Husserl established phenomenology as a method, and of the implications of this for reflection on the sense of God.

There are two preliminary points which need to be made. The first is that the whole project is clearly absurd. There is no way in which the ground and the specializations involved could possibly

[3] Talmon, p. 126.

be covered. Furthermore, some topics which would have required very extensive preliminary discussion have had to be omitted— there is, for example, some discussion of Freud, but none of Jung, because the problems of relating analytic theory to experimental psychology are even greater, at the present time, in the case of Jung than they are in the case of Freud; or again, no attempt has been made to discuss the contribution of relatively new tech- niques, such as those which occur in locational analysis—even though in my view, in the case of that particular example, the insights gained are likely to be of real importance in understanding the human senses of God; but it would require a very extensive discussion to indicate what the methods and insights of locational analysis are. Yet the underlying issue, of whether separate disciplines can be integrated to any degree at all, is serious if what used to be referred to as 'comparative religion' is to develop as a subject. What is suggested in this book is one possible framework within which this could occur, but at school and at university level. But this will not in any sense diminish the number of mistakes any individual is bound to make in undertaking such a task. All I can do is make my own the words with which a former Master of my own College, George Thomson, prefaced his book, *The Fore- seeable Future:*

In some of what follows I have gone outside the studies of which I can claim any professional knowledge. For this rash act I claim forgiveness of those into whose coverts I have trespassed. If some of the game I have reported exists only in my imagination, at least this kind of poaching does no harm to the rightful owners, while the onlooker may occasion- ally see something that is both unexpected and real.[4]

That final word 'real' leads to the second preliminary point. In this book, the ideas of a great many different people are discussed, and as far as possible I have tried to quote the salient points of their arguments in their own words, in case these are unfamiliar (and this explains why such lengthy passages have been quoted, in the notes and in the text). But throughout I have been haunted by the reaction of Phil Fuller (the main character in James Leigh's novel, *What Can You Do?*) as he listens to the lectures of Dr. Brinkman on social science: 'While Dr. Brinkman hacked away at one theoretician after another, I said to myself, *All right,*

[4] Thomson, Preface.

what is there?[5] What is really there? I, too, will have to hack away at theoreticians, but I have tried to keep alive that question, what is really there? It is not a bad question to ask in relation to the sense of God:

> Elizabeth Ann
> Said to her Nan:
> 'Please will you tell me how God began?' . . .
> And Nurse said, 'Well!'
> And Ann said, 'Well?
> I know you know, and I wish you'd tell.'
> And Nurse took pins from her mouth, and said,
> 'Now then, darling—it's time for bed.'
> Elizabeth Ann
> Had a wonderful plan:
> She would run round the world till she found a man
> Who knew *exactly* how God began.[6]

I am not sure whether we will be any more successful than Elizabeth Ann, but let us at least set out on the journey, running, if not on six-year-old legs, at least with an inquisitive mind.

[5] Leigh, p. 154.   [6] Milne, p. 78.

NOTE OF THANKS AND
ACKNOWLEDGEMENT

I would like to offer my thanks to all those who contributed to
these lectures, and in particular to the following: to the electors,
who took the risk of allowing me to do this 'thinking aloud' in
public; to Miss Gurley and Mrs. Goddard, who typed the lectures
from almost illegible notes under great pressure of time; to
N. Tennant, who made important corrections and suggestions,
particularly suggestions of further reading; to the many people
at the lectures who took the trouble to comment, both at the time
and later—where possible (and where I accept their points) I have
incorporated their comments in the book; to the Clarendon Press,
for their efficiency and help in producing these lectures in much
less than a year—in ordinary circumstances I would not have
considered publication at all, or at least, not without much more
time for correction and change; but since the next two years of
the lectures are dependent on the first (those represented in this
book), there seemed to be some sense in making them available
as early as possible; and this could not have been done without
the real contribution of the Press.

Finally and supremely, my thanks go to Margaret, my wife,
who not only undertook nearly half the typing herself in the midst
of her own work but who supported and encouraged the completion of these lectures at times when the amount of work and
reading involved in the time available came close to defeating me.
However inadequate the result may be, there would have been no
result at all without her.

The publishers and I gratefully acknowledge permission to
to reprint extracts from copyright works:

A. J. Ayer: *Bertrand Russell and G. E. Moore: The Analytical
Heritage.* © 1971. Reprinted by permission of Macmillan,
London and Basingstoke, and Harvard University Press.

P. L. Berger: *A Rumour of Angels.* © 1969. P. L. Berger. Reprinted
by permission of Penguin Books Ltd., and Doubleday and
Company Inc.

E. Durkheim: *The Elementary Forms of Religious Life*, trans. Swain. Reprinted by permission of George Allen and Unwin Ltd.

E. Husserl: *Paris Lectures*, trans. P. Kostenbaum. Reprinted by permission of Mouton and Co., Publishers.

A. A. Milne: *Now We Are Six*. Decorations by E. H. Shephard. © 1927 by E. P. Dutton and Co., Inc. Renewal © 1955 by A. A. Milne. Reprinted by permission of Mr. C. R. Milne, Methuen and Co. Ltd., McClelland and Stewart Ltd., Toronto and E. P. Dutton and Co., Inc.

D. Nauta: *The Meaning of Information*. Reprinted by permission of Mouton and Co., Publishers.

Jean Piaget: *Structuralism*, trans. and ed., C. Maschler. © 1970 by Basic Books Inc. Reprinted by permission of Routledge and Kegan Paul Ltd., Basic Books Inc., and Presses Universitaires de France.

A. S. Romer: *The Vertebrate Story*. © 1959 A. S. Romer. Reprinted by permission of The University of Chicago Press.

Poems without attribution are my own—with the perhaps obvious exception of the stanza on the cheese-mites.

CONTENTS

CONTENTS

I

EXPLAINING HUMAN BEHAVIOUR

ON the 13th of July 1900 Joseph Conrad sent his wife and child out of his house to London, in order to make what he called a 'desperate' effort to finish the writing of his novel *Lord Jim*. The previous September he had written to Galsworthy to say that *Lord Jim* would be finished in a month; he continued to make similar forecasts during the months that followed, until at last he was able once more to write to Galsworthy:

The end of *Lord Jim* has been pulled off with a steady drag of twenty-one hours. I sent wife and child out of the house (to London) and sat down at 9 a.m. with a desperate resolve to be done with it. Now and then I took a walk round the house, out at one door in at the other. Ten minute meals. A great hush. Cigarette ends growing into a mound similar to a cairn over a dead hero. Moon rose over the barn, looked in at the window and climbed out of sight. Dawn broke, brightened. I put the lamp out and went on, with the morning breeze blowing the sheets of MS. all over the room. Sun rose. I wrote the last word and went into the dining room. Six o'clock I shared a piece of cold chicken with Escamillo. . . . Felt very well, only sleepy; had a bath at seven and at 8.30 was on my way to London.[1]

It is not surprising that Conrad had found it difficult to complete *Lord Jim*: he had attempted, in this novel, to probe the explanation of human behaviour. What, Conrad was asking, is the 'true' explanation of Jim's final act, whereby he stands 'with bared head in the light of torches',[2] waiting for Doramin to shoot him? ' "We ought to know," ' says Marlow, almost as the final words of the book, ' "he is one of us." '[3] *We ought to know: he is one of us:* those are the words which Conrad wrote on that July evening in 1900. They are a magnificent and a prophetic note on which to enter the twentieth century. The regularity of explanation in the natural order and in the universe must surely be applicable to the 'natural nature' of men. He is one of us; it ought, therefore, to be possible to explain and understand how his life has been constructed, what are the causes of his actions, what are the realities or the illusions of his beliefs. By the end of the nineteenth century the possibility of arriving at true explanations of human behaviour, in terms of regularity and law, seemed to be within grasp. The problem had been posed by John Stuart Mill, with his usual clarity, in 1843: 'Are the actions of human beings, like all other natural events, subject to invariable laws? Does that constancy of causation, which is the foundation of every scientific theory of successive phenomena, really obtain among them?'[4]

The pioneers of the new 'social science'—such men as Comte, Buckle, Spencer, Tylor, Durkheim—had little doubt that the answer was yes. Perhaps at last it would be possible, by unravelling the mechanism of cause and effect which has brought all manifest human and social behaviour to its observable forms, to establish a Newtonian science of behaviour. By assembling comparative evidence from as many societies at as many moments in time as possible, sufficient recurrences (or as Hume had put it, in the case of Newtonian physics, sufficient constancy of conjunction) would be discerned which would justify behavioural laws, in much the same way as the observations of other scientists were taken to justify the conclusions of physics. If, as seemed to be the case, Hume had shown that perfect induction (the adducing of all possible instances) is neither possible nor necessary to establish the conclusions even of Newtonian physics (this point is discussed in more detail in ch. VIII), then perhaps sufficient induction (the adducing of a sufficient number of instances) would be enough to establish the laws constraining human behaviour. In this ambition they were reinforced by their belief that Quételet had established the statistical regularity of social behaviour, and had therefore contained the individual within the social. For Buckle, this laid the foundations for a thoroughgoing science of history, and others shared his belief.[5]

But Conrad, in *Lord Jim*, was not affirming, he was deeply questioning, the possibility of ever arriving at an adequate explanation of the real nature of men. No doubt it must be the case that whatever a man does, it will contribute to a statistic. But is this sufficient to explain how men so variously construct their lives? How *do* we build up our ideas of what is true, of what we must do, of what we believe to constitute our peace? How do we arrive at a sense of what is real, at a sense of what is duty, at a sense, even, of God? These are the questions of Conrad in *Lord Jim*, and they are the questions, also, of these Wilde lectures, focused on the sense of God: how do human beings arrive at their sense, or senses, of God? It is this precise question which was the basic and fundamental concern of Henry Wilde in founding these lectures in Oxford.

It follows that there could scarcely be a better introduction to these particular Wilde lectures than to go back to Henry Wilde himself, in order to understand something of what was in his mind when he brought these lectures into being. What Conrad grasped in 1900, and what Wilde also discerned in a quite different way, was that the very ambition to develop a scientific explanation of human behaviour, in the ways which seemed open in the nineteenth century, at once created what may be summarized as a dilemma of individual meaning: if it were to turn out to be the case that the actions and thoughts of an individual are as much constrained by lawful regularity as an apple is constrained by forces referred to as gravity when it falls from a tree, then on what basis can one attribute worth or blame or praise to individual actions or beliefs? But on the other hand, if, as immediate appearances certainly suggest, human behaviour does *not* turn out to exhibit the same steady-state regularity as that of stones or apples when they fall, then where could the embryonic scientists of human behaviour locate an explanation of that behaviour (which was taken, of course, to belong to the natural order, and not to be subject to extra-natural or super-natural influences), which would count as scientific in some available sense? The dilemma may perhaps seem artificial, particularly in the terms expressed. It was, nevertheless, a real and very searching dilemma, not least because the vast extent of the achievements of science in the nineteenth century in other areas of the natural order made the step along mechanistic lines towards a science of human behaviour, conceived as equally a part of the natural order and open to similar procedures of investigation, seem to many to be both correct and necessary. Thus although it may seem strange to begin these lectures by going backwards in time, and although this account must necessarily be over-brief, it is in fact highly important to understand to what extent in *some* nineteenth-century approaches to the explanation of human behaviour an extreme mechanistic ambition seemed legitimate. Only then can one adequately grasp how important—indeed revolutionary—are the changes in explanatory ambition (particularly in relation to the sense of God) which have been occurring in the last few years. Something of this change is summarized in Runciman's graphic phrase 'idiographic explanation', which seemed to him to be demanded if justice is to be done, in explanation, to individual and contingent circumstances, including a psychological component.[6]

Wilde was born in Manchester in 1833—the Manchester to which, at almost exactly this date, Disraeli's Coningsby arrived.[7] Coningsby came to Manchester, 'because a being, whose name even was unknown to him, had met him in a hedge ale-house during a thunderstorm and told him that the age of ruins was past'.[8] When he arrived, 'He saw all . . .; he beheld, in long-continued ranks, those mysterious forms, full of existence without life, that perform with facility, and in an instant, what man can fulfil only with difficulty and in days.' In other words, dismantling the prose of Disraeli, he saw machines: ' "It haunts me", he said, "in my dreams; I see cities peopled with machines." '[9] Wilde, also, was fascinated by the age of machines. He was the eldest son of a working mechanic, and he kept his home in the north, where he became one of the great private scientists of the nineteenth century (he retired in 1884, at the age of 51, in order to devote himself to research), working particularly in the field of electricity, which to him was the key to the understanding of many phenomena. In 1868, for example, he applied the synchronizing property of alternating currents in order to control the rotations of a number of dynamos. He had thus discovered that alternators can run in parallel when synchronous. This made possible the breakthrough which facilitated such massive installations as the one at the Niagara Falls. On a smaller scale, it was Wilde who applied his knowledge to the production of the first searchlights for the Royal Navy. The *Minotaur*, the *Alexandra*, and the *Temeraire* were fitted with Wilde's searchlights in 1874. His achievements, therefore, were real and practical. But he also speculated on much wider issues. It was here that he seemed, to some of his contemporaries at least, idiosyncratic; no doubt some would have put it more bluntly by calling him downright eccentric, particularly since he spent much of his time engaged in lawsuits over patents. After he died, in 1919, the President of the Royal Society, Sir J. J. Thomson, clearly found it difficult to know what to say of him. In the obituary speech, he referred to him as 'a man of pronounced individuality'.[10]

If he *was* idiosyncratic, it was because of his determination to probe the possible electrical component of any problem. He suggested, for example, that the explanation of shifting magnetic poles, as indeed also of 'the principal phenomena of terrestrial magnetism',[11] required rotation within the core of the earth, making it almost into a kind of generator. The idea seemed eccentric at the time, as certainly in some of its details it is, but it no longer looks wholly foolish, as a recent description of research on magnetism makes clear.[12] Or again, to take another example which comes closer to the explanation of human behaviour, Wilde was certain that there must be an electrical component in the mechanism of brain behaviour.[13]

There was nothing novel in this. Ever since Galvani, at the end of the eighteenth century, had watched his wife preparing frogs' legs for supper it had been known that electric currents were the key to understanding nerve conduction and muscular action.[14] Wilde, like many others in the nineteenth century, had moved beyond this, in order to ask what might be the electrical component in brain behaviour itself (that is to say, in 'thinking'). Experimental Psychology, particularly on the Continent, set out to unravel the complexity of brain behaviour, including conceptual and emotional behaviour, on the basis that the brain must be understood as a physical energy system. Helmholtz, in particular, who had so pervasive an influence (not least on Freud), insisted on a rigidly physiological basis for thinking and experience: already by 1850 he had measured the speed of the nervous impulse—and he had, appropriately, used frogs' muscles for his experiments; in 1851, he invented the ophthalmoscope and located three receptor mechanisms in the eye sensitive to the wavelengths in the spectrum, red, green, and blue, from which other mixed colours are constructed. These experiments seemed to be spectacular examples of the physiological basis of mind, of the brain converting energy to thought and action. It was a programme which captivated the young Freud, as he set out to make more systematic the explanation of even the most private and abstract features of human behaviour: all thoughts, including thoughts of God, must ultimately be reducible to physical-chemical activity.

Freud was taught by a close friend and associate of Helmholtz,

Ernst Brücke, a man to whom Freud (to use his own words) 'stuck like glue' for six years. It was Brücke who had taken the famous oath with du Bois-Reymond,

... a solemn oath to put into effect the truth: 'No other forces than the common physical-chemical ones are active within the organism. In those cases which cannot at the time be explained by these forces one has either to find the specific way or form of their action by means of the physical-mathematical method or to assume new forces equal in dignity to the chemical-physical forces inherent in matter, reducible to the force of attraction and repulsion.'[15]

It is a question whether Freud spent the rest of his life attempting to escape the baneful influence of this mechanistic physiology, as those who are psychotherapeutically inclined suggest,[16] or whether, as the physiologically inclined neurologist Pribram suggests,[17] the work of Freud is still worth attention because his work was, in its own way, an attempt to realize Brücke's commitment. The debate is complicated. But the fact that the debate can occur indicates how deeply Freud was caught in the dilemma which the intuitive genius of Wilde recognized, that on the unquestioned basis of physical-chemical activity, ideas and programmes are generated, which the physiology of the process does not wholly capture. Freud recognized that the individual, when regarded as a centre of conscious activity, informed and influenced by roots or memory traces in unconscious resources, constructs a personal universe of meaning, which physiology (the mechanism) alone will never wholly explain: there is a component of individual circumstance which must be integrated *as of effect* within and through the common mechanisms of the brain. It is this which makes one person's 'universe' different from that of any other person; and it is this also, in part, which creates the dilemma of individual meaning.

How then *do* we, on the basis of the mechanisms of sensory perception and internal organization, build up our senses of the world? How do we construct our sense of there being other persons, of there being obligations and duties, of there being experiences of beauty and of love, of there being, in reality, God? '*We ought to know: he is one of us.*' But comparative physiology and experimental psychology did not yield the answer to Conrad; nor did they yield it to Wilde. Wilde, therefore, founded in the university of Oxford, not only these lectures but also a Readership in Mental Philosophy and the John Locke Scholarship in Mental Philosophy. 'Mental philosophy' was defined as 'the study of the human mind based on observation and experience *as distinguished from* Experimental Psychology'.[18]

From this point of view, the name of John Locke was a good one to choose. Wilde by no means accepted Locke's explanation of how ideas are constructed: indeed, he believed that Locke had simply described the problem and explained nothing. Locke, it will be remembered, had argued against the view that human beings are born with some innate ideas, and had concluded that the mind starts, much as Chairman Mao has described the Chinese people, as a clean, blank sheet of paper without any blotches:[19] ideas are built up from experiences and from reflections on them.[20] Wilde did not doubt the foundations of knowledge in experience, but he also observed that ideas are generated with such novelty and profusion that a great deal more reflection on the nature of the mental process is required if Locke's empiricism is to become even remotely plausible: if ideas have to be constructed from building-blocks of experience, in the strictest sense, then an individual would have to live to the age of Methuselah if he is to have any chance of arriving at a sense of almost anything. There was, therefore, an uneasiness in Wilde's mind about strict empiricism and about the way in which it was being allied to experimental psychology in order to explain how human beings think and how they arrive at their senses of the world and of reality—and Helmholtz was absolutely specific about his reliance on British empiricism, particularly on Locke, in contrast to what he called the 'absolute rubbish' of Hegel.

This uneasiness of Wilde is important because it anticipates, in a curiously exact way, the uneasiness that Chomsky feels about the account which Skinner and other strict behaviourists give of language acquisition (that verbal behaviour is acquired through stimulus, association, and reinforcement in the parental or comparable environment).[21] Chomsky's arguments are perhaps familiar, but if they are not, the quoted passage[22] summarizes some of the salient points. What emerges in that argument is that the issue of innateness is no longer dead, but that it is not in the least to be equated with the issue as it occurs in Locke. Because of the speed with which language is acquired and understood, without necessary reference to experience, it is likely, in Chomsky's view, that there are, not innate ideas, but innate brain structures, which are, by the fact of birth, universal. It is this which enables language competence and thus also language performance. What Chomsky conjectures is that the rapidity through which language competence is acquired suggests that certain innate structures or organizational principles in the brain delimit the class of learnable languages and thus enable the process of internalizing a grammar (that is, of acquiring a language).[23] If, in fact, transformational linguistic theory is able to yield adequate grammars of natural languages, then because the theory imposes universal constraints and characteristics on admissible grammars, it suggests that there are underlying innate structures which predispose an individual to the learning of a natural language. On this basis, through an actual language, almost unlimited sentences, and senses of meaning, can be generated.

Wilde also believed that the real problem is how, on the basis of what is indeed experience and 'physical-chemical activity', ideas are *generated*. Wilde, with his strong electrical predisposition, meant by 'generated' something a good deal different from Chomsky's 'generative' grammar:[24] yet the possibility of the same word in both cases again demonstrates the kind of intuitive skill with which Wilde guessed that severely empiricist accounts would not be adequate on their own for total explanation. When, therefore, he endowed the Lectures and the Readership, he focused his unease on an ultimately metaphysical issue, about as far removed from immediate empirical experience as possible, on the human sense of God: how do human beings *generate* their ideas of God? So far as the *Readership* which he founded was concerned, the Reader was put under the obligation to lecture on 'the illusions and delusions which are incident to the human mind, and, so far as practicable, on the psychology of the lower races of mankind as illustrated by the various fetish objects in the Anthropological Museum of the University and in other museums'.[25]

In the *Lectures*, Wilde intended that the *developed* ideas of God should be considered as they occur in what were then called 'the higher religions'. On this basis, it should now be a little clearer why 'the sense of God' has been chosen as the title and theme. It concentrates attention on these central questions: how does a sense of God originate in human consciousness, and what light do sociology, anthropology, psychology throw on that question? Can such senses 'make sense' or will they turn out to be 'illusions and delusions', to use Wilde's phrase, without reference in reality?

There is an immediate and very curious point to be made: if we had asked those questions about the origins of the sense of God at any point from a hundred to fifty years ago, we would have received confident and unhesitating answers. Sociology and anthropology (which in that period were just becoming established as disciplines) both provided crystal-clear answers; so also did psychology, at least after the arrival of Freud. The majority of those who were working to establish those disciplines *as* disciplines had no doubt that the origin of the sense of God could be identified, and that all subsequent theistic phenomena could be explained as derivations, through the mechanism of cause and effect, from whatever was claimed to have been the origin or point of departure. What kind of answers, in briefest possible summary, were they suggesting?

For Durkheim, one of the greatest of the early figures in establishing sociology as a subject, the origin of the sense of God lay in the origin of the sense of society. Religion is the elementary social form: 'dans le principe tout est religieux'.[26] 'In the beginning all is religious.' The elementary original act which creates both a sense of society and a sense of God is totemism. In the totem a social group symbolizes itself: it 'objectifies' (makes an object out of) both its unity and the cohesion it feels when it assembles as a group (the excitement, so to say, of a football crowd). That cohesion—society itself—is held together by the power of the symbol. Men are thus as much constrained by the symbols through which the social is objectively expressed as an apple is constrained by gravity when it becomes detached from a branch.[27] For Durkheim, the origin of the sense of God lay in the endeavours of men to objectify (that is to say, give an objectivity to) the social forces which constrain their individual lives.

For Tylor, one of those who did most to construct anthropology as a subject in the nineteenth century, the origin of the sense of God lay in the endeavours of men to account for phenomena which are common in experience but difficult to explain—in particular, the experience of dreams, in which one's 'self' seems to wander out of the body, but also the experience of visions and trances, even to the extent of seeing someone, or the impression of someone, whom one knows to be absent or dead. The primitive 'natural' explanation is that an *anima*, soul, lives within the body and is able to be detached from it, and hence may be able to survive death. This is the basis of animism, and animism is the basis of religion. On this basis, an entirely naturalistic explanation then posits a 'supernatural' world, a world full of effect on this world, even though it cannot be wholly seen. From this point of view, it is not difficult to populate the supernatural world with hierarchies of spirits, with gods, and hence, eventually, with God. For Tylor, the origin of the sense of God lay in animism,[28] in the attempts of primitive men to explain the 'animation' of their bodies, as also of trees, animals, clouds, rivers, and all other moving (and eventually even immobile) objects.

For Freud, the origin of the sense of God lay in the projection on to the universe at large of the situation in which every human being learns that it cannot continue its life without dependence on others; and that is the situation in which the infant is dependent on its parents. Those who cannot face the fact of ultimate *non-*continuity (that is, oblivion in death) project into the universe a father figure on whom they can be dependent, and live *as if* this comforting illusion is true, and *as if* there will be continuity of some personal existence in relation to that figure, even through and after death.

In the new science of mythology, Max Müller was also advancing equally confident claims. In what he referred to as his 'Copernican revolution' (his discovery that the Sanskrit Dyaus equals, philologically, the Greek Zeus), he gave semantic precision to an argument already long established that India was the original home of mankind, and that from this centre the variations and conflicts of men diffused.[29] At the earliest stage of human development, according to Müller, men expressed their observations of nature anthropomorphically: instead of saying 'It is night,' they personified the observation into some such form as 'The moon (*silene*) has kissed the setting sun (*endymion*) into sleep.' The personifications then became detached into myths, so that myth was created by early man's inability to disentangle concrete and abstract meanings: it is in this sense that myth is, in Müller's famous phrase, a disease of language.[30] Müller then looked for a single, catalytic, point of origin, and believed that he had located it in the sun: 'I look upon the sunrise and sunset, on the daily return of day and night, on the battle between light and darkness, on the whole solar drama in all its details that is acted every day, every month, every year, in heaven and on earth, as the principal subject of early mythology.'[31]

In these different ways the proponents of sociology, of anthropology, of psychology, of mythology would all have answered with confidence if they had been asked what was, and is, the origin of the sense of God. More offensively, another worker in mythology and anthropology, K. T. Preuss, identified the origin of God in what he called *Urdummheit*, 'primitive stupidity'.[32] Yet if the same question is asked of those who work in the same disciplines *now*, not only is it unlikely that any answer will be given, it will also be explained with some sharpness why it is not particularly sensible even to ask the question. There is only one area in the contemporary scene where an answer *will* be given with a kind of nineteenth-century assurance; and this answer we will come to in due course.

The question is thus worth asking why this shift of emphasis has occurred. It has not occurred simply because the errors and the inadequacies of those early theories can, without much difficulty, be specified. That is true, but trivial. In point of fact, there was not much difficulty in making fun of the early theories even at the time. Andrew Lang was already doing this before the turn of the century, pointing out that there are as many theories as theorists,[33] and he wrote on one occasion to Robertson Smith saying that if only the orthodox theists had someone on their side with a sense of humour, they would decimate the ranks of their opponents—he even thought of offering himself for the excitement of the chase.[34] Or again, a Frenchman, Gaidoz, took on Max Müller, and turned Müller's method against himself, proving that Müller had never existed, but was simply a corrupted solar myth—in an article 'Comme quoi M. Max Muller n'a jamais existé'.[35] He had equally little difficulty in proving that the University of Oxford has never existed but is a solar myth of a particularly degenerate kind.

But that kind of attack on the early theorists does not do justice to the extreme complexity of the problems which confronted them as they attempted to establish an account of human behaviour which would qualify as scientific, nor to the extreme skill with which at least some of them tackled those problems in the terms in which they conceived them. What is much more to the point is to recognize the difficulties into which their conception of what would count as scientific led them, particularly in the *naïveté* of its understanding of induction and of the related notion of law—the kind of approach to evidence, for example, which tended to search for common features (for sufficient 'constancy of conjunction'), and which necessarily disregarded variant elements in particular contexts: it was this kind of approach which enabled Conybeare to advise Frazer that he should regard Epiphanius and other ancient authors as 'a mine of folklore' to be quarried,[36] and Frazer to answer a query of Robertson Smith by saying that he would 'empty out his notes higgledy-piggledy' in the hope that it would serve his purpose.[37] Equally misleading, to give another example, was the hope that all developed phenomena can be adequately explained by identifying a point of origin (a point of departure) and by tracing the stages through which, by cause and effect, the developments have evolved. It was this ambition that led Tylor to search for primitive stages in phenomena which happen to have survived into the present age—what he called 'survivals', or in a far more graphic phrase 'unchanged savagery':[38] what he meant by this was that developments have passed through stages, and that some phenomena happen to have 'stuck' at a certain point; this means that those phenomena, being open to direct observation, allow the anthropologist to observe evolution in its actual stages. It is here, incidentally, that one must remember, if one is to understand the origins of sociology and anthropology, that the important influence was not Darwin, but historiography: Darwin served as a confirmation and as a reinforcement, but the real drive was already long established (and was influential on *him*) to discover the laws operating through history which had caused the evolution of societies. The equation is much more that of Alfred Marshall, who wrote in 1897: 'Social science or the reasoned history of man, for the two things are the same, is working its way towards a fundamental unity.'[39]

The project of reconstructing the stages of evolution, and of thereby explaining the significance of all phenomena, including conceptual beliefs, no longer seems so simple. Yet the ease with which one can collapse the massive nineteenth-century theories about the origin of the sense of God, in all their earnest variety, does not take us very much further in understanding why we have become less certain about the possibility of identifying the solution; after all, it might presumably be possible simply to improve on their theories. But what makes that an improbable way to proceed is that the nature of the human subject matter has compelled a change in the goals of explanation—not the goal of including human behaviour within the natural order, but the goal of arriving at single, simple laws which govern the emergence and occurrence of all manifest behaviour. At the heart of *this* problem stands Conrad. To Conrad, struggling to explore human behaviour in ways which appear to be open to a novelist alone, there seemed to be something profoundly inadequate in the nomothetic ambition (meaning by nomothetic, analysis directed to the forming of general principles, and the explanation which seeks to identify the behavioural and social law which constrains an individual into a particular action, and which therefore becomes the explanation of that action). Certainly, the novel *Lord Jim* articulates two fundamental doubts about the nomothetic ambition, even though it is unlikely that this was a particularly conscious intention in Conrad's mind.

The first doubt is perhaps more a question, whether one will ever be able to specify the constituent elements of constraint which make two individuals act differently in exactly the same situation, or which make two individuals derive from the same event different memories, different interpretations, and different consequences in the construction of their lives. Jim was not the only white officer on the *Patna* who deserted the passengers when it seemed that the ship was sinking. The desertion was an occurrence, a serial item, in which several individuals participated; yet only Jim was subsequently haunted by the fact; only Jim had his subsequent life constrained by that fact. Conrad meant his readers to be in no doubt about the explanatory power of the fact, the desertion of the *Patna*, in Jim's subsequent life. He spelt it out in the opening pages:

His incognito, which had as many holes as a sieve, was not meant to hide a personality but a fact. When the fact broke through the incognito he would leave suddenly the seaport where he happened to be at the time and go to another—generally farther east. . . . He retreated in good order towards the rising sun, and the fact followed him casually, but inevitably.[40]

'*Inevitably*': one of Herbert Spencer's favourite words in arguing for nomothetic regularity in the history of societies. But not *all* the white officers were *inevitably* pursued by this fact: there was no single, inevitable meaning in this serial occurrence. But even supposing one argued that the memory of the *Patna* desertion was coded in the brain, so that it could become of effect in Jim's subsequent behaviour, and thus, at least in part, be the cause of that behaviour, we are still left with Conrad's second doubt, the possible innovatory effect of the reality of the objects of our belief, which are disruptive of steady-state regularity in the sequences of human life. Intransigent realities—realities which cannot be evaded—are capable of creating new effects within the sequences of ordered behaviour, which may indeed be 'lawful', in the sense that they are not wholly random, but which create such complex novelty that the specification of the laws in question seems impossible. Jim had 'ability in the abstract' which would have given him, as Conrad puts it, adequate occupation as a water clerk:[41] but his stone-falling regularity, his ability to be a clerk, is invaded by his belief that he has deserted the *Patna*, and the *reality* in this belief works its new and disruptive effect. If it had been possible to convince Lord Jim that the desertion of the *Patna* was not culpable, that it was not really a desertion, because the ship did not sink and the passengers survived, he would not have been pursued or constrained for the rest of his life by the fact. But the reality in the object of his belief, that he *had* deserted the ship, could not be dissolved: and that reality, by being constituted in his life *as reality*, worked its effect.

In principle, this might still be open to nomothetic explanation; but in practice, the identification of the effect of the sensed reality of the objects of belief is, or so it seemed to Conrad, eternally elusive. The variables which enable men to initiate change and direction are a compound of high complexity; and in a sense, the man who throws away the least scrap of paper, let alone the least thought, eludes our final and certain grasp. But what happens if these considerations are transferred to the reality or the unreality of God? Conrad was well aware that truth can be disclosed in a moment of illusion: this is made specific at the very centre of the book, when Marlow is explaining why he is telling the story at all.[42] But this leaves open the possibility that truth can be disclosed in a moment of reality. What becomes a matter for concern is the possible effect in the construction of human lives of the reality of the objects of belief, or conversely the difference that might be made in effect if the objects of belief were shown to have no reality in existence.

It is of course obvious that this phrase, the possible reality in the objects of belief, is far too brutal a short-hand with which to refer to problems which require extreme caution and refinement for their adequate discussion—not least because the phrase at once precipitates us straight into the centre of the controversy about the non-cognitive thesis of avowals; and if that topic is unfamiliar, there is a very clear introduction to it in the chapter entitled 'A Cloud of Philosophy Condensed into a Drop of Grammar' in Hacker's book on Wittgenstein, *Insight and Illusion*. There is no doubt that the unqualified introduction of the words 'reality' and 'object' confuses almost all the issues involved. 'Reality' is one of those words which refuses to lie down and be stunned to death by definition. Similarly, it is far more accurate, in many instances, to use the phrase 'the objects (or apparent objects) of human attention', rather than 'the objects of human belief', because in that case belief is a particular mode of attentiveness to the possibilities involved in particular situations, occurrences, or persons (including oneself). It is certainly possible for 'God' to be an object of human attention without the involvement of belief; and the question then would become a question of the possible independent reality of this 'object' of attention. The appropriateness of independent reference within the term 'God', and thus of belief as the proper mode of continuing attentiveness, would then have to be justified within the quality of the very complex mosaic of cues which arise within the universe and which present themselves for attention to the human subject. All these are points which will be developed in due course. But for the moment, although there are real difficulties in both these phrases, the objects of attention and the objects of belief, it will be helpful to continue to use them, because they do at least focus attention on the issue of criteria—criteria, for example, to which appeal is, or might be, made to justify particular uses of language or particular organizations of overt behaviour.

It follows that no attempt is being made at this point to advance a concealed argument for the existence of God—that beliefs have effects, and that at least to that extent 'God' is constituted in the reality of existential construction. But what is undoubtedly the case is that the possible reality of the object of beliefs (which includes the possibility that there may be sufficient criteria) cannot be ruled out *a priori* by the procedures of behavioural analysis *alone*; it has to be established on other grounds as well. What has made us more cautious in defining, with absolute certainty, the origin of the sense of God, is the realization that *a priori*, in behavioural terms alone, the possibility cannot be excluded that God is the origin of the sense of God—a possibility which to Tylor, Durkheim, and Freud was simply inadmissible. Undoubtedly Jim may be persuaded that he did not in reality desert the *Patna*, and we may be persuaded that the term 'God', despite its many uses in the various theistic language games, does not and cannot refer to anything that has existence in reality. But this does not alter the fact that these disciplines, sociology, anthropology, and psychology, have returned, each in its own way, to a very central concern with the reality and the unreality of the objects of our perceptions and our beliefs, and to the consequent differentiations in effect which are dependent on the issue of reality or unreality. They have returned, in more technical terms, to a serious concern with ontology. But the trouble with ontology is that it is easy to state as a problem, highly difficult to handle in practice. This point is beautifully compressed by Quine in the famous opening to his essay, 'On What There Is':

A curious thing about the ontological problem is its simplicity. It can be put in three Anglo-Saxon monosyllables: 'What is there?' It can be answered, moreover, in a word—'Everything'—and everyone will accept this answer as true. However, this is merely to say that there is what there is. There remains room for disagreement over cases; and so the issue has stayed alive down the centuries.[43]

The 'distinction among cases' is precisely what has led sociology and anthropology and psychology to become more hesitant about arriving at universal laws of explanation which make irrelevant the individual appropriation or expression of detail, as though, at the furthest extreme, it would make no *essential* difference whether the objects of encounter or of belief have reality or no reality in existence. This is a point much emphasized by Harré and Secord in their attempt to establish a systems theory of behaviour which involves an endeavour 'to bring into behavioural science the phenomenal experience of individuals: the things that people say about themselves and other people should be taken seriously as reports of data relevant to phenomena that *really exist* and which are *relevant* to the explanation of behaviour'.[44] This does *not* mean that because someone reports something it necessarily has a reality in existence external to the belief; obviously not. But the report is a datum, and the grounds of that report cannot be examined unless the report itself is taken seriously as a datum. Faith and credulity, vision and delusion can only be distinguished provided that in case-studies the issue of ontology is kept alive. As will be seen when we come to consider Lévi-Strauss (who comes as close as any to what Leach has called 'contempt for the empirical phenomenon'),[45] the case can no longer seriously be defended that we are constrained by depth structures *alone* (by the innate structures, or by the chemical-physical *grundlage* of Brücke and Helmholtz), but that in realizing our competence for thought, the effect of what is external to that thought has its own, inevitably *sui generis*, contribution to make in our actual performance. Thus no one presumably doubts the nomothetic regularity of brain *competence*, the regularity of structure, for example, in the human brain, which forms a basis for behavioural science: 'He is one of us: we ought to know.' There *is* a common subject matter. But in *performance*, the nomothetic explanation of human behaviour is increasingly elusive, as Marlow finally comments in *Lord Jim*.

'And that's the end. He passes away under a cloud, inscrutable at heart, forgotten, unforgiven, and excessively romantic. Not in the wildest days of his boyish visions could he have seen the alluring shape of such an extraordinary success! For it may very well be that in the short moment of his last proud and unflinching glance, he had beheld the face of that opportunity which, like an Eastern bride, had come veiled to his side.

'But we can see him, an obscure conqueror of fame, tearing himself out of the arms of a jealous love at the sign, at the call of his exalted egoism. He goes away from a living woman to celebrate his pitiless wedding with a shadowy ideal of conduct. Is he satisfied—quite, now, I wonder? We ought to know. He is one of us—and have I not stood up once, like an evoked ghost, to answer for his eternal constancy? . . .

'Who knows? He is gone, inscrutable at heart, and the poor girl is leading a sort of soundless, inert life in Stein's house. Stein has aged greatly of late. He feels it himself, and says often that he is "preparing to leave all this; preparing to leave . . ." while he waves his hand sadly at his butterflies.'[46]

What has happened, in the years since Tylor and Durkheim, is that the goal of explanation has been shifted. The target is no

longer an ambition to identify a point of origin from which all
subsequent variations can be explained as derivations; it has
become much more an attempt to map with increasing precision
the parameters, or boundaries, within which particular instances
of human behaviour are likely or probable or even predictably
certain to occur. The parameters of behaviour can ideally and
often actually be given precise mathematical or statistical formulation. But within those parameters, a wide range of individual
effect is still clearly possible:

> '. . . Bear my greetings to the senators
> And tell them that I will not come today—
> *Cannot* is false, and that I *dare* not, falser;
> I *will* not come today . . . . .
> The cause is in my will: I will not come.'[47]

No one presumably doubts that even the will of Caesar is constrained. Let us even say, for the moment (in order to avoid being
diverted as yet into arguments about free will), that his will is
wholly constrained; let us, in other words, agree with Caesar:

> 'What can be avoided
> Whose end is purposed by the mighty gods?'[48]

Even then, the means through which those constraints are brought
to bear which take him to the Senate (the dreams of Calpurnia,
the auguries, the persuasions of Brutus, Artemidorus, the sooth-
sayer—and these are only the most immediate) are innovatory in
the sequential construction of Caesar's action. Yet if that is so,
then it would be quite impossible, on behavioural grounds alone,
to exclude an effect within the individual of the reality (supposing
there is one) of the objects of his belief. The question then will be
where or whether those beliefs are grounded, and from what
resources they are derived. Protestants or Catholics in Derry are
living within parameters of behaviour, which can be mapped,
sociologically and psychologically, and which constrain the likeli-
hood of their actual behaviour. But this does not in itself provide
a comment on the reality of the objects of their belief, however
much the situation in Northern Ireland may suggest to some that
the claimed object of their belief (in this case, God) has no
specifiable reality *in effect*, or that as a concept the notion of God
seems to be divisive.

In saying this, no attempt is being made to establish 'Man' in the gaps of statistical evidence. The nineteenth century was no doubt mistaken in attempting to create a god of the gaps, a god in the gaps of mechanistic explanation; but it would be an equal mistake to attempt to create a man of the gaps—a 'manness' of man somewhere in the gaps of physical, chemical, and statistical explanation, as though this is the only feasible defence of distinctively human qualities. If the scope of behavioural explanation is misunderstood in this way, it then becomes simple for those who believe (quite rightly) that the gaps will be increasingly closed to argue—in tones quite as strident as those of certain anti-theists of the nineteenth century—that man is 'nothing but' the accumulation of physical, chemical, and statistical explanation, and that the idea of 'distinctively human qualities' is a *folie de grandeur*.

The attempt to locate man in the gaps of evidence is by no means overt, but it is pervasive at the present time. I am not in any sense attempting to do this. I believe we need to look very steadily and without apologetic agitation at the way in which as a whole the sequences of human lives are actually constructed, including what Lashley has called, and what is clearly fundamental, 'the implicit grammars of sequentiality'.[49] This certainly includes the observation that the individual may act within the statistical parameters of behaviour in a way which evades the explanation which those statistics offer, principally because effects externally derived may make an innovatory contribution to the sequences of human behaviour. This point is made very clearly by Kitzinger, in his recent analysis of voting patterns in the Commons over the issue of the Common Market entrance. The theme of his analysis is clear in the sub-heading of his article: 'In the crucial E.E.C. vote last year, one M.P. in five opposed his party's line. Rebellion of this sort is rare. What are the root causes?'[50] Kitzinger tried several correlation runs, and those which emerged are clearly of importance in mapping the parameters of likely behaviour in this case. But Kitzinger concluded with these words:

My own conclusion from these data is twofold. First, they explode various current myths. Second they put anecdotal material into perspective, reducing, on occasion, the alleged typical case to the only possible instance. Beyond that, statistical tabulations are no substitute for treating each M.P. as an individual, with his own problems: for, in the last resort, the rebels were the chaps who wanted to rebel, and had the guts for it—the chaps who, whether they wanted to rebel or not, had boxed themselves in by their earlier declarations. Actuarial tables or political science correlations are useful in their way; but only documents and interviews can give us the feel of how events really happened, and of what compound of heroism and villainy individual human beings are made.[51]

Words, as well as numbers, are still required to 'catch' the meaning of a man, and how a man arrives at a sense that there can be meaning for him: 'Perhaps', wrote Conrad, as an introduction to *Lord Jim*, 'my Jim is not a type of wide commonness. But I can safely assure my readers that he is not the product of coldly perverted thinking. He's not a figure of Northern mists either. One sunny morning in the commonplace surroundings of an Eastern roadstead, I saw his form pass by—appealing—significant—under a cloud—perfectly silent. Which is as it should be. It was for me, with all the sympathy of which I was capable, to seek fit words for his meaning. He was "one of us".'[52]

'Fit words for his meaning': this remains the elusive goal; but we are at least closer to it by refusing to accept the *a priori* assumption that there cannot ever be any reality in, or approximately referred to by, the objects of human belief:

> Could I catch my shadow
> If I knew where to run?
> Could I catch another one
> Statistical as I?
> His progeny of two point five
> His code, his papers through the door,
> His homeward thought at half past four:
> All this. But is his life alive
> To laugh as I do, and to sigh?
> To flare with feeling in the transient sun,
> To be the sum of all that I have done?
> Could I catch my shadow
> If I knew where to run?

The answer is that there now exist the techniques, in sociology and in psychology, to catch many shadows, and thus to explain how, comparably, human lives and human senses of the world are constructed. Is it possible by those same techniques to catch the shadow of God within those human constructions? And if so, can it be shown that the shadow is thrown by some reality in existence, or that it is nothing but a shadow, an illusion of reality which cannot ever be substantiated outside ourselves? These are the questions with which these lectures are concerned. We will begin with sociology, by asking whether a thoroughgoing sociological explanation of the origins of theistic belief is as possible as Durkheim believed.

II

SOCIOLOGY AND THE SOCIAL CONSTRUCTION OF REALITY

In the first chapter, brief reference was made to Durkheim, one of the men most instrumental in establishing sociology as a separate discipline in the nineteenth century. What seemed important to him was that if any serious understanding of the constraining power of social forces is to be established, it is essential to look at what actually happens in society. This was the great principle which made sociology possible: the social must be explained by the social, not by appeal to some external method, still less by appeal to the supernatural, or to the interpretations of the individuals concerned. The point is concentrated by Durkheim in his review of some essays of Labriola, *Essais sur la conception matérialiste de l'histoire*:

I believe that this idea—that social life must be explained, not by the notions of those who participate in it, but by more profound causes which are unperceived by consciousness—is fruitful; and I think also that these causes must be sought principally in the manner according to which the associated individuals are grouped. In this way—and in this way only—it seems to me, can history become a science, and sociology itself exist.[1]

Durkheim, therefore, rejected the Marxist explanation of conceptual phenomena (for example, of religious beliefs), that they reflect the obtaining relations of production,[2] and concluded: 'Not only is the Marxist hypothesis unproven, it is actually contrary to the facts which appear to be established. Sociologists and historians tend more and more to agree in this common affirmation that all other manifestations of collective activity—law, morality, art, science, political forms, etc.—emerge through successive transformations. In the beginning all is religious.'[3]

Thus, not only is religion *not* 'a late starter' as Marx might have held, in the sense that religion is a distorted reflection of the social realities that already exist to be reflected, 'the heart of a heartless world',[4] but rather, religion is the aboriginal social phenomenon from which all others, including Marxist society, are derived. Religion is 'aboriginal' because it was religiously that individuals first recognized the power of social forces as a reality, a reality transcending their individuality and constraining them as individuals. This recognition of super-individual, super-natural reality they made objective: that is to say, they made an object to represent these forces, those very evident powers. They set up, in other words, a totem; and this is why Durkheim went to the 'aborigines' in Australia, because it was being claimed that they had preserved the earliest forms of totemism.

The social, therefore, must be explained by the social. If this is taken as the proper point of departure, it follows that if there is to be a sociological explanation of theistic phenomena (for example, of the many different guises under which belief in God has manifested itself throughout the world), it would be necessary to identify the social facts which are idiosyncratic to the situations in which those differences occur. If any other factors are brought in (the feelings of the individuals who participate, for example, or the reality in effect of the object of belief, as, for example, a reciprocally affecting presence of the actual totem, as an object, in itself), then a thorough-going sociological explanation, in a Durkheimian sense, has failed; it has failed because more factors than the social alone would have contributed to the construction of further social reality. Thus, a contrary argument would be that even if Durkheim's suggestion about the origin of totemism were accepted (that the totem is 'objectified' society), it would still be possible for an individual to contemplate the totem as an object and for its affecting presence to become entirely independent of its original social constitution: it is possible for a whole range of other feelings, other responses, other ambitions, other hopes, to be evoked by the object. It was this which enabled Clive Bell to invert the (in his time) popular assumption that art is an expression of emotion, and to suggest that if in fact emotional responses occur, then the task of aesthetics must be to locate what he called 'significant form' within the object itself.[5] That there are problems in this theory will be obvious—even Bell himself came to regard it, forty years later, as impetuous.[6] But it nevertheless drew attention to the fact that there is not a single significance in an object, but a very wide range of affective consequences, which may have little or nothing to do with the intention for which the object was first designed or produced. It was this which led Armstrong, more recently, in *The Affecting Presence*, to explore precisely this relation between anthropology and artistic expression.[7] It follows that if a thoroughgoing, Durkheimian explanation is to be achieved, it can indeed accept the affecting presence of objects on individuals, but it would have to discount any feedback from those affects into the subsequent construction of social reality.

This may seem an over-stringent interpretation of the dictum 'the social must be explained by the social', but it is, nevertheless, indispensable for sociology that this dictum be tested to the very furthest limit of its applicability. Only then can one know whether or not any other component factors help to constitute the social.

The exploration of whether such a Durkheimian explanation of the human senses of God is possible can be focused on two examples: the first is G. E. Swanson, the second is Berger. Swanson is an inevitable example, because he is one of the very few sociologists who have actually tried to give a specifically Durkheimian explanation of 'the origin of primitive beliefs'. That phrase is in fact the sub-title of his book, *The Birth of the Gods*. Swanson was well aware that very few of his colleagues were doing much more than describe religious phenomena:

It is true that one could fill a sizable library with the studies which describe religious beliefs and organizations, or which comment on them. By contrast, it would take but a single shelf to hold all the books which, from the view of natural science, contain distinctive explanations of religion's nature and origins. On that shelf would be a monograph by Emile Durkheim entitled *The Elementary Forms of the Religious Life*. . . . Its point of view is part of the foundation on which I have built.[8]

Swanson, therefore, was deliberately and self-consciously setting out to establish a full sociological explanation of the human senses of God, based on the principle that only the social will explain the social. If, therefore, there is to be a sociological explanation of the origin of the sense of God, it must achieve two things: first, it must identify the social realities which have brought the diverse senses of God into being; second, it must then argue that 'the world of the gods' is constituted by those social realities in such a way that it reflects the obtaining social structures and, in reverse, confirms and strengthens them. In other words, the 'world of the gods' must be something like the mirror of the Queen in *Snow White*: it must not only reflect what is there; it must also confirm and reinforce the image.

These two points are exactly what Swanson attempted to establish, on strict Durkheimian lines: a super-natural world is constituted, because men experience in the natural (i.e. immediate) world of society controls and emotional forces which are independent of their own individuality. As individuals, they are immersed in these social controls and forces, which are so real as to be 'objective'.[9] This means that they are able to be 'objectified' as belonging to a super-natural order of reality. In his own words: 'The argument to be outlined here states that people experience "supernatural" properties in social life not merely because men are unwittingly controlled by social norms which they learn, but because social relationships inherently possess the characteristics we identify as supernatural.'[10]

This means that there is, or has been, a supernatural world, only because in the natural world the experience of living in society discloses to men forces and constraints which seem so real that they have to be given an existence. But since those experiences of the social have no ground except in society (they are constituted by the experience of being social), any putative independent existence of those forces has to be projected into another non-natural, or super-natural, world. Is it possible to identify the actual social realities in which different kinds of control and emotional force are experienced and which thus form the basis for constituting a mirror-image (a correspondent super-natural order), in which those controls and forces are made into existent objects, into spirits or gods or even impersonal *mana*?

So far as the sense of God is concerned, Swanson suggested (as indeed he had to suggest) that the different characterizations of the world of the gods reflect different constitutional structures in actual societies. More specifically, he argued that belief in a high god, especially monotheistic belief, will always be found to occur in societies which have three or more hierarchies of sovereign groups. By hierarchies Swanson meant, roughly, three or more 'layers' of authority through which control is mediated, as, for example, Monarch, Parliament, and Local Authorities.[11]

Here is a clear, Durkheimian hypothesis, that the sense of God, and in this particular case the sense of a high, supreme God, is constituted by the experience of hierarchical authority in actual societies. The experience of control which transcends the individual's feelings or inclinations is so real that it is believed to have an objective reality in existence and is therefore constituted *as* objectively real in another world. If so, there is no need to bring in additional explanations for the origin of the sense of God: the sociological explanation is complete and adequate.

Does the hypothesis stand? Swanson took as a sample 50 societies which have been described anthropologically. In testing this hypothesis about the high god, 11 of the 50 societies had to be left out, because of the ambiguity of the evidence in their case about monotheism. Of the remaining 39, 19 have fewer than 3 sovereign groups in their social structure and, of those 19, 17 do not have monotheistic beliefs, according to Swanson's definition of monotheism.[12] Of the 20 societies which do have 3 or more sovereign groups, 17 possess a high god. As Swanson then put it, 'The probability of so great a difference occurring by chance is less than .0005.'[13] However, 5 societies fail to fit: 2 have less than 3 sovereign groups and yet have a monotheistic belief; 3 have the requisite groups but no monotheism. Of these 5, Swanson suggested that 2 do not conform to his prediction, 2 'may be due to misclassification',[14] 1 is difficult to appraise because 'many professional anthropologists doubt the validity of the available descriptions concerning the presence of a high god':[15] perhaps, therefore, it should belong to the 11 ambiguous cases. Does, then, this sociological explanation of the origin of the sense of God— that it originates in, and is directly constructed by, human experiences of the social, and by nothing else—stand? Is this sufficient to confirm the hypothesis, and to establish a complete sociological explanation of the sense of God? If so, Swanson has achieved his ambition to implement Durkheim's principle, that social phenomena must be explained within the social, not by appeal to extraneous sources of explanation.

If Swanson's argument is to be accepted, it depends on two things: first, that his definition of monotheism adequately contains and refers to those beliefs and practices which have in fact been associated with belief in one god, since otherwise his identification of monotheism in a particular society will simply mean that he has identified in that society *his* definition of monotheism, leaving other senses of what a high god might be to slip away unnoticed into the scrap-yard of ambiguous cases; and secondly, and even more seriously, the establishing of his hypothesis depends on the adequacy (and on the adequate handling) of the evidence on which he draws for his knowledge of the sample societies. On both these points, Swanson is fundamentally weak.

So far as the definition of monotheism is concerned, it is not even certain that his basic assumption is correct, that there has always (or almost always) been a radical separation between two environments, two worlds, the natural and the supernatural.[16] What seems far more likely, from the point of view of surviving anthropological evidence, is that the majority of men have lived in a single environment which has different modes and opportunities of existence. The world seems more usually to have been experienced as a whole, including the so-called 'world' of invisible forces and spirits. Some men have certainly found no difficulty in believing that such forces or spirits belong to a single environment, just as some men live on another island, or in another part of the forest, or on the other side of the hill, and yet occasionally make their presence felt. That some men consequently arrive at a clearly conceptualized supernatural world does not mean that such a concept is a necessary and invariable fact of consciousness, which a sociologist can assume in order to develop an exchange theory of the construction of religious or theistic concepts. Yet these and other limitations of definition are nothing like as serious as the problems of evidence, the second point on which Swanson is suspect.

Swanson was faced with the problem that anthropological evidence has been gathered by diverse people at diverse times, and with very different understandings of method and of what was worth recording. For example, a great deal of anthropological evidence, for periods before the disruption caused by contact with Western expansion, comes from such (to the twentieth-century mind) prejudiced people as missionaries: what is one to make of their evidence? Tylor had attempted to handle this problem by arguing that provided sufficient reports corroborate each other, it makes no difference what kind of person made each report, nor what his prejudices might have been. He therefore arrived at his principle, 'non quis, sed quid'.[17]

But what of the situation where a single report is uncorroborated, where the informant cannot be established as trustworthy, and where the report cannot be falsified or confirmed because the people and their situation have been disrupted and changed? That last possibility is obviously extremely frequent in the case of anthropological evidence. Frazer encountered this when he was attempting to collect all the known instances of fire-drill, and wrote to Annandale for evidence from Malay. Annandale replied:

I am sorry that I can give you no information regarding the fire-drill among the tribes of the Malay Peninsula. Even among the Semangs it is practically obsolete. As regards the reliability of Vaughan Stevens, we obtained evidence that certain of the specimens he sent home were forgeries and that he was frequently under the influence of morphia to such an extent that his observations were absolutely unreliable. Still, when he makes a statement such as you refer to, I would be inclined to believe him. He certainly had a knowledge and experience of the wild tribes of the Malay region which few or none have excelled, for he lived literally as one of themselves.[18]

Frazer, as was pointed out earlier, dissolved the problem by the higgledy-piggledy principle;[19] and it is not difficult to see in retrospect that the results in *The Golden Bough* were inadequate to establish the conclusions which Frazer attempted to draw.[20] Higgledy-piggledy merges, all too easily, into hocus-pocus.

In this respect, Swanson is closer to Frazer than to Tylor, but Swanson made the acceptance of evidence without reference to its source, context, or reliability sound more respectable by referring it to Zelditch:[21]

On another matter, we have adopted the decision of Zelditch.
'... It was taken as a policy decision of some importance, for this paper, that all ethnographic reports would be accepted as accurate. This is not 'epistemological realism', it is merely that to question one is to question all. It is for this reason, in fact, that a crude analysis depending for its significance primarily on replication was made at all.'[22]

This unqualified and undiscussed decision is in fact fatal to Swanson's argument, principally because he violated it himself, in explaining exceptions to his hypothesis. There is, for example, one particular people, the Yaghan, who have few sovereign groups, but who *do*, apparently, have belief in a high god:

While we cannot eliminate the possibility that the Yaghan provide a case for which our prediction does not hold, it is worth noting that our information about them comes primarily from Martin Gusinde, a follower of Father Schmidt, whose theory would lead one to expect mono-theism among this simple, isolated people. As in any research, one would have more confidence in Gusinde's report if it were given in-dependent and impartial corroboration.[23]

So much for Swanson's 'policy decision': for, what now could possibly count as 'independent and impartial corroboration'? What about the presuppositions or prejudices which affected the anthropologists on whom Swanson in fact relied for other soci-eties? It would be very hard to maintain that theoretical con-siderations did not influence Margaret Mead (in 1938), Ruth Benedict, Max Weber (on the Israelites), or Geoffrey Gorer (again, in 1938), all of whom were used by Swanson as source-material. One of the hard lessons which anthropologists have had to learn is that much of their evidence (perhaps strictly *all* their evidence, once field-observations have been committed to writing) is *historical* evidence, and must be approached with all the caution and expertise which that implies. This is particularly true where the peoples observed have disappeared or have been disrupted, since in that case the observations are unrepeatable. But unless the evidence can be rigorously established, a complete sociological explanation, in Durkheim's sense, remains out of reach, because the possibility cannot be excluded that the sense of God is consti-tuted by experiences of realities other than, or in addition to, the social.

The argument here is not that in principle the sociological explanation might be established but in practice cannot be because of the state of the evidence. That, in any case, certainly seems to be so. The more important argument is that, because the evidence even as it stands is ambiguous and contradictory of the hypothesis, it is extremely likely that the correct interpretation of the evidence is that there are resources of meaning in the construction of human senses of reality in addition to the social as such. This does not in the least invalidate Swanson's correlations between particular conceptualizations and particular social, constitutional realities. What it does suggest is that what Swanson is analysing is not the *origin* of the sense of God, but the ways in which some senses of God, which may well be derived initially from *other* resources of meaning, are expressed or clothed imaginatively. Once a 'signifi-cant form' is discerned in, for example, the process of time or of

ageing, or in the regularity of seasons, or in the incidental occurrences of sickness, or of famine, or of earthquake, the possibility
of God may be suggested; and it may be suggested, not in intellectual terms, but in what Emerson referred to, in making this
identical point, as 'the awe and wonder of men'.[24] This is not in
the least to suggest that men have necessarily labelled such experiences correctly when they have labelled them as 'theistic'.
But if one is attempting to understand how men arrive at the
sense of a reality or realities which they refer to as God or gods,
then the suggestiveness of these and other experiences can only
be ruled out *provided* the sociological evidence is absolute and
unambiguous. At the moment, it clearly is not. This means that in
any of these cases which are, or have been, suggestive of God, the
existing social realities then function in a quite secondary way:
they become a resource from which ideas and concepts can be
drawn with which to clothe imaginatively the supposed reality
which is *already* working its effect. In that case, Swanson's correlations will frequently, but not invariably, obtain, which is exactly
what his evidence suggests. They will not invariably obtain because, although most social groups may well imagine that the
world of invisible reality resembles their own, some social groups
may feel that it has quite other characteristics, as, for example,
characteristics of the world of animals.

The fact that Swanson's evidence does not establish exact or
invariable correlations suggests that the inversion of his argument
is in fact the more likely—that the experience of social reality is
not the only or invariable resource from which the sense of
'another world' is constituted, but that there are other resources
which have seemed to suggest to men that there are realities which
touch their lives, and which in some instances can appropriately
be referred to as God. What Swanson has in fact analysed is the
way in which the apparently factual nature of 'another world' is
imaginatively constructed and is made plausible by being made
sufficiently recognizable. A world of the gods, to be plausible,
must have at least some features which men can imaginatively
identify. Jerusalem on high may have streets of gold, but they
are at least streets; God may have a voice like thunder, but he
has at least a voice. As an analysis of plausibility, of how beliefs
can seem convincing, Swanson's work is at once important, because if there are any correlations at all between a particular

example of social realities and the theistic beliefs which obtain in that society then this suggests that one of the supports of plausibility in the case of theistic belief lies in the extent to which the world of the gods can be imaginatively envisaged as corresponding to the present order, though no doubt, in the hopes of men, an improvement upon it. What cannot be established, unless the correlations are absolute, is the argument that social realities are *absolutely* sufficient, without reference to any other resource of experience, to constitute (to bring into being) the entire sense of God as such.

This does not mean that sociology cannot 'explain' at all how people arrive at a sense of God. On the contrary, sociology can explain very powerfully exactly how virtually everyone who maintains belief in God arrived at his own particular belief. He arrives, putting it far too crudely for the moment, because he is constrained into the particulars of his conceptual and actual behaviour by the social and cultural context in which he was born and in which he lives. There is plenty of room for individual variety within those parameters, or boundaries, of behaviour, but the possibilities of *all* behaviour depends on what is made available in the process of social and cultural transmission. No one, to take an example, could be a Christian before Christ was born (except in the rather tortuous sense of Hebrews and the Fourth Gospel). The possibility was not socially available. After A.D. 30 it becomes a possibility of conceptual behaviour, and in some contexts the constraint towards belief becomes much higher than in others: it is more likely in Rome than in Rangoon, more likely in Rome in 1572 than in 1972. It is part of the task of sociology to identify these constraints and to map the boundaries of the behaviour which is likely to occur in the identified contexts of constraint.

This is what made Berger suggest that sociology poses a greater threat to any 'absolute truth-claims' in religion than perhaps any other discipline, because it can always specify the cultural relativity of any particular belief. It was on this basis that Berger wrote (in *The Social Reality of Religion*, first published as *The Sacred Canopy*) his rigorously sociological account of how human beings arrive at a sense of God. Yet Berger also came to recognize that even the strictest sociological account could not exclude the possibility that the sense of God is constituted in part from resources outside the strictly social. It is this which makes Berger so important an example in relation to Swanson, because although Berger shares with Swanson a rigidly orthodox sociological intention, he felt compelled to change his mind, in his understanding of the social construction of religious reality, when he came to write his slightly later book, *A Rumour of Angels*. The point which compelled this change of mind is exactly the point which has emerged in the discussion of Swanson, the question of whether there are resources of meaning in addition to the social which contribute to the human senses of God. What exactly is involved in this 'change of mind', and what are its consequences for understanding those senses of God?

If we look first at the earlier book, we can see, from the opening pages, that there is no doubt about Berger's sociological 'orthodoxy':

Man is a product of society. Every individual biography is an episode within the history of society, which both precedes and survives it. Society was there before the individual was born and it will be there after he has died. What is more, it is within society, and as a result of social processes, that the individual becomes a person, that he attains and holds onto an identity, and that he carries out the various projects which constitute his life. Man cannot exist apart from society.[25]

But Berger also tried to defend the creative possibilities of men as they appropriate whatever is socially and culturally available to them, so that men can become prior to *some* social realities by directing them and giving them shape. The sentences which come just before the passage quoted above are these:

Society is a dialectic phenomenon in that it is a human product, and nothing but a human product, that yet continuously acts back upon its producer. Society is a product of man. It has no other being except that which is bestowed upon it by human activity and consciousness. There can be no social reality apart from man. Yet it may also be stated that man is a product of society. . . .

The rest of that opening chapter continues to balance these two elements, the priority of social forms and the value of individual appropriations of whatever is socially available:

The two statements, that society is the product of man and that man is the product of society, are not contradictory. Rather they reflect the inherently dialectic character of the societal phenomenon. Only if this character is recognised will society be understood in terms that are adequate to its empirical reality.[26]

But here Berger is locked in a fundamental dilemma, the dilemma of individual meaning which was already apparent in the nineteenth century and which was surveyed briefly in the opening chapter: on the one hand, individual behaviour must be able to be explained by the laws which operate through history in the forming of societies; on the other hand, it seemed important to be able to say that individual actions transcend those laws, since otherwise it would be difficult to attribute worth or merit to moral effort or altruistic behaviour. There would be no point in even Samuel Smiles's self-help, if all is actually governed by invariable law.[27] There is a brilliant statement of this dilemma by Durkheim in the final paragraphs of *The Elementary Forms of the Religious Life*.[28] It hardly needs to be pointed out how fundamental this dilemma is in Marxism, as Plekhanov so rapidly and so clearly grasped, a point which is summarized in my book on *Problems of Suffering*.[29]

Berger is still locked in the same dilemma. On the one hand, as a true descendant of empirical sociology he must maintain that men are formed socially: 'It has by now become a social-scientific platitude to say that it is impossible to become or to be human, in any empirically recognizable form that goes beyond biological observations, except in society.'[30]

But on the other hand, he desperately wants to retain a high value-status for the internal appropriation of what is socially made available to particular individuals—a value which is somehow independent of the social realities which have made internalization possible, and which always precede it. How can the two be related? Absolutely nothing is gained by leaving the matter at this point and doing nothing more than producing that pervasive and mesmerizing word 'dialectic'—'the inherently dialectic character of the societal phenomenon', as Berger put it.

But if there *is* a 'dialectic partner' in relation to the social process of cultural transmission (the creativity with which human beings make use of the materials that are socially and culturally available to them) then perhaps that partner, that 'creativity', gains access to realities in existence which are independent of that cultural relativity which is undoubtedly the foundation of its gaining access to *anything*. Once again, the possibility cannot be excluded that men draw on resources of meaning which exist apart from the social. We are back, yet again, with Emerson's blue and silver world:[31] granted that the words through which Emerson and everyone else interpret their sense perceptions are culturally given, nevertheless the cues, the signals, which arrive from the apparently external world have a sufficient existence to act *as* cues (*as* signals), quite apart from the particular social contexts which enable men to label them appropriately.

In *The Social Reality of Religion*, Berger completely missed this point. He got diverted into sociological orthodoxy—which in itself is not surprising, since sociologists, like all others, have to earn their way in the world, and are thus deeply constrained by norms and conventions of expectation in the sociological community. Thus Berger, instead of exploring the possibility that there might be a sufficiency of reality in existence in the external universe for there to be a groundwork of perception on which interpretation can be constructed, suggested that the more important reality is the one which individuals confer on the external universe: individuals 'pour out meaning' into it, on the basis of the language and concepts which they have culturally acquired. Having internalized, or appropriated, what is culturally available, men can then externalize and construct different sorts of meaning. In his own single sentence: 'In the course of externalization men pour out meaning into reality.'[32] But this means that interpretation is always an inaccurate approximation towards understanding. It is this which led Berger to emphasize 'the precariousness of all humanly constructed worlds': 'The difficulty of keeping a world going expresses itself psychologically in the difficulty of keeping this world subjectively plausible.'[33] In other words, all men at all times construct universes of meaning which depend for their continuity on the extent to which they remain plausible (not *true*, but plausible); and plausibility depends, to a very great extent, on social and cultural support. This is why sociology, in Berger's view, pronounces the death sentence on absolute truth-claims, not only in religion but anywhere: *veritas requiescat in pace*. Religions, on this view, are particular constructions of possible meaning. In addition, religions (whole complexes of traditional belief and action) then become highly important as contexts of plausibility, whole areas in which individuals can be held and reassured that the universe—*their* universe—has meaning. It follows that internalization is necessary (it is, after all, what it means to be alive as a human being), but that its content is always possessed of a high degree of artificiality: it is not itself 'real' in the way that the 'outsideness' of the universe is accepted (but then immediately discounted) by Berger as real. It must always be an approximate account of 'reality', constantly threatened by its formulations being shown to be unreal and illusory; and yet nothing apart from itself can be known 'really' to be the case. The point was put by Berger in this way:

In other words, the marginal situations of human existence reveal the innate precariousness of all social worlds. Every socially defined reality remains threatened by lurking 'irrealities'. Every socially constructed nomos must face the constant possibility of its collapse into anomy. Seen in the perspective of society, every nomos is an area of meaning carved out of a vast mass of meaninglessness, a small clearing of lucidity in a formless, dark, always ominous jungle.[34]

This is a thoroughgoing Freudian view of projection—even the language is exactly reminiscent of the opening pages of *The Future of an Illusion*:[35] how can we face the unfaceable universe, unfaceable because *it* has no face, and certainly no personality, unless we choose to give it one? We can face it by 'pouring meaning' into it, even though the universe is strictly speaking 'a vast mass of meaninglessness'. On this basis, religion pours out (and thus makes culturally available) a particular quality of meaning, by attributing sacredness to the universe, or to aspects of it. In its theistic forms, religion also faces the universe in the other sense: it gives it a face or a personality, by making it the stage, or the garment, or the consequence, of God. This is exactly Berger's conclusion: 'Religion is the human enterprise by which a sacred cosmos is established. Put differently, religion is cosmization [i.e. a making meaningful of the world] in a sacred mode. By sacred is meant here a quality of mysterious and awesome power, other than man and yet related to him, which is believed to reside in certain objects of experience.'[36]

It follows from all this that God is an artefact. God is as much a part of what Berger calls 'cultural facticity' as the most primitive Stone Age axe. What men term 'culture' is, at any particular moment, 'shared facticity'.[37] It is the assemblage of shared creations, non-material as well as material. Men learn to share facticity by being born into a particular cultural situation. This means that God, as an artefact of this facticity, is an end-product of socialization, one stage further out than the thinking process itself, in the sense that 'God' is a building brick in the projected construction of meaningfulness. Any attempt on the part of demythologizers to bring God down from 'up there', where projection has put him, into here, into the thinking process, into the ground of our being, does not alter what is socially and humanly happening: it simply tightens up the scale of projection. In a way, it elides it. It simply establishes a much closer connection between the process of socialization and its symbolic consequences. It does not alter the fact that 'God' is a symbolic construct, whose 'reality' is constituted, both by the degree of meaning which that symbol enables us to pour out into the external world, and equally constituted by the extent to which as a meaning-enabling symbol he (i.e. the symbol as constructed) remains plausible: that is to say, the extent to which we are able to pour meaning into *it*.

This, then, is a clear statement of sociological orthodoxy. Berger does not specify, as Swanson attempted to specify, the social realities which (and which alone) demanded a construction of supernatural world; to that extent, he is not so strictly Durkheimian. But he *is* strictly sociological in arguing that belief in God is enabled and controlled by sociological conditions, conditions of context, transmission, and plausibility. In general terms it is hard to see how the truth of this could seriously be doubted—the truth that men construct their lives out of the materials available to them in the contexts of time and space in which they are set. And yet it is at exactly this point that Berger began to realize that something was radically wrong, and that his massively orthodox sociological account of how religious realities are constructed was insufficient. What now seemed wrong, and what were these doubts?

The point can best be taken up by emphasizing that in *The Social Reality of Religion*, Berger applied a general sociological theory of the way in which human senses of reality are constructed to the construction of religious reality.[38] We have seen that for Berger this construction depends on a dialectic relation between the social contexts in which individuals are born and live (and which make available to them the materials from which the construction of meaning is possible) and the individuals themselves who appropriate the socially and culturally available materials and internalize them. But we then saw that Berger implied another dialectic relation, between the whole human process, individual and social together, and what he referred to as externality, a somewhat abstract external universe, which men attempt to interpret. In the earlier book, Berger tended to stress the movement in one direction only: there is indeed reality 'out there', but as a sociologist his focus of interest must be on the means through which men learn to 'pour meaning *into* reality'[39]—the means, in other words, through which men construct their ever-moving, ever-threatened, ever-disintegrating[40] senses of what that 'out-thereness' is approximately like.

There is no need to deny the validity and importance of that particular 'dialectic relation', the interaction between the social and the individual by which alone an individual can enter into a heritage of knowledge, value, and belief, for this alone enables him to live as *homo sapiens*. But what needs to be more carefully considered is whether, within the constructions of what the externality, the 'out-thereness', may approximately be like, the features of that externality may themselves have a contribution to make. What Berger, in *The Social Reality of Religion*, found difficult to integrate was the possibility that, granted that men pour meaning into externality (that which surrounds them), externality (that which is externally the case) may perhaps pour meaning into them. This is the other 'dialectic relation' which Berger took for granted but did not adequately explore. But what is clearly the case is that if what Quine refers to as 'the externally observable cues' arising in the universe offer evidence for the construction of what may in reality be the case about itself, that 'evidence' is by no means simple to handle. If it were so, there would be no need for 'social constructions of reality'; men would already have come, where some of the Encyclopedists of the eighteenth century perhaps hoped to arrive, at a knowledge of all knowledge. If, to put it more seriously, the construction of reality could be built up simply by ostension, whether direct or deferred, and by procedures or steps derivative from self-evident truths, there would be virtually no work for philosophers, and probably even less for theologians, to do. It may be, for example, that sentences describing subjective appearances or beliefs must always in the end be 'parasitic upon the sense of sentences about the objective'.[41] But this simply emphasizes the extreme importance of reflecting on the way in which the intricate mosaic of cues arriving from the external universe does not constrain us into a single, one-for-one response, but enables, or is suggestive of, interpretations and semantic explorations of great (and no doubt frequently bizarre) diversity. We arrive, therefore, at statements which 'vary in the directness with which they are conditioned to non-verbal stimulation'.[42]

This does not mean that suddenly anything becomes nominally true, but rather that we need to reflect very carefully indeed on the way in which 'externality' offers criteria which are suggestive of particular constructions of reality or of particular universes of meaning,[43] and why, in some cases, the criteria no longer appear to justify the weight which has, in the past, been placed upon them—the crises of plausibility, for example, to which Berger referred. But what is obvious is that neither of those reflections is possible if the contribution of the externally observable cues is dissipated by an exclusive emphasis on the other dialectic relation, the process through which all knowledge and all belief is established and transmitted, as though the process is all. It was a glimmering of this point which made Berger change his mind when he came to write his later book, *A Rumour of Angels*.

In this book, Berger, quite rightly, did not move a single inch from what he took to be the norms of sociological procedure—the assumptions on which sociology proceeds:

One of the fundamental propositions of the sociology of knowledge is that the plausibility, in the sense of what people actually find credible, of views of reality depends upon the social support these receive. Put more simply, we obtain our notions about the world originally from other human beings, and these notions continue to be plausible to us in a very large measure because others continue to affirm them.[44]

Berger did in fact draw attention to exceptions. He immediately continued: 'There are some exceptions to this—notions that derive directly and instantaneously from our own sense experience—but even these can be integrated into meaningful views of reality only by virtue of social processes.'[45]

Yet the exception is important, if we are to take seriously the suggestion that the universe does as a matter of fact offer cues of understanding. This is in fact the line which Berger then developed. He accepted that sociology has tended to understand religion as 'a human product or projection'.[46] But now he glimpsed the possibility that this argument may have to be turned back on itself, if it turns out to be the case that some human projections (including religious projections) do as a matter of fact correspond to a reality external to the human projector, and are reinforced from that externality. Berger suggested an example from mathematics:

Put crudely, the mathematics that man projects out of his own consciousness somehow corresponds to a mathematical reality that is external to him, and which indeed his consciousness appears to reflect. How is this possible? It is possible, of course, because man himself is a part of the same over-all reality, so that there is a fundamental affinity between the structures of his consciousness and the structures of the empirical world. Projection and reflection are movements within the same encompassing reality. The same may be true of man's religious imagination.[47]

It so happens that mathematics was a disastrous example to choose, because the issue between a formalist and a platonist understanding of mathematics is by no means decided; this is an issue which will be taken up in more detail later on (see pp. 110f.). In this passage, Berger has simply assumed that the platonist position has prevailed. But leaving that particular issue on one side, let us accept, in order to follow his argument, the correspondence theory of meaning which Berger is here attempting to establish. This means that for one reckless moment Berger could even resurrect the notion of truth, when he asks the question of the cultural relativist: 'Once we know that all human affirmations are subject to scientifically graspable socio-historical processes, *which affirmations are true and which are false?*'[48]

Berger knows perfectly well that some affirmations which are empirically false may nevertheless be lived with as true: 'Human thought seeks to unify, to reconcile, to understand how one thing taken as truth relates to another so taken.'[49] But one can in fact establish a criterion of discrimination among affirmations, including religious affirmations, if one looks for degrees of correspondent coherence. Obviously one may prefer to value incoherence, as some modern forms of Californian Buddhism have done; real insight lies through, or beyond, the apparent order which men project: it lies in a quite different perspective. In one sense, this is very likely to be so, as much in the natural sciences as in religion. But that does not alter the possibility of the particular criterion of discrimination which examines the relation between the cues of understanding which arise in the universe, and the interpretation, whether of the religious or of the scientific imagination, which is built on them. Here, incoherence is of a different order from the incoherence valued in the context of Californian Buddhism. It is precisely this principle of correspondent coherence, between interpretation and that which gives rise to it, which Berger grasped hold of in his belief that the universe itself contains (or perhaps better transmits) 'signals of transcendence'.

I would suggest that theological thought seek out what might be called *signals of transcendence* within the empirically given human situation. And I would further suggest that there are *prototypical human gestures* that may constitute such signals. What does this mean? By signals of transcendence I mean phenomena that are to be found within the domain of our 'natural' reality but that appear to point beyond that reality . . . By prototypical gestures I mean certain reiterated acts and experiences that appear to express essential aspects of man's being, of the human animal as such. I do *not* mean what Jung called 'archetypes'—potent symbols buried deep in the unconscious mind that are common to all men. The phenomena I am discussing are not 'unconscious' and do not have to be excavated from the 'depths' of the mind; they belong to ordinary everyday awareness.[50]

The important word in that final sentence is the word 'ordinary'. What Berger is in effect attempting is an argument against too diminished an understanding of what is ordinary, or of what belongs to the capability of this particular architecture of atoms, this 'human being'.

There are, in fact, many different ways of resisting the diminishment which an acquiescence in ordinary, everyday reality imposes: one can break through that diminishment scientifically, as Frisch has recently suggested;[51] one can break through artistically, as Eliot glimpsed;[52] and one can break through religiously, as Berger is here suggesting; but in all these cases, criteria of coherence and incoherence can be applied. The question which Berger wants to keep alive is simply this: what are the capabilities of this particular organization and assembly of matter which makes us what we are? We know that we are capable of walking, eating, talking, drinking; we know that we are capable of experiencing feelings, which we label (culturally) as beauty, truth, love. Is it also possible that we are capable of God—capable of experiencing feelings and effects which we label theistically? If one approaches the human sense of God from this angle, then it follows obviously that the 'discovery' of God may be as possible as the discovery of penicillin, or of America, or of perspective, a point which Berger specifically made: historically and empirically God *has* been discovered.[53] Thus, taking the example of ancient Israel, Berger argued: 'It is possible, with all deliberation and full awareness of the immense cross-cultural range of human religion, to speak here of a *discovery of God.*'[54]

Berger went on to state that the God thus discovered was 'an unheard of novelty in the context of the religious world of the ancient Near East'. But this, to some extent, was to forget himself. Socialization occurs, not simply in individual histories but in the continuities of social groups as well. Thus a critical focus of the sociological and anthropological study of religion must always be the inner logic through which a sense of God develops in relation to its previous context; it is never wholly 'unheard of'; there is always enough precedent for disagreement to take place. But this does not alter the general point that even though it may have become a part of the sense of God to state that 'he discovers men, men do not discover him' (and this is a perfectly feasible thing to say, if we are to take seriously the possibility that the sense of God is suggested by particular cues of understanding in the universe), it is an equally fundamental part of the sense of God that men *do* discover him, men *do* discern 'the outskirts of his ways'—that borrowed phrase which caused Lightfoot so much trouble when he used it, with reference to Christ, at the end of his Bampton lectures in 1934,[55] but which now seems an inevitable phrase if the notion of faith is to be defended, and which is in fact explicit in the actual structure of that work so profoundly influential in the Christian tradition, the *Summa Theologiæ*.

Berger's argument is then developed along the line that particular characterizations of the nature of transcendent reality locate themselves historically in particular actions, or individuals, or sequences of occurrence. So, for example, Jesus characterized a meaning of redemption; or putting it in reverse, a characteristic meaning of redemption was worked in and through his life:

The discovery of Christ implies the discovery of the redeeming presence of God within the anguish of human experience . . . It follows that the community (or, more exactly, communities) in which Christ becomes manifest cannot be identified with any particular 'names' or traditions ... The presence of Christ will have to be determined not by a direct succession from a certain point in the past, but rather from such evidence as can be found in the empirical reality of communities whose actions can be called redemptive.[56]

But what is undoubtedly the case is that the possibilities of transcendent interpretation are differently characterized in different traditions. This means that theology must have as much an inductive, or as much an empirical, base as other forms of human inquiry. It must also be based on comparative study, since otherwise it destroys its own subject matter:

The traditions, all the traditions, must be confronted in search of whatever signals of transcendence may have been sedimented in them ... History provides us with the record of man's experience with himself and with reality. This record contains those experiences, in a variety of forms, that I have called signals of transcendence. The theological enterprise will have to be, first of all, a rigorously empirical analysis of these experiences, in terms of both a historical anthropology and a history of religion ... The theological enterprise will go beyond the empirical frame of reference at the point where it begins to speak of discoveries and to explicate what is deemed to have been discovered—that is, at the point where the transcendent intentions in human experience are treated as realities rather than as alleged realities.[57]

So we come round, in full circle, to the word 'reality'; and here, at last, we have an expression of the dialectic which actually does obtain, not the dialectic constructed from the Victorian dilemma (social process and individual appropriation) but the dialectic between the process through which a sense of anything arises, internal and external together, and that which gives rise to interpretation as such. But, if we are seriously going to look at all the resources of meaning from which human beings have constructed senses of transcendence, and in some cases senses of God, as opposed to saying that 'social process is all', then sociology is at once pointing beyond itself to anthropology for a more realistic estimate of the ways in which those senses arise and of the ways in which they become characterized in relation to the whole setting of cultural groups. This is not in any sense to diminish the importance of what sociology can achieve. The possibility, for example, that correlations will be established, as Swanson argued, between particular hierarchical structures and actual characterizations of the sense or notion of God remains highly likely. But even so, it could not be explanatory of the *origin* of the sense of God, as Swanson hoped. It could only be explanatory of the process whereby the characterizations of God are developed and extended in time. If sociology hopes to explain how a sense of God came into being, the furthest it can proceed is to the hypothesis that the degree of correlation between structure and concept is so great that in point of origin the latter must have been dependent on the former, and dependent to such an extent that the former must be regarded as the cause of the latter. But as Berger came to realize, this hypothesis is too restricted to be even remotely probable, and for one essential reason: structure is not a sole and exclusive cause of concept. In many instances, not least in the natural sciences, it represents a means through which concepts, which may have other resources of meaning than the social alone, become plausible and are continued from one generation to another.

To say that sociology points to anthropology for more adequate explanation is not to deny that sociology may claim to incorporate the whole context in which societies occur as indispensable in explaining the characteristics of any social group, nor is it to deny the difficulty of drawing a dividing line between sociology and social anthropology. The point is much more simple, that anthropologists are (or should be, in terms of their discipline) less likely to attempt single-minded explanations of complex phenomena, of the kind attempted by Swanson, while at the same time accepting all that sociologists establish about the processes of acculturation. It is, perhaps, easier for an anthropologist to recognize the coalescence in concepts of multivariate factors in any cultural situation. The range of resourcefulness in the process of conceptualization may in fact be very wide, and this, from an anthropological point of view, certainly seems to be the case in the characterization of God. It is this recognition of the resourcefulness of objects which suggests the importance of the phrase 'the affecting presence',[58] and the importance, also, of investigating the exact nature of those objects and of that 'presence'. But it is through anthropology that those issues must be approached.

III

ANTHROPOLOGY AND THE
EXPLANATION OF RELIGION

THE question we come to now is whether anthropology has any
light to throw on the possible origins of a sense of God or gods. If
the question is put in a cultural or descriptive context, the answer
is clearly yes: if we are looking at the ways in which cultural
groups variously characterize the sense of God, or the ways in
which those characterizations of God are conveyed in ritual or in
object or in sacral personification, or the ways in which the particular
characterizations of God contribute to the viability of the group
in question, then obviously anthropology has a great deal to
say, because it is precisely in the areas of sacral presence and of
structure and function (particularly as observable in surviving
cultural situations) that anthropology has been concentrating its
attention for some decades.

Even though 'structure and function' is now under strain, it is
worth bearing in mind the very considerable fruits which that
particular tree has borne. One of the consequences which unquestionably remains important for those reflecting on the sense of
God is that there is no such thing as the sense of God. There are
only senses of God, or senses of gods, whose characterizations can
be entirely contradictory of each other. This is a more important
point than it perhaps immediately sounds, since it implies that at
the present time an essentialist approach to the sense of God is
not the most fruitful way to proceed. By an essentialist approach
is meant the kind of approach governed by the consideration that
if there *is* a sense of God it must be a sense of *God*, and that consequently if there is a sense of God, there must be an essential
'core-meaning' of the term God, namely, 'what God is'; with the
further conclusion that no matter, therefore, how different approxi-
mating conceptualizations of God may be, they must essentially
have the same referent, namely, whatever in reality the words for
God refer to.

But does the word 'God' refer at all? Certainly no 'core-meaning' has yet been satisfactorily disentangled, from the multitudinous conflicts of God-language, which might help to identify the reference of that word. The inscrutability of reference, as Quine once observed, runs deep;[1] and it is possible that, despite the many credal affirmations which obtain in the world, we are here in the realm of unactualizable impossibilities, round square cupolas on Berkeley College. Quine's attack on Wyman's 'overpopulated universe' is certainly one way of destroying the essentialist argument.[2] Less drastic is Gastwirth's argument, though it comes to the same conclusion, the rejection of an essentialist argument.[3]

There is certainly no doubt that anthropological evidence supports that rejection, at least at the present time. The diversities in what is actually observed amount, in some instances, to radical incompatibilities in what is claimed to be the case. What is required, therefore, is a much more careful reflection on how such incompatibilities can arise, and in particular on how and why groups living in similar (in some cases virtually identical) environments have arrived at wholly different characterizations of God, and what differences those differences have made. Here, one can think of such relatively obvious examples as the Heiban and Otoro groups in the Nuba mountains, or the Apa Tanis, in contrast to the Daflas and Miris, in the Eastern Himalayas. These two particular examples are chosen because they are different sides of the same coin: the two Nuba groups are very close indeed ethnographically, and yet as Nadel put it, 'It is in the field of religion that the crucial "variations" occur',[4] whereas the Apa Tanis are very different, politically and economically, from their neighbours, yet the religious beliefs are very similar. von Fürer-Haimendorf commented: 'This similarity between the world-view of as stable a community as the Apa Tani tribe and the insecure and turbulent society of the Daflas must appear as a challenge to the theory that religion is basically a reflection of social situations and suggests the possibility that an ideology rooted in a specific cultural background can persist with little modification in societies of very different structure and character.'[5] This, in a sense, returns us to the dilemma of the sociologists, because the juxtaposition of those two examples raises yet again (albeit in a slightly different way) the question, first, of how much weight one must give to the *sui generis* contribution of the external cues, and now, also, of the experience generated by belief, to the construction of religious reality; and second, of what exactly the resources of experience are, once *generalizations* about the affecting presence of sacral objects or persons (or, for that matter, of hallucinogenic drugs) begin to be broken down by more detailed observation. Are they generated entirely within the social, as an experience *of* the social, as Durkheim and Swanson argued? Or are there resources of experiencing outside the social? *In detail*, one must begin to ask what differentiating effects occur as a result of the very different modes through which the possibility or the plausibility of a world of transcendent reality is affirmed.

What emerges is that no matter how much anthropology may contribute to the anti-essentialist argument, this does not in itself dissolve the problem of the reality of the objects of human attention, including the objects of belief—not simply the actual sacral objects which serve as *deliberate* cues of the transcendent or of the paranatural, but the possible realities in existence to which those beliefs approximate. Once again, it has to be emphasized that men may be mistaken in the ways in which they characterize what may in reality be the case, and may equally acquire the means with which eventually to specify their mistake. Men may characterize the earth as flat, but by failing to sail over the edge, and for other conceptual reasons, they come to characterize it as more approximately round. On the other hand, there is a controlling and contributing reality in existence to which those developing characterizations endeavour to refer. There is nothing in the current stance of anthropological research, despite the enormous light it throws on the effects of cultural relativity, to rule out an analogous possibility in the characterizations of the senses of God.

If, therefore, one asks an anthropologist how a sense of God originates in human consciousness he can answer very graphically and very illuminatingly in terms of acculturation, in terms of how cultural groups make available diverse senses of God or of gods, or in terms of what particular senses of God mean in the life of such a group or of the individuals who belong to it. But this is not actually scrutiny of reference at all, a question which much anthropological research avoids, and frequently even evades, as not belonging to its subject matter.[6] Yet anthropological evidence, by careful description of what actually obtains in the varied senses of God, might well throw light on the question of reference, particularly if it could specify the conditions which bring, or brought, those senses of God into being. Certainly anthropologists can tell us a great deal about how and why senses of God are at times stable and at other times on the move. But can they help to illuminate the question of *what* is on the move? Is it possible to press the anthropologist further and ask him whether he can throw light on the origins of the sense of God in the more obvious meaning of that phrase, whether anthropological evidence throws light on the origin of the sense of God in the early history of human consciousness and development?

It is certainly possible to ask. But it is extremely unlikely that any answer will be received. Indeed, an anthropologist so asked will probably fuse with indignation at the improper *naïveté* of the question. His main reason for indignation is clear and legitimate: virtually no evidence has survived which could possibly throw light on that question; and even the early evidence which has survived, of burial, of cave art, of first human settlements, of fire, carries no unequivocal indication of associated concept or ritual. Hence, if we are *really* talking about origins, everything must be entirely speculative. He might also, of course, have doubts about the wisdom of reiterating the attempts of nineteenth-century anthropologists to make the identification of origins one of their principal ambitions, and to regard the principle, 'one event is the father of another' as a sufficient definition of the notion of causality.[7]

Tylor at least wore his heart on his sleeve in this respect: 'Happily, it is not needful to add here yet another to the list of dissertations on supernatural intervention and natural causation, on liberty, predestination, and accountability. We may hasten to escape from the regions of transcendental philosophy and theology, to start on a more hopeful journey over more practicable ground.'[8]

We may indeed hasten to escape, but in fact we cannot, because we now know that the notion of causality is nothing like so simple as Tylor was able to assume, and that the sense of 'definite law' in cultural change is not yet so well established that we can argue back from survivals to original forms. A contemporary anthropologist might well, therefore, doubt the wisdom of regarding a Tylorean programme, of tracing cause-and-effect sequences, from origin to present-day developments, as a proper task for anthropology. But his more specific doubt, about the wisdom of even asking questions about the origin of the sense of God, lies in the fact that no evidence has survived which could possibly contribute to a credible answer. Any speculation, therefore, about origins would indeed be speculation, usually reinforced by the words 'sheer' or 'mere'. Here, for example, is R. G. Lienhardt's expression of this rejection, the opening of an essay he contributed to a volume edited by H. L. Shapiro, *Man, Culture, and Society:*

Less than a hundred years ago, scholars discussed with interest such questions as how men could have come to conceive of Gods, whether there might be tribes so primitive as to have no religion, and how far the faiths and superstitions of savages could properly be related to the great universal religions. No one who studies tribal religions today is interested in trying to answer such questions, nor even thinks that satisfying answers to them could be found. There is no evidence for any theory of an origin of religion in time or place; and most anthropologists have ceased to take their bearings in the study of religion from any religion practised in their own society.[9]

In view of the peculiar history of anthropology in the last 100 years, one can well understand the reasons why this refusal has to be so emphatic. Yet it may be that this sensitive legacy from the modern origins of anthropology has made anthropologists *too* sensitive and their rejection of reflection on origins too emphatic. Consider this expression of the same rejection, by William Goode, in *Religion Among the Primitives:*

First of all, it [his book] is not a new attempt to probe the 'origins' of religion. Whether the beginnings of religion arise from the ultimate revelations of some Divine Being, or from an apocalyptic experience, will not be considered relevant . . . Inevitably and forever, we are barred from obtaining the needed data for non-literate tribes which have disappeared. Even when we can make intelligent guesses about these matters, we are not even close to a knowledge of a phenomenon which perhaps appeared with the very first men. To make a surmise about even the religion of a Neolithic tribe is to fall far short of an analysis of religion still earlier. And to speculate about how, under what conditions, man began to believe in divine beings nearly a million years ago must remain sheer speculation.[10]

Once again, the general point, about inadequate evidence, is not in question. What *can* be 'in question' is the force of the word 'intelligent' in the sentence: 'Even when we can make *intelligent* guesses about these matters . . .' No one doubts that they remain guesses; but what would constitute an intelligent as opposed to an unintelligent guess? It would certainly require some reference to whatever evidence has survived, set in the context of what is known in more general terms about the conditions of evolution and the emergence of that line of development which has led to the existence of the hand that writes this book and of the eye that reads it—the line which has led, in other words, to the emergence of *homo sapiens sapiens*. Almost any palaeontological reconstruction or interpretation is speculative, but that does not mean that no speculation is either rewarding or illuminating. No doubt much speculation is absurd. There has been no shortage of lunatic speculation on human origins in recent years; and frequently the state of the evidence makes almost *any* speculation possible. This point is well made by Jepsen, reviewing the reasons which have been advanced why dinosaurs have become extinct, a question on which almost everybody is prepared to offer an opinion.[11] But the general 'palaeoweltschmerz' to which he refers does not mean that no speculation is admissible, still less does it mean that speculation is without value, since it is in fact the only conceivable way in which one could reflect on the little evidence which *has* survived in order to reorganize one's understanding of its significance. It may be conceded that there are some differences between dinosaurs and God; for one thing, dinosaurs used to exist and now do not, whereas the sense of God once did not exist and now does. More seriously, in the case of the sense of God we are dealing, at least in part, with concepts, and concepts, in preliterate days, leave even less trace than dinosaurs. Nevertheless, it is possible that some speculation, in the restricted sense in which it is now being described, is necessary if we are to arrive at any seriously adequate understanding of the ways in which a sense of God occurs in those cultural situations which can be, or have been, observed. This is not a concealed argument for Tylor's 'survivals'. It is a suggestion that reflection on origins, however speculative, is an important way of reviewing the evidence which has survived, and particularly of reviewing current methods and interpretations. This means reflecting on the senses of God in the context of what seems, so far, to be established in the understanding of human origins and human evolution. Granted that we never arrive, even there, at final truths, we arrive at certain points of reference which themselves unlock the way to further understanding.

From this point of view, the anthropologist would have a great deal to contribute, as well as a great deal to learn, at the present time. His point of departure would have to be what he has established in his discipline beyond doubt, the universality, and yet at the same time the extreme diversity, of senses of God. If this is assimilated to what is now better known about the homeostatic and conservative nature of human life-ways, it becomes clear that one important way of reflecting on the human senses of God must be to explore their survival value in selective and adaptive terms. It is the complex fact of universality in combination with extreme and often very subtle diversity which suggests that, at least at some stage, human senses of God have had a high survival value. The crucial question then becomes, survival in relation to what? The hypothesis must at least be tested that an answer can be given in terms of anthropological 'orthodoxy', survival in evolutionary terms. From this point of view, evaluations of the sense of God should be set initially in the context of the necessity for living organisms to continue their lives long enough for the reproduction of themselves, since otherwise that particular evolutionary sequence ends in extinction.

The acquisition of language and the emergence of culture as an adaptive environment fundamentally transform the nature of continuity in the human case. The actual life-ways, the paths which men trace from birth to death, become vastly diverse, and it at once makes sense to talk of 'continuity' in terms far more extensive than simply the necessity to reproduce or disappear. Yet basically one is still talking about the capacity of an organism to recognize, and initiate responses to, the limitations which circumscribe the possible continuity of its existence. It is in this sense that one can talk of 'the homeostatic and conservative nature of human life-ways', and it is on this basis that one can analyse theistic beliefs from the point of view of the contributions they make to the continuity of human life-ways through, or in relation to, particular limitations. However true, therefore, it may be that it will never be possible, definitively and finally, to write the book of the genesis of God, any more than it will be possible ever finally to write the book of the genesis of man, both tasks can legitimately be explored.

What is thus being suggested is that this question, *as a question*, of the contribution of the sense of God to homeostatic and conservative life-ways must be asked, as, in fact, it *is* asked of virtually all other anthropological evidence. What, then, does this phrase 'homeostatic and conservative life-ways' mean?

'Homeostasis' is a term which has been much filled out in recent years in systems analysis, or in more general terms in cybernetics, and it now has quite a high mathematical component. In general terms, a homeostatic system is a system which is goal- or state-seeking; that is to say, it is a system which tends towards a goal or state and which frequently relies on positive or negative feedback to direct it (i.e. to converge its oscillations) towards that end. Examples of such a system would be a guided missile or a thermostat or a mechanical governor. One could put this a little more precisely by saying that if the feedback loop regulates the matrix of transition probabilities and controls future states of the system, and if the set of stable system states is limited, then the system will tend to oscillate around and converge upon successive stable states.

If that sounds somewhat complicated, then one can only say 'si exemplum requiris, circumspice': if you want an example, look around you, or—even better—look within you, because the human body was the stable state system which first evoked the term 'homeostatic'. The term was used by a physiologist, Cannon, in 1932, in order to extend a basic observation of Claude Bernard, that in mammals a constant composition of the blood is maintained in spite of changes in the surrounding environment; indeed if this did *not* happen, there would not be any mammals.[12] Bernard focused the importance of this in a very famous sentence: 'La fixité du milieu intérieur c'est la condition de la vie libre.'[13] What he meant initially by the 'internal environment' was the blood, but homeostatic analysis can be applied in a much more extensive way, as Cannon realized when writing *The Wisdom of the Body*.

Homeostasis turns out to be a fundamental principle around which we can begin to organize better our understanding of the way in which a living organism maintains, or endeavours to maintain, the continuity of its life, particularly in relation to those circumstances which threaten to limit or extinguish that continuity. Obviously, some limitations, like those of ageing or of death, cannot be resisted for ever, or at least, not as yet. It is necessary, therefore, to build into this homeostatic observation the realization that the stability of the organism is actually maintained not, usually, for short periods, but frequently for millennia; and that by the process of gradual adaptation the main features of living organisms are maintained and continued, despite changes in the environment: either that, or a line of adaptive response becomes extinct. Technically, of course, one could argue that adaptation is a second means through which whatever has gone before becomes extinct. Thus one can argue homeostatically that the system being maintained is not any particular life but ultimately life as such on this particular planet, and probably an ecologist would so want to argue.

It is at this point that one can see the force and meaning of the term 'conservative' in the suggestion made earlier about the reorganization of anthropological understandings of religion—'the homeostatic and conservative nature of human life-ways'. Once again, this is a way of pointing out the obvious, that unless an organism can maintain the prevailing circumstances (or can cope with any change in the circumstances) of its ecological niche (not absolutely but sufficiently for itself to reproduce itself), it will not reproduce itself and in that particular example will become extinct. If the ecological niche is disturbed, then the slight 'nudges' which occur in the transmission of the genetic code, or even the more drastic 'shoves' of mutation, may well be rewarded, and in this way 'natural' selection can occur. These points must obviously be linked to the current explorations of genetic diversity within the gene pool of many species, and of genetic variation within natural populations. The consequences for evolutionary theory could be extensive, since variation would not depend on disturbance alone (whether of environment or of mutation), but could occur within the continuity of environmental conditions, and could thus enable at least marginal exploration of other conditions. This would represent the opening up of a new environment, provided the changes involved are reflected genetically in the offspring of the 'selected' individual.[14] At the same time, it will remain the case that for the majority of the natural population continuity of environmental conditions is matched by continuity of adaptation even though increasing specialization to that environment may well continue —indeed, it probably will.

All this is to point out, if not the obvious at least the familiar: organic life-ways tend to adhere to the circumstances which have enabled their continuity up to that point. But there is an additional implication here, which comes out very clearly in the work of A. S. Romer—so clearly, in fact, that Hockett and Ascher proposed the formulation of a 'Romer's Rule':

The initial survival value of a favourable innovation is conservative, in that it renders possible the maintenance of a traditional way of life in the face of changed circumstances.[15]

If this is substantially correct—and to Dobzhansky it was *so* correct as to be virtually tautologous and scarcely worth stating as a rule, though he also doubted its generality[16]—then it suggests that whenever we find ourselves drifting into speaking about evolution as though organisms seek out new environments or new lifeways, we should reverse this and understand an adaptation as the reward in terms of survival offered to those genetic shifts or mutations which were in fact able to survive. Romer's basic example is the famous Devonian lung-fish, which represents the transition from aquatic to land life.[17]

In that particular example, it is clear that Romer has not yet become sufficiently rigorous in terms of the implicit principle derived from his ideas, because the 'newly-developed land limbs'[18] apparently *precede* the Devonian droughts; in which case the droughts cannot be a 'cause' of that adaptation, but a circumstance in which that adaptation is rewarded. What one must therefore argue is that adaptations towards the development of limbs had already been sufficiently rewarded for those adaptations to capitalize on the Devonian situation. It therefore seems clear that the more stable compound of limitation which would threaten the continuity of inshore aquatic life would be tidal and high wind conditions; and by 'stable' is meant more continuously present than drought. Those conditions would clearly deposit some examples in pools which dried out, or even on dry land. Either the examples would be rewarded in terms of survival by having sufficient means to struggle back to water, in which case those 'means' could be genetically coded for the forms of subsequent generations, or they would become extinct. This indicates how salutary it can be, in reflecting on the evidence of evolution, to eliminate, even if only as a procedural device, any primary sense that organisms seek out new adventures and new environments, unless these are compelled (though that procedural device would clearly have to be modified to the extent that the observations above, about the genetic diversity in the gene pool of many species, is substantiated, and it is in any case an argument which will be further qualified below). Hockett and Ascher made a beautiful application of it in their speculations on the origins of man, by arguing that instead of seeing the proto-hominids as energetic pioneers who became dissatisfied with the trees and dropped down to explore the new environment of the savannah, it is more likely, in view of the homeostatic and conservative principles in combination, that they represent those who were the *least* energetic and the *least* able to continue themselves in the trees and who were in fact expelled by those who were stronger and better adapted for life in the trees. The human ancestors, in other words, were not even drop-outs, they were throw-outs.[19]

It is from this point on that the filling-out of the new ecological niche would represent a reward to those forms of adaptation in the primate line which made survival possible—particularly gait, stance, the release of what became hands, and co-operation in hunting. Without those degrees of adaptation, that particular ecological niche would have been filled with many other forms adapted to it, but not with proto-hominids. There were and are many other possibilities of life in the savannah, many other variations on the theme of survival, but the human line represents the rewards offered, not primarily to aggression but to co-operation, not primarily to territorial imperatives but to territorial exploration.

This necessarily is to over-simplify, but it does at least emphasize that the filling-out of an ecological niche, although it may well be a highly conservative exercise in which an existing life-way maintains its continuity with only gradual change as the genetic pool of the better adapted possibilities builds up and becomes numerically superior (or, if one prefers it, simply survives by having more opportunities to reproduce itself), the changes in adaptive response can be, but are not always, dramatic. It is the failure to give sufficient weight to distinctions in the degrees of change which actually obtain that makes the over-direct connections between animal and human behaviour implausible. But having got this far, and having accepted the homeostatic and conservative nature of evolving life-ways as primary and fundamental, we can now accept the legitimate sense in which one can also talk of purpose, and can thus qualify the statement above. It lies in the way in which living organisms *endeavour* to maintain the continuity of their own existence and in the extent to which they are able to initiate certain muscular actions in order to achieve that end.

Again, it must be emphasized that no 'occult principle' is being introduced here: one can, in fact, reverse even that statement along the lines of Romer's rule, in order to say that in the course of evolution those organisms in which even the most rudimentary initiatives had developed had better chances of surviving and reproducing themselves, and that they were rewarded in exactly that way, by surviving. Yet it is clear that we are now building into the picture a high survival value for co-ordinated activity directed towards the penetration (or, if one prefers to put it the other way round, the denial) of a particular compound of limitation which threatens the continuity of that example of organic life. Even the Devonian lung-fish, rewarded by survival because in some circumstances only those examples which could regain the water could remain available for genetic reproduction, must be understood, from this other point of view, to be exercising purposeful behaviour. There is a perfectly proper sense in which the lung-fish *endeavoured* to regain the water.

This may seem a limited sense of purpose, because one may want to say that, unless there was sufficient genetic coding and environmental learning, no organic survival of any sort is possible. Yet still, one has to insist that it is survival *with this component* of ability to recognize and to initiate action in defiance of particular compounds of limitation. It becomes important, therefore, not to rule out too energetically the exploration of environment, despite the earlier statement which seemed to suggest the contrary (p. 53). When we come to the emergence of men, to the emergence of the proto-hominids within the hominoids, thrown out of the trees, and either finding a means to continue their existence or else not continuing to exist, we arrive very rapidly at highly co-ordinated activities for which the development of language was clearly critical. What became possible was co-operation in a wide range of exploration into different environments, with an equally wide range of responses, increasingly constructed with an end in mind, with which to resist the limitations (the threats to the continuity of existence) in different environments. Those who like to draw lines of direct continuity between the past and the present are inclined to suggest that there is no distinction, beyond that of specialization, between the first Gravettian shelters and the first men on the moon: both are responses to the limitations which threaten the continuity of an existing life-way in circumstances in which existing life-support systems are absent. In the case of the early settlements, there were no caves, in the case of outer space, no oxygen—amongst much else. The 'nothing butterer' might therefore conclude that *Eagle*, the first lunar module to land on the moon, was nothing but an elaborate Gravettian shelter.

Granted the necessary truth that there is a continuous line of descent (since otherwise none of us would be here), the weakness of the 'nothing but' case lies in its inability to catch within its net the effect of man's extension of himself, through the building process which culture makes possible, on the possibilities of being human; and in particular his ability to scan the components of limitation which circumscribe a projected activity, or even the continuity of his life as such, and set up hypothetically, and often co-operatively, possible 'ways through'. It is perfectly legitimate to observe that 'there is a continuous line of improvement from the human-like ape with a stone chopper to the astronaut in orbit and the pianist delighting his listeners in a concert hall.'[20] Perhaps the word 'improvement' is unfortunate, since living on the moon is not necessarily an improvement on living in a cave, in all senses of the word 'improvement'. Nevertheless, some evaluation must be given to the transition from a situation in which an organism is adapted to its environment to a situation in which it is still *that*, but is also scanning its environment and adapting it to its own needs, in ways far more complex and far more extensive in effect than, for example, the use of a stick by an ape in order to retrieve a banana, although the base-line of muscular co-ordination towards an end may well be there. In the human case, there is a more extensive and more complexly co-operative scanning of the limitations which circumscribe particular activities or life itself. This co-operation is not simply within a group or hunting horde: it extends both across time and through time. It is, in the jargon, both synchronic and diachronic; and it is this perception of *time* which becomes fundamental in the human sense of God. What is thus needed is an evaluation of the effect of this transition on the orientation, the possibilities, the *self*-consciousness, of the organism in question, as it transcends the comparative base-line of instinctual behaviour.

What all this suggests is that the common link between the

human-like ape and the concert pianist lies, not in the hypothesis that the latter is instinctually (in terms, for example, of innate aggression) nothing but the former, only now he has to carry round a complicated accumulation of cultural luggage, but in the observation that the ape and the pianist have in common, both with each other and with all life in an evolutionary context, an ability to find a way through the compounds of limitation which threaten the continuity of their existence; either that, or they perish: 'For most species, evolution is a long, twisting road with only death at the end.'[21] Certainly; and no doubt for our species that will be the end of the road one day. But it makes a profound and radical difference in the life-ways which open up if the limitations can be scanned, discerned, conceptualized, and to some extent understood, and if the experience in seeking a way through is built up both traditionally and culturally (both diachronically and synchronically), as is the case with human beings. The real common factor is not any particular achievement, but the necessity of any organism to find a way through the limitations which threaten the continuity of its existence. In this way an organism extends its life. But when one talks of man's extension of life, reference is being made to achievements of perception and organization of such complexity that the difference is much more illuminatingly interpreted as a difference not simply of degree but of kind. Life-ways are opened up which are not remotely possible, even in analogous terms, to any other species. It may be that the high rewards of co-operation became so rapidly apparent to emergent consciousness that this explains why, for example, the cripple of Shanidar, so many millennia ago, was cared for, even though his injury in youth may have made him a liability in terms of defence or of hunting, and why he was buried with equal attention and care:

> There he stood by the cave entrance
> Naked, arm severed,
> Regarding the cave and our decision.
> Another mouth to feed, and food dangerous:
> Animals would leave him where he lay
> Without uses or defence.
> Yet we said, those years ago,
> For this man broken from use,
> Let there be occasion.
> For this man

Who cannot extend our territory,
Who cannot stun prey,
Who cannot heave fuel and defence,
Who cannot do other
Than watch our departing from the cave and our returning,
Let there be occasion.
When, just now, we came back,
Rich with survival,
A roof fall had caught him with no arm to resist it.
He died where we had given him
Occasion to continue.
Where we bury him
The ground will signify:
More than aggression, more than territory,
We belonged in this cave together,
And to him we gave occasion.[22]

Where is all this leading? It is leading—indeed, has already led us—to a highly important point. We now are in a position to see, ironically, how close the embryonic anthropologists and sociologists of the nineteenth century came to finding what they were looking for, regularities in social and cultural process which could be defined in terms of 'law'. They missed what they had in fact observed, no doubt for many reasons, but at least in part because they had an over-mechanistic understanding of law. They were still, not surprisingly, under the influence of Newton; and that particular frame of reference is by no means dead.[23] What they meant by law, principally, was the mechanism of change, the mechanism of cause and effect, the fact that ' "One event is always the son of another, and we must never forget the parentage" ', as Tylor summarized it.[24] Tylor was particularly specific:

None will deny that, as each man knows by the evidence of his own consciousness, definite and natural cause does, to a great extent, determine human action. Then keeping aside from considerations of extra-natural interference and causeless spontaneity, let us take this admitted existence of natural cause and effect as our standing-ground, and travel on it so far as it will bear us. It is on this same basis that physical science pursues, with ever-increasing success, its quest of laws of nature.[25]

It seems likely that Tylor regarded his work as complementing that of Darwin and Spencer, both of whom had attempted to establish explanations of change and development in different fields. Thus in a Preface to a later edition of *Primitive Culture*, Tylor observed:

It may have struck some readers as an omission, that in a work on civilization insisting so strenuously on a theory of development or evolution, mention should scarcely have been made of Mr. Darwin and Mr. Herbert Spencer, whose influence on the whole course of modern thought on such subjects should not be left without formal recognition. This absence of particular reference is accounted for by the present work, arranged on its own lines, coming scarcely into contact of detail with the previous works of these eminent philosophers.[26]

What Tylor clearly hoped to demonstrate was a complementary mechanism of change in the history of primitive cultures, a law as explanatory of the evolution of cultural species as natural selection had proved to be explanatory of the evolution of natural species. What Tylor, so close to Darwin, could not recognize was that even natural selection does not apply as a law in his Newtonian 'cause and effect' sense. It is not genuinely explanatory of particular incidents of change in that way. It is, rather, the context in which all detailed explanation of the emergence of species has to be set. Natural selection does not 'explain' the mechanism of cause which brought a hawk's bill to a form and structure sufficient to tear meat; nevertheless, it is the context in which that development took place, and without which it could not have occurred at all. As MacRae put it: 'A peculiarity of Darwinism, both in biology and in other fields, is that it explains too much. It is very hard to imagine a condition of things which could not be explained in terms of natural selection . . . Natural selection explains why things are as they are: it does not enable us, in general, to say how they will change and vary.'[27]

Nor, one must add, does it explain how in detail they *have* changed in the course of time. Natural selection is not so directly and immediately explanatory of every detail as it seemed when it was first advanced. Nevertheless, it is the absolutely indispensable context without which explanation of detail could not occur.

By looking for single great 'laws', comparable to the supposed laws governing the phenomenon of gravity, which would be explanatory of social phenomena, the nineteenth-century exponents of anthropology and sociology missed the fact that they had virtually identified a 'context of explanation' almost exactly comparable to 'natural selection', which, if it had been recognized, would have made explanation of detail much more possible. The regularity for which they were looking—the 'regular' feature always present as a factor in the forming of any social or cultural reality, just as 'natural selection' is the regularity always present as a factor in the forming of particular adaptations—is exactly what has so far been under discussion, the compound of limitation which circumscribes a projected life-way. This means, putting it in reverse, that social or cultural realities can always be analysed in terms of their relation to a particular compound of limitation, but that this alone is not adequate to explain the details of each case. It is, rather, the context in which more adequate explanation can occur, or at least be attempted.

It may be helpful, at this point, to take an example of what this might mean. A more detailed example will be given in the next chapter. But in order to give a preliminary illustration, we can take the example of these lectures. The possible words and combination of words which might have been spoken in these lectures is virtually infinite. What constrained these lectures into their audible and now manifest form? Why *these* words, rather than the many others which might have occurred? In order to answer that kind of question (which would be, in effect, to analyse these lectures as a cultural artefact), it would be necessary to specify the component elements of limitation which have exercised constraint. It would be necessary, that is, to analyse them in terms of their relation to the particular compound of limitations which applies in their case. Compounds of limitation are derived at three different levels, from limitations which are continuous, contextual, and contingent. These levels can be illustrated with reference to the example of these lectures. First, the lectures are constrained into their present form by general or humanly continuous limitations, for example, the structure and physiology of communication itself, in this case of speech; or the unforeseeability of the future, so that it is possible to comment on the work of Tylor, but not on the work of Tylor's great-great-great-great-grandson, who has not yet (supposing there could be one) been born. Second, they are constrained into their present form by contextual limitations, limitations which are not oecumenical or global, but which obtain in a particular or cultural context: not simply the physiology of speech, but speaking English, for example; or again, the development of conventions concerning lectures as a means of communication, including the convention, firmly built into the structure of timetables, that they will not last more than an hour. Third, they are constrained into their present form by contingent limitations, limitations which circumscribe far more specifically the projected endeavour to write these lectures: the terms, for example, of Wilde's bequest; or again, the actual form and content of these lectures is contingently constrained by the fact that they had to be written *de novo* between January and October, with two university terms intervening. They are contingently constrained also by the limits of the information-storage in a particular brain, on the basis of which the interpretations which flow into these lectures can be constructed.

If, therefore, we wish to arrive at as full an understanding as possible of any manifest cultural phenomenon, ranging from these lectures to council-houses, from sealing-wax to string, it is necessary to specify, as exactly as possible, the *whole* compound of limitation (not simply some aspects of contingent limitation, which is in effect—life being short—where most social and political analyses are focused) which has constrained the phenomenon into its particular observable form; and this involves an analysis, both of the limitations towards which it is directed (if these can in fact be specified), and of the limitations which have controlled and constrained the attainment of that direction.

A word that has now begun to recur frequently is the word 'constrained'. The use of it is to anticipate one of the crucial insights of information theory, that instead of looking at an item in isolation as a kind of inevitable fact and then looking, in Tylorean fashion, for immediate antecedents which might be explanatory of that fact, it is far more illuminating to look at the whole range or repertory of possible eventualities, and then to ask what has constrained this particular item into its actual expression. This is a somewhat crude over-simplification; a more detailed account of information theory will be given when we come to structural accounts of human behaviour. At the moment, the issue may perhaps become clearer if we take as an example the spinster status of Queen Elizabeth I—that is to say, the historical observation that Elizabeth did not marry.

If one isolates that item as a kind of 'given fact', the tendency is to assume that Elizabeth was faced by a straightforward either–

or: either she would get married or she would not. She did not, so one must look for antecedents which might have caused that fact. One would assume that she was wholly free to marry, but did not do so because . . . Because what? Because, for example, 'the execution of her own mother and the subsequent execution of Katherine Howard made such an impression upon her as a child that she was unable to bear the idea of marriage or of child-bearing'.[28] She began, therefore, to manifest symptoms of hysteria whenever marriage was imminent, and she thus remained unmarried, despite the many marriage schemes which occurred. This argument about Elizabeth's failure to marry has in fact actually been advanced, and it is on these general lines that it has seemed possible to *some* to psychoanalyse the characters of the past. But if we look at the same question from the point of view of the general theory which is now being proposed, we would first ask, what was the repertory of possible eventualities in Elizabeth's case, so far as we can discern them, and what were the limitations which set a boundary on those possibilities—the compound of limitation in her case which circumscribed the possibility of marriage. Instead of assuming that apparently obvious, but actually very misleading, either–or form of the question (Elizabeth was free either to marry, or to remain unmarried), what has to be explored is the actual range of possibilities open to her, and thus the limitations which perhaps meant that she was *not* free to marry. In that case the position might be, not that Elizabeth could have married but did not, but that she would have married, but could not. Of course, if few discernible limitations constrained her into the one outcome 'Elizabeth did not marry', then one may, more legitimately, suggest that psychological factors were themselves the major limiting factor. But if the constraints of the political situation were paramount (if, to put it crudely, she had no room to manœuvre),[29] then the appeal to psychology is less legitimate, because one can only infer psychoanalytic reasons provided one can be sure that sufficient options were open. If not, then the constraint into the actual eventuality might or might not have the suggested psychological component. It would be impossible to know, because the other limitations were themselves sufficiently constraining, and the eventuality might be *with*, but equally might be *against*, the grain of the psychological disposition in question. It is, therefore, far more illuminating to look at the repertory of possible outcomes if one wants to understand how an actual eventuality has been constrained into its particularity.

It is in this context that the principle of the compound of limitation becomes so important, because what it amounts to is the analysis of the constraining factors. As was stated briefly, with reference to the example of these lectures, the components of limitation are partly continuous, partly contextual, and partly contingent: continuous, in the sense that, for example, human activities cannot ignore what has come to be described as gravity (though they can certainly seek to find a way through that limitation for particular purposes); nor can human beings evade what came to be described as the first and second laws of thermodynamics; nor can they dissolve the virtual unknownness of the future (though once again many attempts have been made to penetrate even that limitation)—these are continuous limitations; contextual, in the sense that they belong to a particular social or temporal situation, the particular limitations, for example, of living in a desert, or of not having enough land available to build the kind of housing which is believed to be socially necessary; contingent, in the sense that particular limitations obtrude on the direction, or on the continuity, of immediate life-ways, ranging from letters from the bank manager saying that the overdraft must be repaid, to Germans and Italians entrenched on the Mareth line.

There are three important points about this principle of the compound of limitation: first, it is really nothing more than another way of stating the principle of natural selection, but it admits the adequate integration of a social and conscious component; second, it is no more genuinely explanatory than natural selection: it explains nothing about the details of any particular social reality, any more than natural selection in itself explains the hawk's bill or the sparrow's song; on the contrary, it supplies the context of explanation, the frame within which explanation can occur, and without which explanation is improbable; and third, it includes within itself an individual or, perhaps better, a psychoanalytic component, that the individual in any social context is seeking, and sometimes failing, to maintain the continuity of his own life-way, and that social realities and events conceived as responses to particular compounds of limitation are always interlocked with the limitations which individuals feel or inarticulately perceive (or frequently scarcely perceive consciously at all) to be circumscribing the maintenance or continuity of their own on-going function. Provided we keep a prior and very steady eye on the notion of limitation we will find that the interaction of the social and the individual becomes very much easier to handle than Berger, for example, found it, because the focal point of analytic reference lies outside a decision about the priority of the individual or the social in absolute, or abstracted, terms.

What can now be suggested is that those social and cultural realities, those beliefs, rituals, concepts, activities, which have subsequently seemed able to be defined as 'religious' (even though a universally acceptable definition of religion has never been achieved), those realities which have later seemed able to be defined separately as religious, should in fact be analysed in relation to the particular compounds of limitation which can be specified in their case. On this basis, the hypothesis would be that religious beliefs tend to cluster around particular compounds of limitation. It would seem that the focal limitations, which constitute 'religion' so that it seems eventually to be a separable phenomenon, are those of a particularly intransigent or opaque nature—such as, death itself, the unforeseeability of the future, the irretrievable nature of the past (so that one can do little to retrieve or undo what one has already done), the apparently random or fortuitous nature of some events, such as disease, or earthquake, or madness. These are specific limitations on the range of possibility in the construction of human life-ways. In the case of death, it is a limitation on the continuity of life itself, in present circumstances and in the present body. What seems to be the case is that religions as they have come to be, in manifest form, are consequences of projected 'ways through' the limitations which circumscribe human activity, and that these are focused at points of particular intransigence. This means that 'religion' need not (indeed should not) be regarded as always having been a separable phenomenon, open to uniform definition. What we now define (or attempt to define) as 'religious' represents the consequences of the ways in which men have scanned the limitations (*all* the limitations) which surround them. But whereas men have scanned some limitations with relatively direct success, and have moved from the wheel to the moon, other limitations seem, and perhaps are, impenetrable; and it is this which may have led to the increasing division between 'science' and 'religion'. Religions continue to wrestle with limitations which science has abandoned or left, for the moment, on one side: and if science did attempt to penetrate the limitation of, for example, death, it would not be in an existing religious way. Nevertheless, it is not difficult to imagine a situation in which consciousness scanned the many limitations circumscribing the continuity or the possibility of its projected actions, and did not particularly distinguish among them, but regarded them as pertaining to a single environment (that of which consciousness is conscious). The reason why some phenomena have subsequently seemed able to be defined separately as 'religious' appears to lie in the fact that some of the limitations against which men set themselves do not yield as easily as others. Faced with the problem of getting a mammoth up a hillside to a cave, one can penetrate the limitation of gravity by means of levers and pulleys, and one can eventually arrive at Archimedes realizing that if only he had a place to stand he could move the earth. But some limitations do not seem to yield in that way. What seems to be the case is that those activities which have subsequently enabled religions to be identified and roughly defined are the activities which are directed towards such limitations. This is not to deny (indeed, it is to emphasize) that the constructions of meaning and action, which result in religions, cover the whole of existence and of life. But they are themselves a consequence of the ability of consciousness to scan *all* limitations, and to recognize, eventually, that some are more intransigent, or less easy to penetrate, than others. Of these, death is an obvious example. It may, therefore, be helpful to look more closely at the example of death, in order to understand this principle of limitation more clearly, and its importance for the human senses of God.

IV

DEATH, BURIAL, AND CREMATION

IT has been suggested so far, in very general terms, that it may be possible to gain a better understanding of religions and of the sense of God, from an anthropological point of view, if religions are set in the context of the endeavours of men to find a way through the limitations which circumscribe their projected activities or which ultimately circumscribe their lives as such. The suggestion is, therefore, that the identification of the compound of limitation is the correct general context of explanation: it explains nothing in itself, but it makes explanation of detail more possible. The identification of the correct general context of explanation would be as important here as it was in the case of natural selection, because it would make it unnecessary to look for generality where it cannot in fact obtain: instead of looking for invariables (points in common) among the many variations of custom or belief, we are set free to value the variations as highly important in their variety. What this means may perhaps become clearer if we take the example of death, and of the religious ceremonies which surround it.

The basic anthropological observations are, first, of the universality of burial procedures (hardly surprising, because everybody dies) and, second, of the diversity of ceremonies, customs, and beliefs. How does one explain or interpret this diversity in universality? Is there a single frame or context of explanation which will unify the diversities of belief and custom? We have already seen that it is no longer possible to adopt a Tylor–Frazer selection of items out of context in order to discern a controlling law. Two main possibilities have seemed open since that time: one is the factor-analytic approach which establishes the correlations that actually obtain in the diverse customs and beliefs; the other is the structural-functional approach, which comes much closer, theoretically, to suggesting a single unifying frame of explanation.

Roughly speaking, a structural-functional explanation tries to unlock the interaction both ways between, on the one side, the function of beliefs and ceremonies for society and, on the other, the structures of ceremony and personnel which enable those functions and which in reverse are constituted by them. Obviously this is an over-simplification, and structural-functionalism has in any case been much criticized in recent years. Nevertheless, it offers one of the few unifying frames of explanation, and it does in fact 'explain' a great deal. How does a structural-functional approach work when applied to the universality of burials and the diversity of burial customs? What has to be specified in this explanation is the social function which all these diverse customs serve. What could this function be? The answer, according to David Mandelbaum, is 'social integration': this is argued in an article 'Social Uses of Funeral Rites' which is an almost perfect example of a structural-functional approach.

Its point of departure is Mandelbaum's opening sentence: 'Rites performed for the dead generally have important effects for the living.'[1] This is certainly not in dispute. But what has to be explained is 'the great variety of ways among the different cultures of the world'[2] in which funeral rites are accomplished. Mandelbaum concluded that the variations in custom are varied ways in which social integration is brought about.[3] But then there arises an almost insuperable problem: among some groups there is virtually no socially integrating effect to be discerned; and this becomes an even more acute problem when *other* group occasions of those particular groups *do* have a socially integrating effect. In other words, the groups in question are perfectly capable of participating in group or ritual occasions which integrate them as groups, but their funeral customs do not have this effect. Of this problem, Mandelbaum took two examples, in order to illustrate the extremes, the two American Indian tribes, the Cocopa and the Hopi. He wrote: 'The Cocopa and the Hopi respectively exemplify extremes of emphasis and of de-emphasis in the observance of funeral rites. Among the Cocopa, death ceremonies are the major events of tribal life; among the Hopi, they are brief and hurried affairs.'[4]

The essential problem, therefore, is that although other Hopi rites have a very pronounced function of social integration, their funeral rites do not. This dilemma Mandelbaum made clear in a further passage.[5] The question then arises: what purpose *do* Hopi funeral rites serve? The only possible answer is in fact the one which Mandelbaum himself stated: 'The sovereign desire is to dismiss the body and the event. The urge is to despatch the spirit to another realm.'[6] But it now becomes clear that other factors of explanation have been introduced, and that the functional explanation of social integration is incomplete. What then becomes equally obvious is that among the Cocopa, where social integration *is* one of the effects of funeral rites, the *same* desire, to despatch the spirit through death, is as much apparent as it is among the Hopi. *This*, in fact, is what they have in common, not 'social integration'. So far as the Cocopa are concerned, it is possible to quote Mandelbaum's exact words: 'The cremation ritual was directed mainly at inducing the spirit of the dead person to go on to the afterworld. To help persuade the spirit to depart, clothes, food, and equipment were destroyed so that the spirit could have these things in the hereafter.'[7] There is, in fact, a second and later Cocopa ceremony in which the dead are apparently impersonated and where the same idea is apparent.[8]

The conclusion is obvious, that a structural-functional approach cannot serve as a general context of explanation. It can only specify particular social functions which perhaps widely, but not invariably, obtain; and to that extent it is much closer to a factor-analytic approach than is sometimes realized. What is here being suggested in contrast is that the correct general context of explanation, which then sets us free to examine the variables as highly important *in their variation* (as opposed to extracting unity in functions which turn out not to be invariable), is the principle of the compound of limitation. What this involves is the attempt to specify the compound of limitation towards which particular actions, or beliefs, or rituals, or personnel, are directed. In this case, the limitation is death. In the general context of limitation and of the endeavours of men to find a way through, the distinctions between the Hopi and Cocopa, in the case of death, become immediately explicable in detail, in a way which they do not if 'social integration' has to be found as an invariable among the variations. The differences between them represent different projected 'ways through' the limitation of death, and the ceremonies represent supports of plausibility for those projected ways. They may also additionally represent much more; they may indeed have a highly integrating social function. But 'social function' is not, and cannot be, the sole or primary context or frame of explanation.

The fundamental mistake of social-functional explanations conceived as primary is that they take as axiomatic Raymond Firth's
argument that funerals benefit the living, not the dead; and Mandelbaum in fact quoted Firth's statement: '"A funeral rite",
Raymond Firth observes, "is a social rite *par excellence*. Its osten-
sible object is the dead person, but it benefits not the dead, but the
living." '9 But this is an over-rationalistic comment to the effect
that the dead clearly cannot be benefited, because in the twentieth
century we happen to know that nothing continues through death.
On the contrary, only if the benefit for the dead is adequate and
plausible (that is to say, if the relating of the dead person to the
universal limitation of death in a certain ceremony makes sense to
the living who attend) can the living *also* be benefited, in ways
which may include 'social integration' (but which do not necessarily have to do so) and which may also include other 'spin off'
advantages in addition.

The variety of burial customs, therefore, reflects the varied
ways in which men have sought to scan and penetrate the limitation of death, as they interpret cues from the universe which
suggest that a way through can in fact be found. A great variety
of cues has in fact been utilized. Burying a body gains suggestive
confirmation from the burying of a seed and the growth of a new
plant—as Paul appreciated;10 burning a body gains suggestive
confirmation from the observation that the burning of anything
releases something (visibly in smoke) into the air, and leaves only a
changed and much smaller part of whatever was there in the
ashes;11 floating a body out to sea, or committing it to a river,
gains confirmation from the observation that salt dissolves in water,
but, from the taste of the water, it is apparent that it has not
wholly disappeared.12 These are plausible responses to the limitation of death, suggesting that there is in fact a way through, with
enormous social and cultural consequences in all directions.13

But plausibility, as Berger emphasized, is almost always under
strain. Death is a limitation which circumscribes the continuity of
men's actions, even more than gravity or a hostile neighbour or the
necessity of finding food. Consciousness can set itself against those
limitations in ways which vastly transcend the possibilities of
instinctually accumulated response, not least because it can begin
to discern something of their nature by observing that different
actions have different effects in relation to them. There is no

reason in principle why, in a single environment (which is what makes Swanson's assumption of men having always had an idea of *two* environments so mistaken), the limitation of death would have to be regarded as wholly impenetrable. In fact on the contrary, the care and variation in burials, from at least as early as the Middle Palaeolithic period, suggest that men set themselves against this limitation, even though virtually no reconstruction of their actual beliefs is possible.

Yet clearly 'death' does not fall down, as a hostile neighbour falls down, simply because one throws a stone at it. In this sense the crisis of plausibility in the projected ways through death goes hand in hand with those projected ways: men have indeed set themselves to find a way through death, but can they be sure that a way exists to be found? Many *have* been sure; but not all; and the crisis of plausibility, in this area, is in no sense at all a modern discovery. To give an example, Gautama, the Buddha, was scoured by this crisis.[14] Or again, the attempt to be certain, and thus to resolve the crisis, was precisely the third wish of Naciketas which Yama, Death, tried to refuse to grant;[15] these are familiar examples in the Eastern tradition. In the Western tradition there are plenty of equally familiar examples, from almost any period and any writer. The point is that doubt is always possible as soon as any consciousness becomes conscious of the certainty of its own cessation in its present, visible form. No matter how strong the projected way through the limitation of death may be—'I know that my redeemer liveth' (perhaps the most important mistranslation ever made)—it is always possible to wonder. Obviously, at particular moments, doubts are focused and reinforced, and the crisis of implausibility may become particularly extensive and acute. This clearly happened in the nineteenth century in the West. One of the most familiar anecdotes in this connection is the story of George Eliot walking with Myers in the Fellows' Garden of Trinity College, Cambridge.[16] What may be less familiar is Robert Edgcumbe's recollection of George Eliot in that same May Week, in which Lady Margaret went head of the river, and in which Edgcumbe and his friend Arthur Hilton, as St. John's men, joined in the celebration:

Hilton and I shouted ourselves voiceless, and when we got back to Cambridge, flags, tablecloths, rugs, parti-coloured shirts, and anything that was conspicuous fluttered from window after window, wherever an undergraduate was housed . . . It was a great week, that boat race week at Cambridge, the most exciting one of my three Cambridge Mays. 'George Eliot' was present, and we undergraduates were interested to know what she thought of it all. When we learnt that the only observation she let fall was 'All human joys are transient', she somewhat fell in our estimation.[17]

But now that the flags, the rugs, the boat that went so bravely up the river, and even Edgcumbe himself, have disintegrated and disappeared, does not George Eliot rise again a little in our estimation, at least for being realistic? What *can* be built on the shifting sands of human mortality? The nineteenth century is saturated with attempts to handle this crisis, from the growth of spiritualism to attempts to capture the passing of time in realistic art. But at the end of the physical analysis of the human frame, what *plausibly* could be believed to endure? Something may endure in the memory of others; but this, as Marlow pointed out in *Lord Jim*, is a somewhat fragile endurance.[18] Something may endure a little longer in the works of one's hands or one's mind. This is certainly one of the answers of Shakespeare's sonnets:

> . . . When rocks impregnable are not so stout,
> Nor gates of steel so strong, but Time decays?
> O fearful meditation! where, alack,
> Shall Time's best jewel from Time's chest lie hid?
> Or what strong hand can hold his swift foot back?
> Or who his spoil of beauty can forbid?
>   O! none, unless this miracle have might,
> That in black ink my love may still shine bright.[19]

But if Shakespeare has answers, it suggests that he also has questions; and what is of importance is not simply that so much of Shakespeare's writing is riveted on the recognition of human transience, but that Shakespeare was just as able as George Eliot to remove the two scrolls of promise, God and Immortality.[20] This is not a commitment to what Shakespeare may or may not have believed in himself. It is simply to emphasize that no matter whose beliefs he is reflecting, doubt and proposal always go hand in hand: radical, fundamental doubt is not a modern invention, nor is it necessarily imposed on religious beliefs from the outside; it may and frequently does occur within a tradition as the plausibility of its proposed 'ways through' are tested: and this point is absolutely vital for any serious understanding of the human senses of God. This doubt about the plausibility of projected ways through death is possible at any time, even in so-called ages of faith. The sound and fury of the idiot's tale, signifying nothing,[21] long precede and anticipate Matthew Arnold's 'darkling plain . . ., where ignorant armies clash by night'.[22]

Why, then, continue to believe anything, particularly when, as Matthew Arnold believed, the traditional dogmatic foundations appear to be in the process of collapse? The answer is, just because doubt goes hand in hand with the proposal, so the proposal goes hand in hand with the doubt. There are in fact certain supports of plausibility, in the cues which arrive from the external universe, and in the process of internal reflection on them. The ways which religions project through the limitations which surround men are never wholly composed of wishful thinking—though, as we shall see, that may form a large part of them. But it is highly unlikely that religions would propose or project anything if all men were not haunted by the ghost of significant action. It is this which gives to the route-finding of religions their fundamental vitality, because they provide the means through which the significance of human actions and lives can be identified. Even in the radical doubt of Matthew Arnold or in the doubt expressed explicitly through Shakespeare's characters, and implicitly in his sonnets, the ghost of significant action is never far away. The importance of that ghost which haunts the lives of men will perhaps become clearer if we take those two examples, very briefly, a little further.

In the case of Matthew Arnold, so deep has doubt, the crisis of plausibility, gone, that it has affected the formal structure of many of his poems. The structure is a literary equivalent to the massive genre of allegorical paintings in which hints of life and hope are set, in the composition of the picture, between unmistakable symbols of the only substantial realities of which we can be sure, time and death. There is a poignant example in the painting by Georges de la Tour, *La Madeleine à la veilleuse*, in the Louvre. In the context of darkness a young girl sits gazing at the flame of an open lamp which is burning down its wick; on her knee, with her hand resting on it, is a skull; glimpsed, and only just glimpsed, between the two is the fact that the girl is pregnant: perhaps something will live on in one's descendants. It is obvious, even banal, in prose; it is incredibly powerful in paint; and for some it is powerful in life.

This device of setting, formally, a glimpse of hope between the symbols of reality, in this case of death, appears in picture after picture, though more frequently the transition has been made, as in Shakespeare's sonnets, from survival in one's descendants to a brief hint of survival in the creations of hand and mind; and birth becomes one of the frames of realism about the inevitability of human transience itself. In van Steenwijck's *Vanitas*, in Leiden, for example, the composition places on the right a basket of fruit and on the left a skull, set firmly on a sealed document. Edging in between the two, are a quill pen, a musical instrument, and two books, brief hints of creativity in the interval between birth and death; and what *is* the book on which the skull and the sealed document rest? Is it a Bible? Its size suggests it. Is this a hint of endurance even beyond the skull?

It is this formal placing of brief hints of hope between massive statements of realism and of doubt about the enduring worth-whileness of appearances which reappears in the formal structure of many of Matthew Arnold's poems, and it indicates how deep the crisis of plausibility had gone. 'Dover Beach' is in fact one of the clearest examples.[23]

> The sea is calm tonight.
> The tide is full, the moon lies fair
> Upon the straits; on the French coast the light
> Gleams and is gone; the cliffs of England stand,
> Glimmering and vast, out in the tranquil bay. 5
> Come to the window, sweet is the night-air!
> Only, from the long line of spray
> Where the sea meets the moon-blanched land,
> Listen! you hear the grating roar
> Of pebbles which the waves draw back, and fling, 10
> At their return, up the high strand,
> Begin, and cease, and then again begin,
> With tremulous cadence slow, and bring
> The eternal note of sadness in.
>
> Sophocles long ago 15
> Heard it on the Aegean, and it brought
> Into his mind the turbid ebb and flow
> Of human misery; we

Find also in the sound a thought,
Hearing it by this distant northern sea.   20
The Sea of Faith
Was once, too, at the full, and round earth's shore
Lay like the folds of a bright girdle furled.
But now I only hear
Its melancholy, long, withdrawing roar,   25
Retreating, to the breath
Of the night-wind, down the vast edges drear
And naked shingles of the world.

Ah, love, let us be true
To one another! for the world which seems   30
To lie before us like a land of dreams,
So various, so beautiful, so new,
Hath really neither joy, nor love, nor light,
Nor certitude, nor peace, nor help for pain;
And we are here as on a darkling plain   35
Swept with confused alarms of struggle and flight,
Where ignorant armies clash by night.

In the opening lines (to 'the night-air' in line 6) there is a perfect
statement of an apparently enduring fact, the beauty of nature on
a moonlit night. But these were the far too innocent grounds on
which some of Arnold's predecessors—and contemporaries—were
erecting a fallacy of hope: 'We feel', as Wordsworth had put it,
'that we are greater than we know'; therefore, we *are*, perhaps,
more enduring than a naturalistic knowledge can dissect. Perhaps
these feelings evoked by nature are themselves intimations of immortality, of transcending the *natural* order—'a hope, beyond a
shadow of a dream'.

But Arnold is clear that 'nature' intimates other things than
immortality. This is beautifully done in the continuing lines of
'Dover Beach': '. . . the eternal note of sadness' enters in. Nature,
more accurately, intimates nothing; or alternatively it intimates all
things. Nature, in fact, is neutral. There is no necessary quality
in nature, particularly after the work of Hume, since what men
see belongs to their way of seeing it; and even if Kant arrived at an
a priori category of critical judgement, he, least of all, allowed of
the possibility that beauty is a substance which 'exists' in nature.
'Nature'—a word of which Arnold was particularly suspicious—
does not lend itself to intimations of one thing more than another,

unless one chooses to look in a partial manner born of despair. Faith *and* despair are equal readings of the natural order. This is clear in the later part of the poem (15–28; 30–end). So at both ends of the poem, as in the two sides of the allegorical paintings, the statements of what is realistic are massive and steady. There *is* beauty, but this does not create an immortal substance; there is death, but this does not deny the experience of beauty. What, more than that, can be said? Almost nothing; yet Arnold, like the allegorical painters, edges into his poem a brief glimpse that all has *not* been said; all is not utterly futile: but this glimpse is compressed into a single line and a half:

> Ah, love, let us be true
> To one another!

Why? We are not told; it is a brief enigmatic glimpse, set between the realities of indifferent nature and transient life, that there *are* some significantly worth-while feelings and perhaps even actions. This structure recurs again and again in Arnold's poems. It is at its most subtle in *Empedocles on Etna*, but the constructions within the structure of that poem make it a complicated example. It is much more obvious in such poems as 'Youth and Calm' (in its separated form) and 'A Question', and it can even be seen at the end of both of Arnold's prize poems, at Rugby and at Oxford.[24]

In Matthew Arnold's case, the crisis of plausibility, about the way which traditionally (in his own culture) had been projected through the limitation of death, has penetrated so deeply that it has actually gone into the structure of composition. Why then is there a *crisis* of plausibility? Why not simply admit the fact of transience? Is it only because we cannot bear oblivion, as Freud was to suggest? Certainly this is a part of the answer, but only a part. What Freud overlooked, as we shall see, is that there cannot be a crisis of *im*plausibility unless the supports of plausibility are, or have been, very strong; and this is certainly true of projected ways through death. The beach at Dover may indeed be neutral, but it is neutral *to someone*, to a consciousness which makes out of its perceptions senses of beauty, senses of reality, senses of God. It is perceived, and the enigma of the construction of varied meaning and of feeling remains. Are these so-varied constructions of meaning and value which are made in the brief intervals between birth and death *so* equal, *so* random, that none has more significance than any other? Maybe. But the ghost of significance will continue to haunt the world so long as the varieties of discerned meaning and consequent action remain so vastly extensive in variety. Dover beach itself can illustrate this: the withdrawing roar of shingle meant one thing to Matthew Arnold; the 'surge of chafing pebbles' on that same Dover beach meant quite another for Gloucester in *King Lear*.[25] It is the composition of individual circumstance which constrains all the many possibilities of interpretation (all that the beach at Dover *might* mean) into a single meaning for one particular person: the single 'meaning' is not given in nature; its particular meanings are composed by circumstance. But that simply enhances their utter significance; if there *is* a single meaning in nature it is presumably what it means to a fish; in other words, virtually nothing. Are the meanings which men discern any more enduringly significant than that? For Gloucester, in *King Lear*, the beach at Dover resolves a life whose meaning has indeed been for him 'a darkling plain, Swept with confused alarms of struggle and flight'. It is in this scene, which follows immediately after the putting-out of his eyes, that Gloucester speaks the much-quoted lines which wrench out of mind the last illusion of hope:

> 'As flies to wanton boys, are we to the gods;
> They kill us for their sport.'   (iv.i.36f.)

Edgar, equally desperately, cries out when he first sees his father, Gloucester, stumbling blind:

> 'World, world, O world!
> But that thy strange mutations make us hate thee,
> Life would yield to age.'   (iv.i.10ff.)

Yet it is Edgar who brings his father to what he is *pretending* is the cliff above Dover beach—

> 'The murmuring surge,
> That on the unnumber'd idle pebbles chafes
> Cannot be heard so high.'   (iv.vi.21ff.)

And Edgar does this in order to give his father a means with which to reconstruct his life—a 'miraculous' intervention:

> 'Why I do trifle thus with his despair
> Is done to cure it.'   (iv.vi.35f.)

But, again, *why*? We need an answer to that answer; for what end 'cure it'? For what end be true in love to one another? For its own sake? But that seems insufficient. What is it, to be as Edgar,

> 'Who, by the art of known and feeling sorrows,
> Am pregnant to good pity'? (IV.vi.227)

Is ripeness *all*?[26] The pressures to answer 'yes' became in the nineteenth century, as in our own, increasingly great; if nature is insubstantial and neutral (indifferent, as Freud was so vigorously to assert, in explaining the origins of religious wishful thinking) then how can we locate a substance of continuity in our own nature, our own feelings, however much they enable us to roam, like Satan among the sons of God in Job, about the earth and even to the limit of the stars?

> 'Fools that these mystics are
> Who prate of Nature! for she
> Hath neither beauty, nor warmth,
> Nor life, nor emotion, nor power.
> But man has a thousand gifts,
> And the generous dreamer invests
> The senseless world with them all.
> Nature is nothing; her charm
> Lives in our eyes which can paint,
> Lives in our hearts which can feel.'

That exercise in Kantian aesthetics is again from Matthew Arnold, 'The Youth of Man'.[27] It is admittedly from the Swinburnian speech of the young:

> 'We are young and the world is ours;
> Man, man is the king of the world!
> Fools that these mystics are. ...'

But the older Matthew Arnold has little with which to correct the strident exaggeration of youth. He can only add that nature has proved consistent. Yet still he is haunted to the very end by the ghost of apparently significant action, by the apparent significance of his own feelings. When he excluded *Empedocles on Etna* from the 1853 edition of his poems, he did so because he felt there must be something more to be said of life than the comment of throwing oneself into a volcano. Poetry, for Arnold, insists that there *are* more situations than those in which 'the suffering finds no vent

in action . . ., in which there is everything to be endured, nothing
to be done.'[28] And yet what *is* Arnold actually offering, in Culture
or in Poetry, as an alternative?

> 'And this great Doctor, can it be,
> He left no saner recipe
> For men at issue with despair?[29]

That, of course, is Meredith's famous 'heels in the air' comment
on Arnold. In the light of it, it is not surprising that the very
structure of Arnold's poems reflects so faithfully the structure of
allegorical paintings, where only brief hints of hope are suggested in
the midst of the more powerful symbols of the transient nature of life.

Now why this long excursion on to Dover beach, where Arnold
and Shakespeare meet? It is to emphasize that the ways which
men project through the limitations which circumscribe them are
always, no doubt, partly wishful thinking, but never wholly so.
Men can wish for wings but by doing so never actually fly; but
the wish itself focuses the nature of the compound of limitation
which prevents them from flying, until, not angels' wings, but
aeroplanes, are built. There are enough cues in the universe to
support the plausibility of the eventual way through. In the case
of death, men have believed that they have discerned cues in the
universe and in their own nature which suggest the plausibility
either of certain ways through, or that there may be some way
through, even though it cannot in detail be described. But since it
is difficult to produce consequences as tangible and unmistakable
as the *Kitty Hawk* or the Concorde, the crisis of implausibility
always lies close at hand.

The crisis becomes particularly acute when the supports of
plausibility are themselves threatened: if, for example, burial
customs are changed, the plausibility of the projected way through
death can itself seem to be threatened. It so happens that both
Shakespeare and Matthew Arnold lived at times when major
changes in burial custom took place, and in both instances we can
see very clearly how threatening, consciously or unconsciously,
the changes appeared; they certainly did not *cause* the crisis, but
they contributed to it.

Shakespeare lived at a time of drastic liturgical revision, in which
Latin was abandoned for the vernacular, and in which many of the
ritual supports of plausibility were prohibited as superstitious.

Quite apart from the requiem itself being replaced by a much starker service of burial, it was no longer permissible to pray for the dead, or even to light candles round the coffin of the deceased, in hopeful vigil before the committal of the body to the earth. It is not surprising that one finds that at exactly the time when the young Shakespeare was reaching maturity, 'the people will not be staied from ringinge the bells on All Souls' daie';[30] and the tenacity of the old supports of plausibility and the need to find new ones when the old were at last effectively outlawed is clearly traced by Keith Thomas in *Religion and the Decline of Magic*.

In the time of Matthew Arnold, a much more concentrated but equally disturbing change in burial custom occurred with the introduction of cremation. The odd thing about the ferocity of the debates and of the opposition to cremation is that they could not have occurred in India, where people had been burning bodies for millennia. But burning, as such, threatened the main support of plausibility in the West, the burying of the body as a seed to be reconstituted in a new and risen form—the conceptual support which had led the character in Robert Louis Stevenson's story to collect all his nail cuttings in a match-box in order to help the Almighty on the day of resurrection.

Obviously, adjustments could be made: pamphlets were written,[31] it was pointed out that some people die accidentally in fires, and that the burial service itself speaks of 'ashes to ashes'. Nevertheless, so inconceivable had it seemed that anyone would wish to dispose of a body by burning it, that it had not actually seemed necessary to legislate against it. It was well known that the bodies of Shelley and Williams had been burned on the Italian shore after they had been drowned; but that, some people reassured themselves, was exactly the kind of behaviour to be expected of such godless reprobates as Shelley. Actually, the cremation took place even then simply and solely because of the Italian quarantine regulations, which made it impossible to move the bodies for the burial that was intended for them. Quite apart from Shelley, it was equally well known that those whose bodies had been burned in the not so distant past were heretics or those who were deemed to be, in this world at least, outside the faith. Ironically, it was precisely the absence of specific legislation against cremation which made the first experiments possible. There is an example of this in Italy,[32] but as far as England was concerned the legal issue came to a head slightly later. The Cremation Society of England was founded in January 1874, but it was not until 1882, eight years after Sir Henry Thompson's argument in favour of cremation had been published, that Captain James Hanham cremated his mother and his wife in a crematorium which he had had built in his own garden in Dorset, and in the following year that his own body was also cremated. The law still made no move. But in that same year Dr. Pryce, the Welsh Druid, cremated the body of his child on an open fire on a Welsh mountainside, thereby defying both public opinion and the instructions of the coroner; he then went on, as Dr. Cameron put it in his speech to Parliament in favour of cremation in April 1884, to announce 'his readiness to perform the same service for anybody who may demand it at his hands'.

The defiance of the coroner at last brought the legal issue into the open in a way which had hitherto been avoided.[33] It led to the famous judgement of Sir James Stephen, that cremation is legal provided it causes no nuisance to others. Parliament still felt able to defeat the Bill for the Regulation of the Disposal of the Dead in 1884, but in effect cremation was legally possible. In 1885 a crematorium was built and put into use at Woking; between 1885 and 1890, 154 bodies were cremated; and by 1891 the Cremation Society was suggesting suitable hours for cremation in order to fit in with trains from Waterloo.[34]

The disturbing effect of this change in burial custom can be seen very clearly in the way in which traditional supports of plausibility were attached to cremation, and also on the way in which cremation disguised itself. An example of the first can be seen in the attempt to retain actual burial, even though it had to be burial of the ashes. There was initially an extreme reluctance to scatter the ashes. The point is summarized by Marshall, in an article giving advice to architects of crematoria in 1945: 'If we go back to the early pioneer days at Woking, we find the public clinging to the old tradition of interment so that the small receptacles, containing the ash residue, were buried. Miniature headstones with curbs or reproductions of typical cemetery work covered or enclosed the spot, thus creating a quaint miniature cemetery in effect.'[35] After that, the miniature cemetery was moved indoors, and the urns were stored in niches, sometimes in special buildings, columbaria, built for the purpose. However, it was soon realized that a large number of potentially redundant buildings would proliferate, and at last the public were persuaded that scattering the ashes and setting up a plaque would be sufficient. Even then, the exuberance of grief had to be controlled, since 'it became apparent that it was necessary to exercise some control if incongruity was to be avoided'.[36]

The disturbance of the change in burial custom is equally obvious in the attempt to disguise crematoria, and in particular to get rid of the chimney. The early crematoria were built almost as caricatures of Victorian Gothic churches,[37] and the chimney was hidden within either the spire or the bell tower.[38] Even recently an architect has commented on his design for a new crematorium, that he designed a long colonnade of arches in order to give the impression of on-going continuity, even in the presence of death, and that he had had the buildings constructed of natural stone in order to suggest permanence and endurance.

What is happening, in these illustrations of committal procedures, is that although the details, through which the 'way through' the limitation of death has been proposed, may come under severe strain, it is still possible to attach some of the old supports of plausibility to the wholly novel means of disposing of the body. Men do not lightly abandon their hopes, their attempts to find a way through even the most intransigent limitations, provided these receive *some* support; and for Christians the underlying support, which enabled very considerable adjustments of details (of demythologizing or of re-mythologizing), was the belief that Jesus had risen from the dead. Thus cremation eventually comes to offer its own suggestions of meaning, and for some it becomes preferable to burial, even when no specific 'way through' the limitation of death is offered. It creates an attitude to that limitation, as in the poem 'Cremation' by Robinson Jeffers:

It nearly cancels my fear of death, my dearest said,
When I think of cremation. To rot in the earth
Is a loathsome end, but to roar up in flame—besides I am used to it,
I have flamed with love or fury so often in my life,
No wonder my body is tired, no wonder it is dying,
We had great joy of my body. Scatter the ashes.[39]

What apparently does not happen is that the *Hindu* projected way through death, which is itself supported by burning (*atman* being reincarnated in another body or attaining *moksha*, release), is transferred to and with cremation. This is because religions as a whole are constructed as route-finding activities, as homeostatic and conservative life-ways, through which *as a whole* human lives are made significant, and in which the meaning of their lives and of the universe is able to be discerned. But this means that religions draw for supports of their plausibility on resources in their own past which have been fundamental in constituting them (the exodus, for example, and the giving of Torah, for the Jews, or the life and resurrection of Jesus for the Christians). At this fundamental level of resource there cannot be any easy interchange without changing an old or creating a new religion.

If this is extended into a more general point, what is being suggested is that religions should be conceived as route-finding activities, mapping the general paths along which human beings can trace their way from birth to death and through death, and that the peculiarly 'religious' quality is evoked by a focus on limitations which circumscribe the continuity of human life-ways, of a particularly intransigent kind. Precisely for this reason, the threats of implausibility are virtually coexistent with the actually projected ways through; and for this reason also the actions and words which surround, for example, burial, become deeply connected (ritualized) with possible supports of plausibility.

In a way, death is too obvious as an example. One scarcely needs the suggested principle (the compound of limitation as the correct general context of explanation) in order to arrive at the somewhat obvious conclusions. But the point of taking an obvious example is to suggest that it will be equally correct when applied to other religious phenomena. It certainly applies, for example, to the explanation of the recent emergence of meditational cults (for example, Krishna Consciousness, Sufism, Transcendental Meditation, Subud), which offer release of the essential aspect of a person into new dimensions of freedom or of experience beyond the bodily here and now. Factor-analytic studies of these cults will draw many of the parameters of the correlations in behaviour of those who join, and thus of those who are *likely* to join. The study of structure and function will to some extent discern similarities of process in these movements. But what is being suggested here is that quite different opportunities of understanding and explanation open up if it is possible to discern the compound of limitation to which they are related—focally, in this particular instance, the sense of factors constraining an individual into his bounded (his not unlimited) actuality. This is a compound of limitation which is as intransigent, for many of our contemporaries, as death; to some of them death is preferable to living within it.

Once the study of religion is set into an anthropological context as a route-finding activity (one which has had a high survival value in enabling the continuity of individual and social life-ways), and once also it is recognized that the procedure which enables adequate explanation in the anthropological study of religion lies in the identification of the compounds of limitation towards which particular rites or customs or beliefs or personnel are directed, then it is possible to see that characterizations of the nature of God or gods will necessarily have reference to the projected ways through particular compounds of limitation. If, for example, there is to be a way through the limitation of death (as various cues in the external universe and in experience used to suggest, and to many people still do suggest), then a sense of God may be suggested as a ground of stability beyond death; and if God is to be stable in that sense, he cannot himself be subject to death; or if he is subjected to it, he must rise above it. This means that the sense of God must relate to (bear an emotionally and conceptually linked relation to) the sense which individuals have of their circumstances, that is to say, of the world in general and in particular. Otherwise, God becomes non-sense, so far as men are concerned; and this is the major crisis of plausibility of which Berger wrote.

It is important to note (particularly in relation to Freud) that it is not the case that the projection of a way through death necessarily constitutes a sense of God as such, nor is it the case that a sense of God is constituted *only* by that projection. One of the crises of plausibility for the Buddha occurred exactly at this point, yet Buddhism still projects a way through death, but now of a quite different nature without the ultimate support of God. In other words, just as the projected ways through the compounds of limitation are very varied, so also are the characterizations of the reality which is believed to lie through and beyond them; not simply different characterizations of God, but even distinctions between personal deity and impersonal *mana*; not simply distinctions between the heavenly city and the Muslim paradise, but distinctions between continuity of relation to God and nirvana, or distinctions between Ramanuja and Shankara. This at once means that the notion of plausibility becomes absolutely central in understanding how any senses of God themselves change in the long sequences of human cultural transmission, within the universes of meaning which religions create and are. It also means that the claimed effect of God within those universes of meaning is equally critical in understanding how any senses of God remain plausible.

Crises of plausibility may be imposed from without, but they occur far more frequently, in historical terms, within theistic traditions themselves. They occur because of the constant probing of men and women, as they seek to find a way through the limitations which circumscribe the continuity of their lives, of what God must be to be God. No matter how 'God' is constituted, if there is no feedback at all into the actual situations and experiences of life, plausibility is under maximum strain; if no effect of God can ever be discerned or specified, then in effect God is nowhere. Thus all theistic traditions have at some point suggested discernible (claimed) effects of God, ranging from trances, ecstasies, speaking with tongues, to individual conviction, answers to prayer, and the slow sea-change of human nature. This means that there must be sufficient feedback into experience, whether social or individual, for plausibility to be maintained: not an invariable answer to prayer, but some answer; not an invariably correct prediction of the future, but some prediction; not an invariable glimpse of dead spirits, but occasional glimpses; not universal visions of the Virgin Mary, but some visions. But where the feedback in effect seems insufficient, or where traditional appeals to effect, like those just mentioned, cannot any longer specify what would count as examples, then the sense of God is under strain; and this can occur within theistic traditions themselves. The two major and obvious examples of this occurring within theistic traditions are the Buddha in an Eastern tradition and Jesus in a Western.

Finally, what this means is that even this approach to the understanding of the sense of God as related to the compounds of limitation which men seek to understand and perhaps also to penetrate cannot in itself dispense with the possible reality of the object of belief. On the contrary, it emphasizes that the reality or non-reality in effect of the objects of belief has been a major factor in the crises of plausibility through which the many senses of God have been broken down and either rebuilt or extinguished.

Whether this process will continue remains, obviously, to be seen. But one factor on which it will depend will be the reality or non-reality in effect of the object of belief, and whether what is claimed to be such an effect can or cannot otherwise be adequately accounted for. Putting it in descriptive terms, the issue, ultimately, is whether accounts of behaviour which *use* the term 'God' are sometimes more correct than those which simply *mention* the term 'God'. It is, of course, quite another (and very difficult) question whether those occasions can be specified. But before we come closer to that issue it is necessary to look more closely at the way in which these route-finding contexts (the theistic traditions through which particular senses of God are transmitted) are themselves constructed. The human senses of God are inextricably bound up with the ways in which religions are constructed, as a result of which they are able to make particular senses of God available. It is necessary, therefore, to look now at structural accounts of human behaviour, in order to see what light they can throw on the construction of those universes of meaning which defend and make available particular senses of God.

V

STRUCTURAL ACCOUNTS OF RELIGION

In the previous chapters it has been suggested that religions can be conceived of as route-finding activities which include the attempt to find routes even through limitations of a particularly opaque or intransigent kind, of which death was taken as an example. If this suggestion is at all correct, it at once integrates the study of religion into the many-levelled structural accounts of human reality, particularly those structural accounts which envisage the construction of human behaviour and of human meaning on the basis of relatively simple coding procedures. This means that *theoretically* one can envisage a hierarchy of increasingly complex structures, from the basic ability of the brain to code and decode information to the extreme pressure of, for example, a poet endeavouring to make words do more than they are apparently capable of doing—'the poet', as Peterkiewicz sub-titled a book, 'at the limits of language'. The main title of the book is equally graphic, in this context: *The Other Side of Silence*.

If religion is seen as the attempt to organize meaning and action in relation to particular compounds of limitation, it can be seen that as goal-seeking behaviour it will operate within particular constraints. On this basis, the possibility can be envisaged of tracing the paths of divergent theistic routes. Eventually, therefore, it may be possible to specify the underlying conceptual grammars which create theistic and religious universes of meaning. In that case, the sense of God might be the emotion generated within the construction of those particular universes of meaning; and that would be the furthest structural deduction about the sense of God which could be made.

That must inevitably sound an optimistic programme, and it is certainly unlikely to be realized for several generations. Nevertheless, it represents a serious and highly necessary way of approach to the understanding of the construction of religious universes of

meaning. Its importance lies in the fact that it relates this particular and specialized inquiry to the far more general and structurally
universal question, how are *any* 'universes of meaning' constructed?
Obviously, it is not possible to consider this in detail, but at least
let us consider the way in which information theory approaches
this question, and then the relevance of information theory and of
structuralism to the understanding of the construction of senses of
God may perhaps become clearer.

The basic conditions of information are put by Nauta in this
way:

One of the outstanding features of the higher forms of life is the capacity
for learning and adaptation. The central nervous system appears to be
the pre-eminent instrument that has been designed for this function in
the course of evolution. Whether achieved by a natural central nervous
system or by an artificial one, *learning* can be viewed generally in terms
of an internal organization which is capable of reflecting the relevant
constraints of the environment. This internal organization, together
with its representation and updating of the relevant cognitive aspects of
the environment, will be called *cognitive map* or 'internal model of the
environment'.[1]

What we are now exploring is whether theistic universes of
meaning represent a form of cognitive mapping which deals with
virtually all constraints, but which is focused and made specific by
its reference to constraints in the environment of a particularly
opaque or intransigent nature—the irreversibility of time, the
occurrence of death, and the other examples already mentioned.
What learning, conceived as the interiorization of environmental
constraints, enables is exactly that route-finding endeavour which
is characteristic of so many human activities (and this includes
religious activities—for example, prayer—as much as scientific
activities—for example, attempting to 'crack' the genetic code),
activities which scan particular compounds of limitation in
order to find, if possible, a way through. The full statement of
this will be found in the continuation of Nauta's argument.[2]
The phrase to be emphasized in that argument is the one which
occurs at the beginning: 'learning is essentially interiorization of
environmental constraints'. The 'learning of constraints' means
that all route-finding represents a choice within a set of possibilities. This is precisely why one of the fundamental procedures

of cybernetics is to ask how a particular case is controlled into its restriction. This point is abundantly emphasized in Ashby:

> Cybernetics typically treats any given, particular machine by asking not 'what individual act will it produce here and now?' but 'what are *all* the possible behaviours that it can produce?' It is in this way that information theory comes to play an essential part in the subject; for information theory is characterized essentially by its dealing always with a *set* of possibilities; both its primary data and its final statements are almost always about the set as such, and not about some individual element in the set . . . Cybernetics envisages a set of possibilities much wider than the actual, and then asks why the particular case should conform to its usual particular restriction.[3]

The point is then emphasized later that constraints are of such high importance in cybernetics precisely because '*when a constraint exists advantage can usually be taken of it*'.[4] This means that the notion of constraint here comes very close to the compound of limitation which has been suggested as of such basic importance in understanding religions. For, what exactly *is* a constraint in Ashby's sense?

First we can notice that the existence of any invariant over a set of phenomena implies a constraint, for its existence implies that the full range of variety does not occur. The general theory of invariants is thus a part of the theory of constraints. Further, as every law of nature implies the existence of an invariant, it follows that *every law of nature is a constraint*.[5]

This corresponds to what was referred to as continuous limitation:

> Thus, the Newtonian law says that, of the vectors of planetary positions and velocities which might occur, e.g., written on paper (the larger set) only a smaller set will actually occur in the heavens; and the law specifies what values the elements will have. From our point of view, what is important is that the law *excludes* many positions and velocities, predicting that they will never be found to occur.[6]

After this, Ashby went on to exemplify 'object as constraint', which corresponds in general terms to contextual and contingent limitation. The purpose of referring to 'compounds of limitation', and not simply to 'constraint', has been in order to include the highly important component of consciousness in human route-finding activities. Men are not *simply* constrained. They may be constrained in a very complicated manner; no doubt they are. But what is constituted by consciousness is the at least partial discernment of limitation. It is probably very rare for consciousness to scan every component of a particular compound of limitation. It is thus not surprising that men frequently turn out to have been mistaken. Nevertheless, the basic fact remains that in the abstract the quantification of information is related to a categorical set of possibilities, a framework which is usually referred to as the 'ensemble' or the 'alphabet' of possible outcomes, the 'universe' or 'repertory' of eventualities. Thus the abstract mathematical theory of finite schemes underlying information theory can legitimately be summarized (and this is in fact Nauta's phrase) as the calculus of uncertainty and constraint. This is exactly the direction in which Khinchin set out when he endeavoured to put Shannon's work[7] (which really established information theory, but which had a very practical orientation and cut a good many mathematical corners) on to what Khinchin called 'a solid mathematical basis'.[8]

How, then, do we arrive at the sense of anything? How do we construct meaning on the basis of the information which arrives at our receptor centres in the form of sensation, or occurs within brain function itself? It is clear, as Chomsky ceaselessly points out, that language competence enables almost infinite variations in language performance. The acquisition of one language, say English, enables any individual to generate an almost infinite variety of actual sentences. Yet in fact meaning is conveyed in conversation or in communication because in the majority of cases the sentences used are controlled into their restriction by two levels of appropriateness. The first control is exercised by grammatical rules. The acquisition of these is what Chomsky believes, at the level of deep structure, makes it likely that there are innate structures in the brain which enable it to code at all and which, therefore, may be universal.[9] The details of Chomsky's arguments are necessarily at a very early stage of testing. In point of fact, Šaumjan may well turn out to be right, that 'recursive rules can only be applied to idealized objects whose elements are well defined; but natural languages when treated, as Chomsky treats them, as directly observable empirical objects, cannot be fully described by recursive rules because they are a mixture of rational and irrational elements which cannot be strictly defined in the mathematical sense.'[10] It may be necessary therefore, to postulate (and in this case attempt to generate) an intermediary 'ideal language' stage. But this does not affect the general point about the first control of appropriateness.

The second control of appropriateness is exercised by the degree of 'match' between the language used and the intention of the user. A user of a language participates in a cultural artefact and heritage, a language which is commonly available and which probably took millennia to construct. The creation of meaning depends on the degree of match between the language available and the intention of the user. At the level of primary specification this is relatively straightforward. If I wish to convey what the sensation of this apparent object is, on which I am sitting, I use the generally available term 'chair'. This, in general terms, is what is meant by isomorphism in information theory.[11] But this becomes much more problematic, and philosophers begin to gain employment, when I wish to convey, for example, an internal sensation, a state of brain arousal which I am labelling as happiness, or misery, or boredom. (That actually is a very controversial form of words, but this labelling account of emotional behaviour will be considered more closely when we come to consider hallucinogenic experiences as a possible origin of the sense of God.) At the moment, we need simply to observe that the further one moves away from primary specification the more difficult it may be to establish isomorphism in informational terms, hence more difficult to establish the sense or the meaning which one is attempting to convey: there is a greater degree of signal loss.

But, provided the conditions of isomorphism are relatively stable and generally agreed, it is not difficult to scan the conditions at the second level of appropriateness which would establish the match or mismatch between the user's intention and the language employed. If someone states, 'This is a chair', and if my perceptual sensation conforms to his and the scan of conditions is affirmative, then I will acquiesce that the sentence 'This is a chair' makes sense in these conditions. Consequently, that sentence acquires and retains meaning even in the absence of a perceived object, and even bizarre and factually *in*appropriate uses of the sentence remain intelligible. The match between intention and use is still established by the fundamental controls of appropriateness. This is even true of those occasions of language-use in which more than one intention is involved, and in which the actual words used conceal one particular intention, as Hodge discovered when he bought several razors from an itinerant salesman.[12] But what is involved here is simply an extension of the range of intention in a particular word-sequence; and it still remains the case that the language-use of (in this case) the pedlar is controlled by the two levels of appropriateness. The problem of extending a range of intention is that one has to choose one's words more carefully, particularly (supposing one is attempting to sell a razor) if one is subject to the Trade Descriptions Act.

At this point, we are still well within range of correspondence theories of language. But this has not taken us very far into actual language-uses. What happens, for example, when we move on to the statement 'This chair is beautiful' or 'This statement is satisfying'? Can we still adopt the procedure of match and mismatch between use and intention as the procedure through which 'meaning' is established? Clearly, the area for disagreement about appropriateness is much more considerable, because the conditions which must obtain for the term 'beautiful' to be appropriately used are not in the least agreed. Therefore, the 'maps' of isomorphic correspondence are nothing like so generally established as they are, for example, in the realm of scientific discourse. Nevertheless, all is not lost, from an informational point of view. It is clearly possible still to have agreement and disagreement in aesthetic judgements, because in principle an individual is able to specify the conditions which must obtain if *he* is to use the term 'beautiful' appropriately, if, that is, there is to be a match between his intention and his use. Another person may well respond that those conditions are very peculiar, and that beauty is in the eye of the beholder, but at least 'meaning' is established between them, because match and mismatch in intention and use still obtain. Admittedly, he has to flounder around in other language-uses, in order to indicate his intention, but that at least helps to quantify information.

This means that from an informational point of view the work of literary or of aesthetic criticism is the work of discerning and evaluating the relation between intention and use in the case of any particular product, so that *meaning* is constantly (and never finally, in the case of many works of art or literature) disclosed. There may be more 'meaning' in a poem than a poet 'meant' by it: his own internal attempt to match his intention with his use of language may startle quite other, unexpected, pheasants from the undergrowth.

All this carries with it a vital implication: 'meaning' can be established, by the appropriateness of match and mismatch in intention and use, in one 'universe' or 'realm' of meaning (for example, a religious universe of meaning), while that whole universe of meaning can be shown to be inappropriate when it is itself matched to the conditions which establish appropriateness in another 'universe of meaning' (for example, the scientific). This is clearly what may be the case of theistic language in religious traditions (religious 'universes of meaning'). No one doubts that utterances can be appropriate or inappropriate according to the conditions established in particular traditions: to say that 'God is three in one' is inappropriate as a Muslim utterance, appropriate as a Christian utterance. However, interreligious dialogue, by testing the relation between intention and use, might be able to establish that the intention of the Christian utterance in referring to God as 'three in one' actually conforms to the Muslim intention of referring to God as 'There is no God but God', and the Christian might be able to indicate the pressures of what appears to have been the case in relation to Jesus and early Christian experience, which led to Trinitarian statements. In other words, the Christian might argue that there is a match between intention and use which establishes meaning of a non-tritheistic kind.

But now relate *both* theistic universes of meaning (indeed, all theistic universes of meaning) to another in which some kind of isomorphic specification is considered indispensible for the appropriateness of putative truth-claims: from this point of view, there is always a mismatch between intention and use; and linguistic philosophers have been pointing out, both temperately and intemperately, the nature of this 'mismatch' for the last fifty years. The intention of the user to talk appropriately about God can be matched as it occurs within a particular theistic tradition (hence the existence of theologians in all theistic religions), but it is fundamentally, and invariably, mismatched if it is brought into a *non*-theistic tradition which requires as exact a specification as possible of the object of belief in order to establish at least some kind of isomorphic map through which to test appropriateness or inappropriateness. It appears not to be possible to talk appropriately about God in those conditions. The intention of the user to talk appropriately about God may be matched to the conditions of appropriateness in a particular theistic tradition, but can they be matched to the conditions of appropriateness in traditions which have their own conditions of isomorphic specification on the basis of which worth-while information, or meaning, is to be discerned? One obvious response is to say, Why should they be so matched? Why should not the validity of different traditions of discourse simply be allowed to coexist? But this version of the language-game is highly dangerous for theological language. This is not to deny the importance of its familiar point of departure: don't ask for the meaning, ask for the use:[13] 'For a *large* class of cases— though not for all—in which we employ the word "meaning" it can be defined thus: the meaning of a word is its use in the language.'[14]

The attraction of this for the understanding of theistic language is irresistible—or at least it has certainly proved irresistible. Here, for example, is an application by Phillips: 'The surface grammar of "There is a table in the room" and "There is a God in heaven" is similar, but their depth grammar is very different. One finds out the latter by exploring the limits of what can and what cannot be said in each case.'[15]

This corresponds roughly to what has been referred to so far as testing the conditions of appropriateness in the match between intention and use in the context of particular traditions of discourse. Phillips added that one can never establish this test by asking the believer what he *means*, because his words may not be able adequately to express his meaning:

Two believers may give the same account of prayer, and yet mean something different from each other by prayer. The ability to pray is not the same as the ability to give an account of prayer. Just because someone gives a naïve account of the existence of God, it does not follow that this is the God he believes in. To find out what belief in God did mean to him one would have to consider the role of such a belief in his life.[16]

This is about the furthest limit to which the 'not the meaning, but the use' advice could be pushed: the life of faith, and the theistic language associated with lives of faith in particular traditions, are finally to be evaluated as existential affirmation, or as the appropriate playing (or rather) living of the language-game in question. In that case the origin of the sense of God is the origin of a linguistic tradition through which a particular existential stance, or affirmation, is enabled. The validity lies in the attractiveness of the affirmation and in its uses and consequences. There is no need to deny the importance of existential affirmation as the locus of meaning in individual cases. But it seems doubtful if theologies would be wise to regard that importance as the beginning and the end of their business. It so happens that as a matter of fact theologies do make putative truth-claims, and these are not simply convertible into dummy counters in some kind of a game—shall we say, Pascal's wager? At some point, not least if Pascal wins, we shall want to know whether the counters have any cash value—if, that is, they are convertible the other way round. One might say that if Pascal wins, then we *will* know: in other words, one might say that verification could only be eschatological, when we cease to see through a glass darkly. That is certainly a possibility. But that does not absolve us from the responsibility of asking whether the putative truth-claims of a 'life of faith' are *intended* to bear a relation to what may in reality be the case or not. If so, then one of the means through which theistic language is controlled into its restriction must be the effect of that claimed reality in the creation of that particular theistic tradition. If the claimed reality is of no effect, it cannot be surprising if 'the life of faith', despite all its extraordinary richness and vitality of language and culture, seems ultimately vacuous.

To put it briefly, theologies can never absolve themselves from the responsibility of wrestling with the problem of the reality or the unreality of the objects of belief. The paradox of theological language is created by the fact that if God-language is to be used appropriately in the conditions of a theistic tradition, the sense of God must actually be indefinitely regressive. What this means will be discussed further in due course, but roughly, what is undoubtedly true, from an anthropological and historical point of view, is that if God is to have *any* appropriate meaning he must always be slightly beyond human attainment: *Deus semper maior*. For God to be God, to do for men what men have needed him to do, emotionally and conceptually and religiously, he must stand beyond the limits of their attainment so far. So, the nearer one comes to getting God within one's grasp, the more he has to be posited beyond that grasp, or else the more it has to be realized that the sense of God has collapsed by being exhaustively grasped. It is at this nexus that the great crises of plausibility in the sense of God and in the ways in which God remains 'sensible' (able to be sensed and to be made sense of) have occurred in the history of religions.

But even if the sense of God is necessarily regressive, this does not alter the fact that no routes of meaning can be constructed towards God and remain widely plausible, unless there is a feedback from the possible object of belief into the reality of human lives sufficient to constitute information in the construction of those routes of meaning. Put more crudely, this means that one cannot construct a way through to God unless there is a sufficient feedback from the reality of the object of belief to keep the whole enterprise going.

We are now in a position to return to the question we were considering: how do we arrive at the sense of anything? How do we construct meaning on the basis of the information which arrives at our receptor centres in the form of sensation, or which occurs in the internal process? The biological and neurological answer lies in the (initially latent) structured ability of the brain to code, store, and decode signals and represent (re-present) them *as* information. This implies that 'meaning' is constituted not by the quantitative amount of information, but by a qualitative selection (control into restriction), which enables meaning, based on a wide range of isomorphic maps, to transcend the mathematical base of its constituent elements; and because the isomorphic conditions which men set up are so varied, the structures of meaning at which men arrive are correspondingly varied.

The way in which 'meaning' transcends the mathematical base of its constituent elements does not mean that there is an automatic, radical disjunction between quantitative (in a semiotic sense) and qualitative information. The comment, once again, of Nauta, may be helpful:

The opposition between information in a qualitative sense and information in a quantitative sense is not an essential one; information in the qualitative sense should be viewed as information which might be related *in principle* to a quantitative frame although its specification is not actually completed. It should be conceded that the actual specification is often very difficult to complete, but *in principle* it *is* possible . . .[17]

But this comment needs, itself, to be approached with caution. If it is taken to imply that qualitative information is in principle *reducible* to its quantitative base, and that its significance is exhaustively contained in that reduction, then 'meaning' and 'meaningless noise' could not be disentangled: there would, in other words, be no problem. A much more accurate description, from an informational point of view, is that of Polanyi, in his attempt to establish how, within the boundary conditions of scientific regularity (the 'laws', for example, of physics or chemistry), certain operations constrain these regularities into consequences which are *additional* to the laws of physics and chemistry';[18] and this is what enables him to argue that 'biological hierarchies consist in a series of boundary conditions':

> The theory of boundary conditions recognizes the higher levels of life as forming a hierarchy, each level of which relies for its workings on the principles of the levels below it, even while it itself is irreducible to those lower principles . . . Living beings comprise a whole sequence of levels forming such a hierarchy. Processes at the lowest level are caused by the forces of inanimate nature, and the higher levels control throughout the boundary conditions left open by the laws of inanimate nature . . . Each level relies for its operations on all the levels below it. Each reduces the scope of the one immediately below it by imposing on it a boundary that harnesses it to the service of the next higher level, and this control is transmitted stage by stage down to the basic inanimate level.[19]

Although this is expressed in very general terms, it nevertheless represents precisely the reason why it is possible for consciousness to scan the compounds of limitation which circumscribe the continuity of its life-way, whether in detail or as a whole.

The immediate implication of this is, once again (see p. 86), that theoretically it ought to be possible to trace the means through which the various hierarchies of meaning in human discourse have themselves been constructed. This is the indispensable point to grasp if one is going to have any chance of understanding what Lévi-Strauss is up to: when we talk about meaning transcending the biological base of language we are not (or should not be) talking about meaning *escaping* the biological base of language (the coding and decoding ability, the means through which, as Lenneberg has put it, the species-specific trait of conceptual thinking is possible), but about the way in which those actual 'coding procedures' enable the construction of highly personal universes of meaning which are nevertheless intelligible to other people. The central problem of information being constituted as meaning lies in the fact that statements can be utterly novel and wholly intelligible, and also wholly intelligible and utterly meaningless—as in Chomsky's example of 'colourless green ideas sleeping furiously'. But the fact that novelty and intelligibility *can* be combined means that language is a potent weapon with which human beings can probe the limitations which circumscribe the continuity or the development of their lives. They can, as Nauta puts it, 'break through the existent informational frames'.[20]

Theoretically, therefore, the more one can identify the isomorphic conditions which obtain in particular areas, the more one ought to be able to trace the various hierarchical structures through which meaning is constructed. One ought to be able to examine the transactions which create and generate particular universes of meaning. If this were so, there would be a chance of creating a genuinely transformational understanding of theistic participation in the construction of meaning. This would be a major advantage for theology, because it could equally well do justice, on the one side, to the participation of men in the symbolling which enables their movement towards God and, on the other, to the *possible* participation of God, effectively and transactively, in the transformation—or better, in the Christian tradition, the transfiguration —of the lives of men. Thus, to give an example, from the point of view of a thoroughgoing structural theology, one can certainly analyse the way in which Jesus generated (contributed) transformations to the obtaining structures which were in his time available for construing the 'godness of God' (what it must involve for 'God to be God'). But equally one must look at the ways in which those obtaining structures contributed to Jesus the form and boundary of his own transacted grammar. In other words, we now see opening up the possibilities not only of a structural theology, which is straightforward in principle, though difficult, as yet, in practice, but also of a structural Christology, in which there is no confusion of the one side into the other (or, in more traditional language, of the two natures). It may even be the case that structural theology creates a quite different opportunity to defend the otherness of the object of belief in the case of God; and in the next series of Wilde lectures I hope to indicate how this might work, and what it could mean for the contemporary exploration of Christology.

If, then, the tracing of conceptual structures is in principle possible, does this imply that the conceptual sense of God, from a structural point of view, is an internal equivalent to the external attempts to build constructions which will reach to heaven, an internal equivalent to the tower of Babel or the spire of William Golding's cathedral? If so, might it not be possible to survey the architecture of both types of construction?

In practice, this seems, at this moment in time, so difficult that one cannot really envisage it being done. But in principle it could be possible; and it is certainly possible to test the principle at a low level of construction—low level, that is, in the hierarchy of structures which constitute the sense of God in a developed theology—namely, in the construction of myths. This is very much what Lévi-Strauss has attempted. Lévi-Strauss came to believe that the vast confusions of mythology (similarities of myth in different parts of the world, for example, combined with different contingent details) could never be organized for understanding so long as one simply looked at the surface contents. The supposed 'understanding' will be correspondingly as confused as the phenomena under investigation. In the case of totemism, von Gennep was already, by 1920, able to list over forty theories. Totemism had been Durkheim's great ab-original social act, the origin of religion and society. But totemism became a happy hunting-ground for other theorists. Lévi-Strauss cut through the theories which were built on surface meaning, and looked instead for underlying structures. Exactly, therefore, as linguistics could not, in Lévi-Strauss's view, break through to a more scientific exactness until it had been realized that it is 'the combination of sounds, not the sounds in themselves which provides the significant data'[21], so the study of myth cannot break through, according to Lévi-Strauss, until it cracks the code which combines at depth apparently disparate surface elements. The focus of study should be, not the surface content but the underlying combinative code. From this arises his central argument, that mythical thought works from awareness of binary oppositions, the fundamental coding possibility of the brain, to their progressive resolution or mediation—'a logic operating by means of binary oppositions and coinciding with the first manifestations of symbolism'.[22]

This harmonizes very well with the procedures of information theory, which also emphasize that one's focus of concern should be on the repertory of possible outcomes if one wants to understand how a particular instance has been controlled into its restriction. The risk involved is that one may then lose all interest in the particular case: the analysis of the code becomes so exclusively the object of the exercise, that whatever importance the surface content may have is unrelated to that study or exercise. This is a point made by Leach:

Note in particular Levi-Strauss' seeming contempt for the 'empirical phenomenon'. The 'general object of analysis' is conceived as a kind of algebraic matrix of possible permutations and combinations located in the unconscious 'human mind'; the empirical evidence is merely an example of what is possible . . . The structure of relations which can be discovered by analysing materials drawn from any one culture is an algebraic transformation of other possible structures belonging to a common set and this common set constitutes a pattern which reflects an attribute of the mechanism of all human brains. It is a grand conception; whether it is a useful one may be a matter of opinion.[23]

It is undoubtedly useful, if it achieves what it sets out to do, namely, to explain how particular instances of myth have been controlled into their restriction from the repertory of available possibilities. But actually, it is possible that Lévi-Strauss's mistrust of surface-meaning makes him unable to achieve that end, because it becomes formidably difficult for him to integrate the real effect of meaning which is externally, perhaps even randomly, derived, on the creation of further oppositions. There is no doubt that Lévi-Strauss's mistrust of surface-meaning is highly understandable. The confusions over totemism were bad enough, but Lévi-Strauss found equal 'superficiality' over the whole field of mythology.[24] Even more to the point, he had to resist explanations from affectivity. But what Lévi-Strauss means by affectivity is the psychoanalytical approach which Freud, for example, brought to bear (Freud being one of the many surface theorists of totemism), and which attempts to explain social constraints 'as the effects of impulses or emotions which appear again and again, with the same characteristics and during the course of centuries and millennia, in different individuals.'[25]

But there is another sense of 'affectivity' which is nothing like what Lévi-Strauss was attacking. The problem is that the formation of structures, even if, for the sake of argument, it is invariably governed by binary coding procedures, can actually be affected by a surface-meaning which may be derived from random or initially unconnected sources. This sense of the affecting presence of objects is quite different from what Lévi-Strauss attacked as affectivity; and in order to make this point clear, it may be as well to take as simple an example of this as possible, the naming of racehorses. In *The Savage Mind* Lévi-Strauss applied his theories to the naming of animals. According to Lévi-Strauss, birds can be named with human names (Tom Tit, Jenny Wren) because they are sufficiently 'far-off' to be considered 'a metaphorical human society',[26] whereas dogs are fancifully named because they are 'domestic' animals, too 'far in' to human society to be conceived as a metaphor of it; so they are named (in Lévi-Strauss's example) Azor, Medor, Sultan, Fido, Diane. But as Leach commented: 'The catch of course, as any pet-loving Englishman will immediately recognize, is that these broad French generalizations do *not* hold up as soon as we cross the Straits of Dover!'[27]

Nevertheless, so far as France is concerned, Lévi-Strauss then postulated the naming of cattle as a half-way house between wild and domestic: 'They are generally descriptive terms, referring to the colour of their coats, their bearing or temperament.'[28] But racehorses are an artificially contrived society, 'the products of human industry',[29] so their names are neither descriptive nor human, but 'display an eclecticism which draws on learned literature rather than oral tradition'.[30]

Part of this is correct, that the naming of animals is governed by conventions. But Levi-Strauss presses on to far more systematic conclusions, based on the underlying codes, without reference to contrary surface facts:

If therefore birds are *metaphorical human beings* and dogs, *metonymical human beings*, cattle may be thought of as *metonymical inhuman beings* and racehorses as *metaphorical inhuman beings*. Cattle are contiguous only for want of similarity, racehorses similar only for want of contiguity. Each of these two categories offers the converse image of one of the two other categories, which themselves stand in the relation of inverted symmetry.[31]

Again, Leach's comment: 'But supposing the English evidence doesn't really fit? Well, no matter, the English are an illogical lot of barbarians in any case.'[32] On the naming of cattle, Leach also comments: 'Here again the Englishman is out of line though we do better when it comes to racehorses.'[33]

But here, Leach is as factually wrong as Lévi-Strauss. The naming of English racehorses does not 'conform better' to Lévi-Strauss's systematics, but it *does* provide a brilliant example, both of Lévi-Strauss's basic method (the mediation of binary oppositions, together with rigid conventions in different areas of animal naming) and of the defects of that method if it does not integrate the affecting presence of meaning.

The naming of English racehorses is governed by a strong cultural convention, whereby the name of a horse constructs a mediating bridge between the names of its parents. This can be seen clearly in the following example:

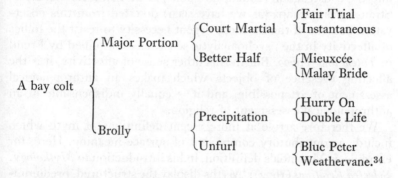

In this example, it can be seen that each name mediates the binary opposition of its parents. The bay colt, foaled on 13 April 1967, had not been named at the time of sale, but one can imagine it might have been named something like 'Partial Cover'.

The naming of English racehorses is thus a very good example of mediation between binary oppositions and of strong convention in the naming of animals, but it does *not* conform to any of Lévi-Strauss's systematic (systematizing) proposals. It does not conform, because, quite specifically, the English naming system exemplifies the affecting presence of diversely derived meaning. Naming by mediation is indeed a strong convention, but *only* a convention. It can be broken into by 'diversely derived' meaning. A name can be supplied from the name, for example, of a husband or wife, or the place where the owner went on honeymoon, or a name associated with something or someone who has brought 'good luck'. In a second example,[35] the bottom sequence exemplifies mediation, but the top sequence is 'broken into' by a name derived from a family relation who is a 'stayer' in chronological terms: perhaps he will be a 'stayer' on the course. But the new term 'Grandad', derived from quite other resources of meaning, then contributes to the coding sequence in 'Old Age Pensioner'.

What seems clear in relation to Lévi-Strauss is that his method should be evaluated in terms of information theory, in which terms it is, in very many cases, highly illuminating, but that his systematic deductions should be treated with extreme circumspection, because they do not, and cannot, integrate the affecting presence of objects, which may well be unique but which nevertheless are of real effect because they are, as a matter of fact, integrated into the construction (coded, no doubt) of human meaning. Lévi-Strauss was perhaps (as we have seen) diverted from this observation because of the far more urgent necessity to resist the follies of affectivity in the psychoanalytic sense, as exemplified by Freud in *Totem and Taboo*. But in this other sense of affectivity, it is the affecting presence of objects which makes an anthropological assessment of art possible, and it is equally indispensable in an anthropological assessment of religion.

We therefore arrive at more recent definitions of myth which include a contributory component of surface-meaning. Here, for example, is Maranda's definition, in his introduction to *Mythology: Selected Readings* (1972): 'Myths display the structured, predominantly culture-specific, and shared, semantic systems which enable the members of a culture area to understand each other and to cope with the unknown. More strictly, *myths are stylistically definable discourses that express the strong component of semantic systems.*'[36] The salient phrases in this definition and in its extension (see ref. 36) are 'to cope with the unknown', and 'structured cognitive guidelines': these correspond to what has been suggested as the correct general framework of explanation, the relation between a cultural artefact (in this case myth)[37] and the compound of limitation which it seeks to recognize, resolve, penetrate, or perhaps simply map. The structures through which men build up resources and routes of action and meaning are precisely the general way in which they are able to set themselves against the limitations which surround them. But in doing so, they are constrained, not simply by the coding ability which alone makes *any* structure possible, but also by effects along the way, which can and frequently do profoundly divert or modify or extend further the actual route and the structure itself—the fact, for example, that Galvani happened to be in the kitchen when his wife was preparing frogs' legs for supper.[38] 'There is no structure apart from construction';[39] and within that constantly moving construction, it is not possible to exclude the contribution either of surface-meaning or of meaning derived from sources which are not wholly contained within the structural process itself. It is no more possible to exclude, theoretically, the possible contribution of the reality in effect of God in the construction of theistic structures than it is to exclude the possibility of Grandad in the naming of a horse in a stable on the Berkshire Downs. Whether such an effect can ever be discerned is entirely another matter. But a strict exclusion of 'the empirical phenomenon' means that an adequate structural account will always be impossible, however illuminating and necessary the analysis of the underlying process may be.

All this brings the structural study of myth exactly into line with what has been proposed as the correct *general* context of explanation, the principle of the compound of limitation. This is equally clear in another passage in Maranda, where he makes the connection between depth and surface: 'The deep structure of a myth is the solution to a problem of a cognitive, sociological, technological, or other central order and, once found, it generates the myth in the codes available to the society.'[40]

Obviously, the listing of problems—cognitive, sociological . . .— misses the generality of limitation which it has been suggested, can in fact be drawn. Nevertheless, in the form in which Maranda presents it, the point about problem-solving is, he argues, as much Lévi-Strauss's definition as his own: '. . . Lévi-Strauss's theory of the structure of myths in general, implies a teleological view. In effect, myths are made to solve contradictions, according to this theory . . . Thus a myth is built from its outcome—like a mystery story.'[41] That Maranda is right in this suggestion is perhaps sufficiently clear in the quotation from James Teit, which Lévi-Strauss put at the head of his famous and seminal paper 'The Structural Study of Myth': 'It would seem that mythological words have been built up only to be shattered again, and that new worlds were built from the fragments.'[42]

If these hints are at all correct, then we can see at once how well the structural approach to myth can be set in the general context of explanation which has here been suggested (the route-finding endeavours of men in relation to particular compounds of limitation, with myth understood as an enabling procedure), and how, much more importantly, it is *only* by being set in that general context that the high value of the analysis of coding procedures can be disentangled from the less convincing systematic generalizations, to which (as we saw in the case of animal naming) exceptions can invariably be found.

Exactly as was the case with burial customs, the attempt to find invariables in the variables will always be defeated. But if a general context of explanation is true, as, for example, it was and is in the case of natural selection, then it sets us free, *not* to seek for generality in the details but to explain how differences have occurred. Differences are valued, precisely because they are differences, not somehow to be explained away as awkward inconveniences. In that particular process, in the case of myths, the coding procedure is of fundamental importance in explaining how myths, both similar and different, are generated, but we will no longer be surprised to find 'differences making a difference', and we will be able to explain more exactly why differences occur.

This is exactly parallel to what happens in explaining the variations in species. How, for example, does one explain the bill of an Everglade Kite, *rostrhamus sociabilis*? If all hawks are lumped together crudely as a species, we observe that the bills of most other hawks are sturdy and hooked, and they are thus able to tear the flesh of the prey on which they live; but the bill of an Everglade Kite is thinner and sharper, and the hook is much more pronounced, like a pair of curved forceps. It is an ideal instrument, one might think, for extracting snails from shells; and water-snails are, in fact, virtually the only food of these birds, so much so that they are often referred to as Snail Kites. How do we explain this variation, and how do we explain the transmission of this adaptation from one generation to another? We would no longer be content to say 'Providence' or '*ab initio* Design on the part of a Creator'. Those explanations were derived from over-attention to the surface-meaning of objects. But we would not be content, either (and this is the all-important point), to say 'natural selection', and leave it at that, because in that case nothing in the detail has actually been explained. What 'natural selection' offers is the correct general context of explanation—the context within which (and within which alone) we are set free to look at the detailed differences *as differences*, and thus to set out on the long road to explanation of how these differences have occurred, and what difference they make. The last thing a zoologist would want to do, presumably, would be to subsume resemblances under a species description in a way which would at once obscure the importance of variant examples.[43] Similarly, if one puts the structural study of myth into a general context of explanation, as suggested, then details do not have to be forced into typical and improbable systems (species descriptions) but can be reinstated as examples of how coding operations *can* produce diverse effects. This means that we can avoid the criticism which Leach made of Lévi-Strauss, of being contemptuous of the empirical phenomenon, while at the same time recognizing that there will be underlying structural rules which enable variant construction.

It thus becomes apparent that the study of the structural 'architecture' of myth along Lévi-Straussian lines is not only possible but already under way, but that it does not produce the whole understanding of 'what a myth really is',[44] as Lévi-Strauss had evidently hoped. But since even this attempt to map the coding procedures which generate meaning at one of the most accessible levels, namely that of myth, runs into difficulties because of the highly inventive capacity of the human brain to introduce fertile innovations from almost infinite resources, what chance is there of successfully 'mapping' even more complex levels of structure in the more developed senses of God? At the moment, very little indeed. But this does not alter what is in principle possible; and already, in very general terms, attempts are being made to map in broad outline the hierarchies of structure through which human meaning is constructed. Of these, Piaget's brief essay on structuralism[45] is probably the most familiar, as equally it is the most ambitious example, because it attempts to trace a hierarchy of structures, from mathematical and logical structures, to physical and biological structures, to psychological structures, to linguistic structuralism, to structural analysis in the social sciences.

Piaget's point of departure is that structuralism enables a relational perspective which seems to be demanded by the constant unlocking of the implications of relativity.[46] Once again, what has been described as the route-finding abilities of men in relation to particular compounds of limitation is extremely clear in Piaget's account of structuralism. At one point he described three derivative properties of 'structure' composition.[47] He then commented:

> The third basic property of structures is, as we said, that they are self-regulating, self-regulation entailing self-maintenance and closure. Let us start by considering the two derivative properties: what they add up to is that the transformations inherent in a structure never lead beyond the system but always engender elements that belong to it and preserve its laws ... These properties of conservation along with stability of boundaries despite the construction of indefinitely many new elements presuppose that structures are self-regulating.[48]

This corresponds to what was said earlier about the homeostatic and conservative nature of human life-ways. Calling a structure self-maintained and closed does *not* mean that it is incapable of generating structures beyond itself in its own sequence. On the contrary, this is precisely what the structuring thrust of structures achieves; and it is this which is of such fundamental importance in the construction (with all its regressive implications) of the sense of God. In order to make clear what this means, it may be helpful to take two, quite separate, examples.

For the first example, let us make our way to the Wigmore Hall, in April 1938. According to the *Musical Courier*: 'A stir was created at a concert by the Philharmonic Trio in Wigmore Hall when James Whitehead, cellist, walked off the stage after playing only a few bars of Webern's String Trio, op. 20. Exclaiming "I can't play this thing", Mr. Whitehead quitted the stage ... He said that it was "a nightmare, not music at all, but mathematics". The majority of musicians will doubtless agree with him.'[49] Indeed, they *must* agree with him: *all* music is mathematics in the sense that it depends on deep structures of what makes 'sound' possible, which are ultimately analysable in mathematical terms; but the more serious question, from the structural point of view, is how specifically the composition is controlled by mathematical considerations. The only ultimately unintelligible music is not Webern's, nor even Cardew's, which sets out—at least in the case of *The Great Learning*—to enable as much improvisation as seems desirable at the time, but music written for any instrument which oscillates vibrations at a frequency of less than 20 cycles per second (the absolute threshold, in Fechner's sense, of pitch in human beings),[50] or at the other end of the scale, the final note for violins in Verdi's *Te Deum* raised an octave. This is the only ultimately unintelligible music because it would be a profound and beautiful silence—so far as the human ear is concerned. But this is trivial: the structural point is that, as Western tonality, with its very formal structures, began to break up, a wholly new level of structure was generated, Schoenberg's serial system of a twelve-note scale. However much Mr. Whitehead may have disagreed, this was in fact conservative of the underlying structure, in the sense that it could be deployed to re-form the classical tradition; and Schoenberg did so intend it to be deployed. Wholly 'free' atonalism seemed, at least to Schoenberg, to be an impractical abstraction, however correct in theory: it would not actually generate *music*. The compromise with tonality is equally clear in Berg. Schoenberg could therefore perfectly properly protest in 1938: 'I expect you will acknowledge, that these works are principally works of musical imagination and not, as many suppose, mathematical constructions.'[51] But this understanding of atonality has in turn generated new structures, total serialization at one extreme, which takes mathematics as deliberately as it can, by suggesting that all features of a composition ought to be deducible mathematically from an original formula; the principle of illocation, at another, which appears to be as 'unstructured' as possible, by introducing, for example, vectorial components. Yet these new structures of musical possibility are by no means divorced from the underlying structures, however much they may, methodologically or at times abusively, repudiate them; and they may, incidentally (and this brings us to the second example of the structuring thrust of structures), incorporate elements from other structural traditions— say, from India, or from Africa—or even, in the case of Messiaen, from bird-song.

Moving, then to the second example of the structuring thrust of structures, the interaction between different hierarchies of structured meaning, it is clear that 'incorporations' from one to another should never be evaluated in abstract terms. They need to be evaluated in terms of their structuring, generative, contribution. They may, for example, produce a new structure closer to the *source* of the incorporation, or closer to the hierarchies of structure which support the universe of meaning in which the 'incorporator' has up to that moment existed. We may be pulled closer to India, or India may be pulled closer to us—as, for example, in the case of Holst, whose opera *Savitri* is a musical equivalent of Yeats's early glimpse of illumination in Indian mythology (mediated, admittedly, via Theosophy, which he later found less resourceful than his own native Ireland).[52] This is a point of the greatest possible importance for the understanding of what has been known, in the Christian tradition, as 'syncretism', and thus for the understanding of what happens when rival senses of God come into contact or collision. Treated as a surface-concept, the confusions and misunderstandings are almost limitless—and anyone who has read the records of the conferences at Jerusalem in 1928 and Tambaram in 1938 will know how utterly misleading it has been to discuss syncretism in surface terms alone. But set in a structural context, one can see that Plato, for example, can indeed be incorporated, or 'baptized', into Christianity, provided that the incorporation generates structures which can be appropriately connected to the already existing hierarchy of structures which have (so far) generated the Christian universe of meaning. This 'universe of meaning' is not itself a fully achieved, static concept, not even by appeal to the New Testament: it is always in the process of construction. But equally the hierarchy of Platonic construction can generate its own universe of meaning—for example, a neo-Platonism which is distinct from Christianity, but which can itself incorporate elements derived from Christian structures. Once again, 'appropriateness' is judged by the degree of match or mismatch between innovatory structures and the already obtaining hierarchies of structure which have constituted a particular universe of meaning up to that point. The decision of 'appropriateness' can go either way. New religions *can* be created: Manichaeans can sing hymns to Jesus,[53] and still be judged eventually to be outside the Christian universe of meaning (the Christian hierarchies of structure) because there is too disjunctive a mismatch between the Manichaean 'sense' of Jesus and the many available senses of Jesus in the Christian universe of meaning. This is not to deny that Manichaeans or Seventh Day Adventists or Mormons can claim to be 'the only true Christians', but this claim can at least be structurally tested, as Augustine intuitively realized by emphasizing the importance of relation to original resources of meaning.

These two examples, musical tradition and syncretism, may perhaps clarify the way in which the structuring process is necessarily conservative, because one particular control of appropriateness must lie in the relation of innovation to the already structured: and yet, at the same time, the structuring process can be constantly creative and innovatory. Piaget, therefore, summarized the process by saying: 'Structure is simply a system of transformations.'[54] The task of structural theology in relation to the human senses of God is to uncover precisely those transformation rules or laws which have generated, constituted, and governed particular theistic universes of meaning. What must always be borne in mind is that no matter how 'fixed' certain resources of meaning may be—Torah on Sinai, Jesus on the cross, the Buddha under the Bo-tree—they do not themselves *constitute* a final or fixed structure of structures. This point is strongly emphasized by Piaget: 'As we have come to see more clearly through Gödel but knew long before, the ideal of a structure of all structures is unrealizable. The *subject* cannot, therefore, be the *a priori* underpinning of a finished posterior structure; rather it is a centre of activity. And whether we substitute 'society' or 'mankind' or 'life' or even 'cosmos' for 'subject', the argument remains the same.'[55]

Does this mean that God, from a structural point of view, is in principle unrealizable? Piaget seems to suggest so:

The basic epistemological alternatives [in the problem of genesis] are predestination or some sort of constructivism. For the mathematician it is, of course, tempting to believe in ideas and to think of negative or imaginary numbers as lying in God's lap from all eternity. But God himself has, since Gödel's theorem, ceased to be motionless. He is the living God, more so than heretofore, because he is unceasingly constructing ever 'stronger' systems.[56]

It would, in other words, be mistaken to leap to a naïve speculation that perhaps 'God' is a term of reference to the structure of structures. Such a concept could not actually exist, because of the relative motion of all structures. It follows that whatever the term 'God' represents would either have to be found within the movement of structures itself, as process theology suggests, or else it would have to be posited as ontologically independent of the movement of structures but creatively involved in those structures as resource and goal. This is actually feasible and possible from an informational point of view, though no doubt one would then have to consider what on earth or in heaven (what in reality) could be represented by such a term.

This means that God may indeed be unrealizable but in a sense quite different from that implied by Piaget. What Piaget was in fact commenting on, in his illustration from mathematics, was the issue between a formalist and a platonist understanding of 'what is really there' in mathematics. A formalist, *roughly*, believes that mathematics is pure form, and that it makes as little sense for a mathematician to ask whether the real-number system really (in reality) contains infinitesimals as it would for a physicist (or at least for some physicists) to ask whether an electron *really* (in reality) has simultaneous position and velocity. A platonist believes that even undecidability (in Gödel's sense) is simply a reflection of the limitations of our present methods of investigating what is 'in reality' the case, but which lies beyond our full comprehension. One of the great paradoxes of the contemporary mathematical scene is that Robinson, who reinstated infinitesimals after their demise and decent burial in the nineteenth century, does not believe they 'really' exist, and has actually written that 'any mention of infinite totalities is literally meaningless'; whereas Gödel, who created so profound a revolution by his principle of undecidability, believed that there are realities in mathematical existence which we do not have the means adequately to discern.[57]

This example must not be pressed too far, as some theologians are tempted to press it. Gödel's theorem is epistemologically relevant only to a system which has attained a high degree of formalization, as was thought to be the case with mathematics before 1931. But since even other sciences are very far from complete formalization, it is clear that some hesitation is required before finding in Gödel's theorem a comment on epistemology or on ontology which can then be generally or extensively applied. The point about Gödel's undecidability theorem is that it is not primarily commenting on ontology. It demonstrates the limitations of formalism. The unprovable formula exhibited (unprovable because it cannot be derived from the axioms according to the rules of inference in the formal system concerned) is nevertheless argued to be true by resorting to an intuitive apprehension of the so-called 'standard universe' of natural numbers. This argument for the truth of the formula, despite its unprovability, is thus a case of theorizing 'as-if' in a platonic universe of ideal mathematical objects enjoying the structure of the standard natural

numbers. The point is that one could not arrive at Gödel's conclusions unless one started from an 'as-if' basis, that there are
ideal realities. But this is *not* a comment on ontology. Thus as
Davis and Hersh comment, on non-standard analysis:

> When we say infinitesimals or monads exist, it should be clear that we
> do not mean this at all in the sense it would have been understood by
> Euclid or by Berkeley. Until 100 years ago it was tacitly assumed . . .
> that the subject matter of mathematics was objectively real in a sense
> closer to the sense in which the subject matter of physics is real.
> Whether infinitesimals did or did not exist was a question of fact, not
> too different from the question of whether material atoms do or do not
> exist . . . Model theory entails no commitment one way or the other on
> such ontological questions. What mathematicians want from infinite-
> simals is not material existence but rather the right to use them in
> proofs. For this all one needs is the assurance that a proof using in-
> finitesimals is no worse than one free of infinitesimals.[58]

In other words, 'as-if' stances have consequences which would
not obtain without the 'as-if' stance in question—consequences of
genuine procedural importance. This is equally true of acting
'as-if' God exists with particular characteristics; and no one doubts
that such 'as-if' beliefs are consequential. But this is *not* a comment on ontology in itself. Therefore, quite correctly, John Hick
has added to his explorations of the 'as-if' quality of theistic
belief a factor of ontological specification, namely, eschatological
verification.[59] Whether this is a successful conjunction is a question which would need to be separately discussed. What is certainly correct is his recognition that 'as-if' stances are not ontological comments.

Nevertheless, it is clear that a structural theology would incline
more to the side of Gödel (supposing the comparison were at all
legitimate, even in a remote sense), that it is not 'literally meaningless' to talk approximately of what may in reality be the case with
regard to God. On the contrary, it is abundantly clear, from a
structural point of view, that the hierarchies of structure which
constitute the sense of God could not possibly function unless this
were so, for one central and all-important reason: for God to *be*
God, for 'appropriateness' to occur at all in theistic language,
'God' must be posited beyond the limitations for whose penetration he seems to be required. Obviously (to take an example), if
God is subject to death he cannot act as a symbol of stability

beyond death. It is in this way that the sense of God is regressive and that God must necessarily be unrealized here and now, but not in principle unrealizable as such. The nearer 'God' comes to being captured, pinned down, ostensively defined, the more he, she, it, or they moves back beyond those points of attainment. The theistic structures which exist in the world, as they *do* exist, could not exist unless this were so. Thus Flew's 'death by a thousand qualifications' is actually also 'life by a thousand qualifications', as Flew himself recognized very clearly in a discussion on 'Creation': 'In any sophisticated theism God has to be conceived as a being beyond all finite human powers of understanding.'[60]

Of course, Flew *then* went on to say: *therefore* it seems doubtful whether anything intelligible can be said about God.[61] But that is precisely the structural and informational issue: it is by pressure on the plausibility of existing 'senses of God' that either one believes that implausibility has been established (as with Flew), *or else* the hierarchies of existing structure constitute a new structure of intelligible meaning.

This means that Nielsen's arguments against Christianity and Judaism could actually be put much more strongly. Nielsen has argued that although Judaism and Christianity make putative truth-claims, their central claims 'remain just *putative* truth-claims':

That they are actually without truth-value does not mean that they are meaningless. On the contrary, religious talk, it is generally agreed, is not flatly meaningless. There are deviant and non-deviant religious utterances. But for all that it remains the case that such utterances as 'God created man in his image and likeness' or even 'There is a transcendent cause of the universe' or 'The universe is dependent on God' have no ascertainable truth-value, and we do not know what we are referring to when we use 'God' in a religiously appropriate way.[62]

But this could—and should, from the point of view of what the notion of God actually does—be put much more sharply. In religious contexts, it is not simply that we *do* not know what we are referring to when we use the term 'God', but that we *could* not know, in any fully ostensive sense, if that use is to be in 'a religiously appropriate way'. If it is 'generally agreed' that there can be deviant and non-deviant religious utterances, then one needs to examine structurally what generates particular theistic languages—

what it is that constitutes particular theistic 'universes of meaning' —and why it must be the case that 'God' stands for the point not yet attained. Anything less than that leads to what the theistic traditions frequently refer to as idolatry.

To make this point clear the example of the Tower of Babel is instructive. In the scriptural account, the offence of the builders of the tower is not specified very explicitly; and God in fact punishes them because they threaten to become too competent— perhaps to rival himself. Christian interpretation has usually accepted that latter hint, that the offence was arrogance—thinking that one could actually build oneself up to God. But the traditional Jewish interpretation is much more subtle: by comparing the word *shem* in Genesis 11: 4 with the same word in Exodus 23: 13, Jewish exegetes concluded that the builders had in fact built the tower in order to put an idol on the top of it to protect them against attack from enemies. The offence lay, not simply in trying to attain God but in pretending they had done so when they found that in reality they could not reach heaven but required a tangible reality on whom they could rely for defence—hence the idol. The offence, both of the literal and the conceptual architecture of idolatry, is that it brings 'God' within our grasp and ostensive definition; and the insistence of all the developed (and still developing) theistic universes of meaning (i.e. those theistic traditions which are still structurally in movement) is that the implication of idolatry is that God cannot *be* God: it is an attempt to arrive prematurely at the goal, in such a way that one actually would not be able to arrive (for example, through death) at all, because God has been so reduced in scale that he is not sufficiently God for that to be possible: 'your God is too small'. This is even true of Hinduism, which incorporates and encourages what would appear, in terms externally of *surface*-meaning, to be idolatry. But this is because Hinduism encourages appropriate action, *dharma*; and for the relatively uninformed villager a wreath of flowers on a tree may be of the most extreme value. But even Hinduism insists that what appears to others (even to other Hindus) as 'idolatry', however necessary in terms of appropriate action, is not the final realization of Being-itself, of Brahman, but rather that it is a means towards that end in the long process of *samsara*, rebirth, through which an individual may hope to move through the hierarchies of structure (of, for example, caste) up to final attainment. In other words, Hinduism, because of the cycle of rebirth, is able to incorporate hierarchies of structure synchronically as well as diachronically (not only through time but also laterally across time). The hierarchies of structure through which Hindu meaning is constituted can be present all at once, at any moment in time; but the much more linear emphasis of the main Western theisms, Judaism, Christianity, and Islam, has made it very difficult for them to incorporate lower structures (idolatry) synchronically; idolatry, even though it *does* occur, ought to lie 'back there', at a time before God revealed that he is 'not like that'.

The recovery of theism, in Jewish tradition, after the expulsion from paradise (in other words, the recovery of appropriateness in God-language), is associated with Abraham, and it is focused in his conflict with idolaters, particularly with Nimrod, the greatest idolater of them all. Some of the stories which relate this are translated in *Targums and Rabbinic Literature*,[63] and these all exemplify the issue, that idolatry is self-defeating because, by being an attempt to arrive at premature and ostensive definition, it destroys the godness of God. It destroys what God must be in order to be God.

The sense of God, then, must be indefinitely regressive—not infinitely, tempting though it is to use that word in connection with God, because it may be that the attainment of the beatific vision is not impossible. But it must be indefinitely regressive, not only in the sense that regression is necessary for any appropriateness in God-language to be established, but also in the structural sense in which the 'sense of the universe' is regressive: final understanding is not attained, it recedes before research in the sense that there is always something more to be known; there are, for this reason, 'structures of scientific revolution'.

But the question immediately presses forward, *what* is regressive in the sense of God? At least as science puts pressure on the boundaries of what is known, it can, to some extent, point to its subject matter. Short of the beatific vision, to what can theological exploration point? Is it not likely (Marx and Freud would have said, Is it not certain?) that the notion of God is constructed in the imagination precisely because without that imaginary construction we know that *some* limitations, particularly suffering and death, cannot be penetrated? 'L'énigme insoluble du monde, l'existence du mal et de la douleur, la folie furieuse de la race humaine . . .':[64]

from this point of view, granted that there must be a logical sense in which 'God' as a symbol retreats in the face of definition, there is no ontological reality whose attainment is regressing in the crises of plausibility: it *is*, after all, death, not life, by a thousand qualifications.

This may well be so; but we cannot decide whether it is so, unless we look carefully at whether or not there is any discernible effect of the claimed object of belief in the construction of human universes of meaning and, if so, what those effects are—the point which has already been repeatedly made: for, supposing there *is* an apparent sufficiency of effect—even if apparent to one person alone—it is life, not death, by qualification: and it is this which took Jesus to Gethsemane and to the cross.

This possibility cannot be excluded simply because Marx and Freud say so, though that, needless to say, *is* sufficient for many people. It needs to be tested very carefully within the theistic traditions themselves. The critical informational point is this: if there were no feedback at all, it is virtually impossible to account for the hierarchies of theistic structures which have in fact been constructed in the world, since these are not invariably stable. The point of access to understanding lies principally in the crises of plausibility, where pressure is put on the implications of the 'godness' of God. But how can this informational and structural point be tested? It certainly requires that we look very carefully at the psychology of claimed experiences of God, as equally at the light which psychology can throw on the pressures which obtain in the human constructions of the sense of God, which give rise to *apparent* senses of God. And since Freud was undoubtedly one of those who believed that the genesis of God occurs within the pressures of psychological demand, and since, more seriously, Freud has been so fundamentally influential in transforming the construction of human understanding, particularly the understanding of religious unreality, it seems advisable to make Freud our next point of departure.

VI

FREUDIAN THEORY AND THE PROJECTION OF GOD

AT the end of the last chapter it was suggested that Freud should be taken as the point of departure for what follows. But this immediately raises a difficult problem: can Freud be taken seriously at all? To many people, particularly those working in experimental psychology, Freud is not only wrong but a real obstruction to any genuine, empirically-based knowledge of psychology—even to the extent of one Cambridge experimental psychologist wishing heartily that Dr. Freud had never been born.[1] The opposition and anger which Freud arouses should not be evaded: if anything of value is to be derived from Freudian method in understanding how the human senses of God are formed, and what functions they serve in the construction of personal lives, the issue of the status of Freudian method and theory has to be faced. But in order to lead into this issue, it may be helpful to summarize, as briefly as possible, some of the main features of Freud's theory of the origin of the sense of God.

If this were anything other than a brief recapitulation it would obviously be necessary to look at the circumstances in Freud's own case which led him to construct his theories as he did: his own, not particularly observant, Jewish family, in a predominantly Catholic environment; his first experiences of anti-Semitism; his inimical relation to Schmidt, which was clearly critical for his own use of totemism; these are obvious examples—indeed, of Schmidt, Freud wrote: 'It is said that the politics of our country are made by a Father Schmidt who lives in St. Gabriel near Mödling and is a confidant of the Pope. Unfortunately he himself is an ethnologist and a religious scholar who in his books makes no secret of his horror of psychoanalysis and above all of my totem theory.'[2] But since this account is not intended to be analytic of Freud himself, it is perhaps sufficient simply to accept that these feelings and experiences were a fundamental means through which Freud arrived at his understanding of religion.

Looking at the theory itself, it is clear that this understanding eventually put together several component elements. The first was his tripartite description of psychic function and process: the basic, quantitatively fixed, instinctual drives represented in the id —'that cauldron of seething excitement' as Freud described it,[3] demanding expression: 'it contains everything that is inherited, that is present at birth, that is fixed in the constitution—above all, therefore, the instincts . . .';[4] then the gradually formed superego articulating restraint on the id ('the successor and representative of the parents (and educators) who superintended the actions of the individual in his first years of life; it perpetuates their functions almost without a change')[5] which thus becomes a 'conscience'; and then, mediating between the steady-state demands of the id and the external world, formed by the conflicting demands of the id and of the restraining superego, determined principally 'by the individual's own experience, that is to say by accidental and current events'[6] (as opposed to the instinctual demands of the id which are inherited as a given quantity), the ego, the organization of a man's drives and behaviour 'the organized part of the id'.[7]

It is the tripartite mental process which constructs religion as it constructs all else; but why *religion*? Freud attempted to answer this question from two different points of view, the one historical, the other psychological; or to put it more precisely, Freud attempted to explain both the phylogenetic and the ontogenetic origins of religion. He thus attempted to explain the beginnings of religion in the history of the human race (the themes, particularly, of *Totem and Taboo* and of *Moses and Monotheism*) and the beginnings of religion in the history of every individual, no matter what his situation in time or space (the theme, particularly, of *The Future of an Illusion*). The vital point to grasp is that the phylogenetic and the ontogenetic explanations are interlocked.

What, then, in briefest possible form, did Freud claim to be the origins of a sense of God? The most familiar formulation is probably the *als-ob*, the as-if, of *The Future of an Illusion*. Here Freud depended on a further postulated universal of psychic formation, the Oedipal situation in which all infants necessarily find themselves as a consequence of being born and of being unable to realize their instinctual drives in relation to the parent of the opposite sex. The family represents the earliest learning situation in which the ego organizes and channels the drives of the id and in which the superego is formed. The resolution of conflict, the continuity of life in clear dependence on parents, and the achievement of a *modus vivendi* in the context of what is rapidly learnt to be a dangerous environment are achieved in the family, in what is in effect a micro-universe. What more natural, then, as one moves into the universe at large, than to attempt to reproduce the patterns which have already led to a more or less successful *modus vivendi*? 'Men cannot remain children for ever; they must in the end go out into "hostile life". We may call this "education to reality".'[8] But this is the basis of projection: the universe *in fact* is not a caring environment. It is indifferent to human feelings. It is impersonal, and at any moment, through earthquake, flood, or fire, it is capable of destroying human life and achievement. How can we face a faceless universe—in both senses of the word 'face'? By giving a face to the universe, by making it personal—or at least by making it an arena in which purpose and care are exercised—we enable ourselves to face up to its terrors and confusions. We create in the imagination (because it does not exist in fact) a father-figure, and we project it into the universe, and live 'as-if' that illusory figure will care for us.

The basis on which the faceless universe is faced is the earliest set of experiences in which men have learnt to resolve conflicts, to organize instinctual drives, and to achieve a *modus vivendi*, the family, which is in character necessarily Oedipal. But of course to achieve that earliest *modus vivendi* a price has to be paid: the drives of the id, for example, have to be repressed; an accommodation has to be found with the father on whom one depends and yet of whom one is deeply jealous. The price that has to be paid, in extreme form, is neurosis. In summary form, 'neurosis is the result of a conflict between the ego and its id';[9] 'the neurotic turns away from reality because he finds it unbearable—either the whole or part of it';[10] 'we cannot escape the conclusion that neuroses could be avoided if the child's sexual life were allowed free play, as happens among many primitive races'[11]—if, in other words, the instinctual drive were organized and channelled, instead of repressed in the Oedipal situation. But equally, 'neurosis seems to be a human privilege';[12] and civilization, for all its discontents and repressive necessities, at least protects us from nature and enables other achievements.

Since manifestly the projection of care and purpose into the universe requires the repression of unwelcome reality (the fact that the universe is not caring or purposeful) and the creation of an imaginary father to correspond to the earliest-learnt source of care and purpose, it follows that religion would be a universal neurosis. It is the illusory *als-ob*, the creation of what one wishes the universe might be; and religion is a consequence of living as-if that wishful thinking is true. So Freud commented:

I am reminded of one of my children who was distinguished at an early age by a peculiarly marked matter-of-factness. Whenever the children were being told a fairy-story and were listening to it with rapt attention, he would come up and ask: 'Is that a true story?' When he was told it was not, he would turn away with a look of disdain. We may expect that people will soon behave in the same way towards the fairy tales of religion, in spite of the advocacy of 'As if'.[13]

All this is familiar to the point of tedium. What may perhaps not be so familiar is that Freud based his 'as-if' projective theory on the very technical *als-ob* of Vaihinger. The dependence is specific in a footnote to *The Future of an Illusion*, in which Freud expressed the hope that he was not doing Vaihinger an injustice by taking him as 'the representative of a view which is not foreign to other thinkers'.[14] In fact this was a fundamental mistake on Freud's part, because Vaihinger was concerned with technical problems in epistemology and in the theory of knowledge, the relation of speculative thought to mechanistic reality, whereby thought can misconceive the reality and yet arrive at correct conclusions. The problem was expressed by Vaihinger in these words: "The course of nature is unchangeable and proceeds according to hard and unalterable laws. Nature has an iron will (*der Wille der Natur ist eisern*); but thought (*des Denken*) is an adaptable, pliant and adjustable organic function.'[15]

But in that case the question arises, to put it again in Vaihinger's own words: 'How does it happen that although in thinking we make use of a falsified reality, *the practical result still proves to be right*?' Vaihinger suggested that even if an idea is later shown conclusively in objective terms to be inadequate in its representation of what is in fact the case, it may nevertheless have great practical importance. What Freud did was to transpose Vaihinger's problem. But in doing so he lost sight of what was in fact problematic: how it is that in 'as-if' behaviour men arrive, on the basis of what was originally falsified reality, at conclusions which turn out to be viable and correct in practice? Freud took it as obvious that religion creates a falsified reality—gods and angels, heavens and hells; he also took it as obvious that the religious believer acts, by definition, 'as-if' these falsified realities are real in existence. What he did not pursue was a strictly Vaihingerian line which might have led him to ask whether, on the basis of what were originally falsified realities, men might nevertheless arrive at correct conclusions—the true, as opposed to the falsified, reality of God. Obviously, since, from Freud's point of view, God does not, *a priori*, exist in reality (and Freud simply took this for granted), the falsified, 'as-if' realities of religious constructions (gods, heavens, hells) must be falsifications of something else, and that 'something else' can only be the 'real' nature of the universe. Thus Freud transposed Vaihinger's question to become: how does it happen that although in religion men make use of a falsified reality, the practical result still proves to be useful—not *correct*, but *useful*?

The answer could only be, because religion enables men to resolve their fears and conflicts on a cosmic scale, and enables them to defy what they know in reality to be the case, the oblivion which awaits them in death.

> What shall be said of me? 'He lived a span—
> Then died.' No more! What more of any man?[16]

This misconception of Vaihinger's problem exposes the poverty of Freud's ontogenetic analysis. It also explains why Freud was not dismayed when his *phylogenetic* explanations of the origin of religion in the history of the human race were dismissed as erroneous speculations. Freud was quite capable of over-reacting under pressure and insisting that his reconstruction, in *Totem and Taboo*, referred to an event that had actually happened. Yet he was equally capable of referring to it as a 'just-so' story, the kind of thing that must, so to speak, have happened even though it actually had not. What Freud did, in effect, was put together a do-it-yourself kit of miscellaneous parts in order to exemplify Oedipal situations as universal. He extracted primal hordes from Atkinson, jealous gorillas from Darwin, the connection between totemism and father-killing from Robertson Smith, and put them together in *Totem and Taboo* as an explanation of the origin of religion: the sons in a primal horde, jealous of their father who reserved the women they desired for themselves, slew their father and devoured him; but then, overcome with remorse and guilt, they set up a totem as a means to expiate their guilt and propitiate the father-figure. Here one has the resolution of an Oedipal conflict in a manner which creates religion (by the setting-up of the totem); and totemism is thus 'the earliest appearance of religion in the history of mankind'.[17]

This ramshackle machine, assembed from odd parts which Freud found lying around in his library, was quite incapable of flying. It bore no relation to the equivalent of aerodynamic facts, namely, anthropological evidence as a whole. But this did not disturb Freud: if the evidence for some situations pointed in other directions, or against his explanation, it simply meant that the Oedipal conflict in those situations was in fact being resolved totemically, even though certain surviving totemic practices did not make this manifest: what in fact is happening in those cases, according to Freud, is that layers of defence and repression have been built up as a way of handling the basic Oedipal guilt. Thus no evidence could possibly shake Freud's certainty that he had identified the Oedipal origin of religion in the history of the human race; and whether or not the event he described, the original slaying of the father, ever actually took place did not really matter. Exactly the same is true of *Moses and Monotheism*, in which Freud relied heavily on the theory of Sellin (a Biblical scholar) to the effect that Moses, who was an Egyptian, had not died, but had been killed by the Israelites, in a way which might be interpreted as the resolution of an Oedipal conflict. When told that Sellin had withdrawn his theory because of the pressure of evidence and argument against it, Freud simply replied that even if it had not happened as he had suggested, it nevertheless *could* have happened that way.[18]

The point is obvious: Freud was concerned with synchronic analysis, not with the possible effects of diachronic process: because the Oedipal situations and the tripartite nature of mental process are universals, they *must* be present at the origin of religion and within every subsequent manifestation of religious behaviour, no matter how deeply the Oedipal conflict and the instinctual drives may have been repressed in the variant forms of expression. This means that no evidence could possibly count against Freudian theory in its classical form. The basic defect of Freud's theory of religion is not that it cannot possibly be right, but that it cannot possibly be wrong: all evidence that superficially appears to contradict the theory is converted to become evidence *for* the theory, because it can be regarded as evidence of repression or of defence against the true nature of what is going on.

This manœuvre appeared in full flower in the Jones–Malinowski debate of the 1920s. Picking up a clue from C. G. Seligman, Malinowki marshalled ethnographic evidence from the Trobriand Islands which suggested that the Oedipal situation did not obtain there. It is important to note that Malinowski was not, as a matter of fact, arguing against Freud as such, but only for a diversification of the way in which 'Freudian' fundamentals happen to be expressed.[19] The alternative nuclear complex which Malinowski postulated for the Trobriand Islands consisted of a triangular relationship between brother, sister, and sister's son, with the emphasis not on a patrilineal but on a matrilineal social structure. In this structure a boy becomes a member of his mother's kin group and is subject to the authority of his maternal uncle rather than to the authority of his actual father. The point here is not whether Malinowski's analysis is correct: kinship studies have moved a long way since the 1920s. The important point is that for Jones, Malinowski *could* not be right; and Malinowski discovered that Freudian formulae, far from being elastic, are made of impenetrable concrete. Jones replied that since parenthood and birth are universal, so also must the Oedipal situation be universal, no matter what subsequently and secondarily happens to have been layered above it as a consequence of social particularities:[20] there may be many 'modes of defence', but the complex remains '*the fons et origo*'.[21]

This is a classic example of the impossibility of falsifying Freudian theory, because evidence apparently to the contrary becomes evidence for the fact. What appears to be contrary can always be assimilated as evidence of repression, or as a defence mechanism. The ultimate deployment of this tactic occurs in the work of Geza Roheim, who argued that the failure to see the Oedipal situation as the universal point of departure for all human beings, and thus for all human enterprises, lies in the anthropologists themselves: their failure to see that the varieties of human culture are simply different repressive developments lies in the fact that they have failed to recognize and resolve their own

Oedipal conflicts. They are so threatened by the suppressed traces of their own Oedipal conflict that they push away violently *all* Oedipal situations and pretend they are 'something else'.[22]

We reach here the ultimate futility of all argument. It is not simply that everything proves the case, but that everything proves to *be* the case, including the anthropologist. It is this which creates the passion and anger of certain anti-Freudians, particularly of those who believe that knowledge of mental behaviour must be in principle empirically, not speculatively, based. Of this argument Max Hammerton, an experimental psychologist, is a good recent example. Hammerton opened a discussion on Freud in 1963 with these words: 'I am an experimental psychologist. My work at the moment is largely concerned with the effects of stress upon human performance. But in spite of all the efforts of many and distinguished colleagues in spreading the truth about scientific psychology, most of the people I meet seem to imagine that my stock-in-trade consists of a couch and a lot of verbiage about libido and id and what-not. Sometimes I heartily wish that Dr. Freud had never been born . . .'[23]

Hammerton did not deny that Freud 'was a shrewd and imaginatively gifted person',[24] but he attacked his theory on two grounds: 'I consider, first, that the whole corpus of Freudian doctrine, considered as a system, stands upon not one grain of scientific foundation; second, that there isn't a scrap of positive evidence that psychoanalysis has ever cured anybody of anything.'[25] What this amounts to is that Freudian theory predicts nothing and explains everything. As Hammerton put it: 'Whatever behaviour a person exhibits, there is a Freudian mechanism to account for it—*afterwards.* They sedulously avoid making predictions which can be put to the test: Freud himself called upon his disciples not to "delude themselves" into thinking they could do so.'[26]

This means that the dead can be explained as much as the living: after all, if there *is* a universal point of departure for all human beings, the dead as much as the living must be amenable to the same analysis. To quote Hammerton again: 'They tackle with equal aplomb the living and the dead. The dead, as a rule, cannot hit back: but there are exceptions even to this rule.' As an exception, Hammerton took the case of Darwin, whose apparent neurosis was frequently analysed, until it turned out that he had probably contracted Chagas's disease, which could have given rise to the same symptoms.[27]

In point of fact, Chagas's disease is much more complicated than Hammerton allows. Its 'symptoms' are more extensive than his brief description suggests, and *some* descriptions of the disease do not include the items which he specifies. The point is rather obvious, that a parasitic disease *may* reinforce or bring into the open dispositions of behaviour which pre-exist the incursion of the parasite. Only in a derivative sense would the 'depression and lethargy' then be symptoms of the disease itself. This may or may not be so in the case of Darwin; but the moral to be drawn is that it may be as difficult, in the case of some diseases, physiologically to analyse the dead as it is to psychoanalyse them. Nevertheless, Hammerton's point could still be argued, that Freudian theory, by insisting on universals of psychic formation, must invariably find what it is looking for. But if there cannot be negative instances, the theory becomes, for practical purposes, virtually non-specific.

This kind of case against taking Freudian theory seriously from a scientific point of view has been made repeatedly and continues to be made: in, for example, *Fact and Fantasy in Freudian Theory*, Paul Kline has set out 'to establish what parts of Freudian theory have been confirmed or, at least, could be confirmed by objective scientific psychological research.'[28] It opens with yet another summary of the anti-Freudian argument.[29] On this kind of basis, it is not in the least difficult to launch a Pearl Harbour attack on Freudian theory and sink the whole fleet without the trace of even a surviving bubble. Why, then, has so much time been spent retracing this apparently unprofitable ground?

The answer is relatively obvious: it is because, to continue the metaphor, the *Lexington* and the *Yorktown* have slipped out to sea; consequently, the real striking force of Freudian *method*, as opposed to detail of the theory, has *not* been sunk, and the battles of the Coral Sea and of Midway remain yet to be fought. Let us revert for a moment to Hammerton's two objections, the first that Freudian doctrine 'stands upon not one grain of scientific foundation', and the second that there is no evidence 'that psychoanalysis has ever cured anybody of anything'. What this means in effect is that in terms of medical specification nothing can count that cannot be counted. Hammerton put it in this way: 'The only way that the efficiency of a treatment can be decided is . . . a statistical comparison of experimental and control groups. As far as I know, no psychoanalyst has ever attempted to do this; and some have quite explicitly refused to do so.'[30]

On this point, Hammerton was factually wrong; an experiment had in fact been carried out (and its results were already in print), which supports the claim to beneficial effects as a consequence of therapeutic and 'insight-promoting' relationships with schizophrenic patients; this was a study undertaken in the University of Wisconsin and in the Mendota State Hospital.[31] But let us suppose that Hammerton is, on this point, factually correct, and that in terms of repeatable specification psychoanalysis cannot identify either an illness or a cure, as, for example, paracetamol can repeatedly 'cure' (or at least suppress the symptoms of) a certain range of conditions which produce headache—but note that paracetamol will not 'cure all headaches'; and more serious conditions can be specified by the inability of paracetamol to effect more than a temporary alleviation of symptoms, a point one can readily observe by reading the small print on the label.

The response of a psychoanalyst might be to say, so what? That may be your definition of illness and cure, but *my* definition is the patient who as a consequence of analysis is able to organize and reconstruct his life in less anguished, more hopeful, ways, and who also knows, in his own experience, the difference between 'before' and 'after'. This is the exact note on which Guntrip ended his recent White Institute seminars on 'Treatment and Schizoid Persons'.[32] If one looks at the last sentence of that passage (which is unquestionably true in human experience), then the term 'cure' in Hammerton's sense can probably be conceded: what is occurring—or is able to occur—in a psychoanalytic relationship is not a 'cure' but a learning-experience, not an elimination of symptoms but a recognition of what they are; and this can be a means through which a person is able to gain understanding of his feelings and his actions, and can perhaps acquire the will to continue his life with greater freedom. No one claims that this invariably happens as a consequence of analysis; but that it does happen is undeniable.

One can even put the case more strongly: it may sometimes be the case that the terms of analysis refer to nothing in the reality of a particular person's experience at all, but that although tangential, they suggest to a person the means through which he can escape the dilemma of his own person by offering acceptable and plausible explanations of his condition. To put the case in its most extreme form, it is possible that psychoanalytic theory has created a mythology of substance in the psyche which enables people to 'grip hold of' their otherwise elusive moods and feelings and emotions, and which thus gives them the sense that they are seeing, if not the world, then at least their own selves, aright: 'Dann sieht er die Welt richtig';[33] and if Wittgenstein can be misquoted a little further, it may be that the propositions of analysis serve as elucidations in the sense that anyone who understands them eventually recognizes them as nonsensical—not in Hammerton's sense of nonsensical, but in the sense that 'when he has used them—as steps—to climb up beyond them, he must so to speak, throw away the ladder after he has climbed up it'.

The shift implied in this is really of profound importance, because it means that what psychoanalysis is ultimately claiming is that each person is (interlocked with others and deriving resources from mutually available environments) engaged in the construction of a personal life and universe, which frequently requires shared insight if it is to be successfully achieved. All of us, to transfer Neurath's famous illustration, are repairing the boat while at sea.[34] The centre of focus for analysis is not—or should not be—the defence of particular mythologies (the mistake of the earlier Freudians) but the enabling of personal construct, particularly (where necessary) through the sharing of accumulated experience and insight. The importance of intuitive mythologies is that they make available a language for public discussion and for the individual learning-experience. Without that intuitive mythology, the founding of psychoanalysis and thus the beginning of this means of learning-experience, would not have been possible. This in itself opens up a more sharply defined understanding of the phenomena in question—in this case the comparability of certain behavioural patterns.

It follows that one of the central problems in assessing psychoanalytic claims is not so much the empirical/non-empirical debate, where the issue is usually focused. The far more fundamental problem is to know how intuitive terms derived from conversational usage can be established as valid when taken over into a scientific, or would-be scientific, vocabulary—a problem discussed by Hempel in *Fundamentals of Concept Formation in Empirical Science.*[35] The problem becomes even more complicated in the case of psychoanalysis, because many of its major terms are not so much derived *from* conversational usage, as contributing *to* conversational usage: terms such as ego, superego, and id; suppression; sublimation; Oedipal; complex; fixation have flowed *into* conversation and become part of the mental environment of many people. They quite clearly seem to possess some sort of meaning, and the question is how that apparent 'meaning' can in fact be given a more precise, specifying, definition. Attempts have certainly been made to test the intuitive mythologies of Freudian theory by other experimental approaches. Some of these are assembled in Lee and Herbert, *Freud and Psychology*, and reference has already been made to Paul Kline's survey; but the correlations are extremely thin. Even at so fundamental a point as the tripartite division of psychic process, id, ego, superego, Kline's conclusion is succinct: 'There is no firm support from neurophysiological studies of brain functions for the Freudian tripartite division of the mind. Brain function is not sufficiently well understood for this to be possible.'[36]

This necessarily means that Freud *may* turn out to be right, in the end; the evidence is not yet sufficient to establish a decision. But this in itself does not alter the fact that Freudian theory is exactly as Farrell has described it, 'a premature empirical [one should perhaps say quasi-empirical] synthesis offered in advance of the evidence'.[37]

In a sense, this is what is meant by suggesting that Freudian theory offers an intuitive mythology—a book of genesis of the human psyche, with all the rich opportunities which such mythologies afford. This does not absolve us from the responsibility of correcting the factual, hypostasizing claims of a mythology (if these in fact are made; Freud was judicious on this point) where these seem no longer to be justified.[38] 'Instinct' is a particularly good example of the confusions which can arise when it is hypostasized as an existent entity ('the territorial instinct'; 'the aggressive instinct'; 'the instinctual sexual drive') which is quantitatively inherited and which must be satisfied. On this point, Gregory Bateson's Metalogue is instructive.[39]

But the points on which psychoanalysis insists are that the individual must be regarded as the centre of his own activity in the construction of his personal universe (consequently, more is required for the understanding of this process than, for example, factor-analytic correlations); and that certainly much more is usually required in circumstances of disordered, or disorientated, behaviour than the modification of that disorder through, for example, appropriate chemotherapy. To say this is not in the least to underestimate the crucial and indispensable importance of such therapy in itself. The point, put crudely, is that a person discharged from a psychiatric ward has actually to go on living, often in the same circumstances which obtained before admission. The personal construction of life goes on, however much undergirded by chemotherapeutic assistance. It was this observation which led Kelly to form his theory of personal constructs, in which the role of the therapist is, in part, to help the patient to visualize alternative routes of construction which lead out of his present situation.[40] This, once again, picks up the threads and relates closely to what has been argued earlier about route-finding and the compounds of limitation. Certainly Freudian analysis can offer help to some individuals as they attempt to discern the compounds of limitation which have constrained them so far into their own particularity. For some people these can be, or can feel to be, constraints of a very tight bondage.

Thus psychotherapy itself moves on, and in some respects leaves the details of Freud far behind. Perhaps the most important change, as we now at last come close to asking what, post-Freud, remains in a psychoanalytic understanding of the origin of the sense of God, is the shift of emphasis implied in the move to an object-relations theory—as, for example, in the work of Fairbairn.[41] What is implied here is that instead of the psychic process being understood as a kind of mechanism driven from behind by the id and the superego, which happens to collide with certain objects in the world of everyday reality, the psychic process is understood as being deeply formed and directed by the very quality of (or alternatively the absence of) relations with the 'objects' which occur; and here the first 'object' with which an infant experiences (or fails to experience) relationship, his mother, is all important. The reality of the object *in effect* is reinstated as being of wholly critical importance.

This has vast implications for the psychoanalytic understanding of the origin of the sense of God. First, it means that projection as a means through which particular characterizations of God occur remains undisturbed—though I would suggest that the word replication, rather than projection, would be much more accurate in this new dimension of understanding. Certainly without replication it is hard to know how one could possibly hope to talk of the untalkable, speak of the unspeakable, and (in certain cultic situations) mention the unmentionable in any other way. The construction both of action and meaning in an individual life necessarily depends on what has been acquired in previous learning-situations, not least those contexts in which one has learnt the experience of one's self in relation to others and to one's environment; and of those contexts the family is clearly fundamental.

But the huge advantage of moving beyond Freud is that we no longer have to assimilate all family situations to one kinship reality, the Oedipal: we are looking instead at the object-relations which actually do (or fail to) obtain. It is thus possible to accept (even more, to emphasize) that 'the family' does indeed generate an infant's first experiences of his self, both good and bad, and that it is suggestive of other contexts of relationship, including perhaps a paranatural one. But here 'the family' has become almost a nominal definition of those people who in different modes furnish the infant's first experiences of a continuous other; and this means that one can pay deeply serious attention to the effects of variables within that definition, because one no longer has to pretend that the Oedipal situation offers a real definition of 'the family'. An obvious example of the profound importance of this shift can be seen in the work of Winnicott, where the importance of the mother as a variable has been disentangled.[42]

The point about the replication of early learning-situations is by no means wholly vague: there are some generalities which appear to be of real effect in the conceptualization of God, of which dependency is the most obvious. The infant cannot continue its own existence without dependence on others. But it is *dependence* which is the generality, not the actual figures which supply it: thus, dependence on an actual father is not necessary as a generality, but dependence is. The psychoanalytic suggestion is that if 'god' is conceived to be necessary for the continuity of one's existence through limitations which one knows one cannot penetrate on one's own (for example, death), then dependency will be replicated in the conceptualization of God. Such replication will occur, not simply in intellectual terms (perhaps least of all in these) but in attitudes, dispositions, and feelings which will pervade all behaviour, but particularly behaviour in specifically religious contexts —in rituals, in the postures of prayer, in ecclesiastical authoritarianism, and the like.[43] But what is clear is that patterns of dependence (for example, of infant nurture) vary considerably throughout the world, and that consequently the actual characterizations of dependence in replication will vary greatly—as indeed they do. If, therefore, a psychoanalytic claim to the importance of dependence in replication is to be substantiated, it could be tested, from an anthropological point of view, by seeing whether correlations obtain between characterizations of God or gods and differently expressed patterns of dependence, much as Swanson tested the correlations between high gods and the number of hierarchies of authority in particular societies.

From all this, there follow three important implications. First, the hypothesis remains plausible and in some respects verified that experiences in initial learning-situations are a resource in memory traces, no longer immediately accessible to conscious reflection, which human beings utilize in the construction of their lives by means of projection and replication; and that in constructing the possibility of a paranatural reality, the characterization of that reality both replicates and compensates for the pleasure and pain of those initial experiences.

So, second, if there is to be a psychoanalytic theory of the ontogenesis of the sense of God it must show sets of correlation between the varieties of theistic characterization and the varieties of learning-situation which in fact obtain; and this is in principle a possible and feasible project.

But, third, there would no longer be any justification on psychoanalytic grounds for claiming that there is only *one* relevant learning-situation (the Oedipal), or that only one learning-situation generates a sense of God: and just as a more variable sense of 'family' has been demanded by the evidence, so a possibility of more learning-situations than the infantile family context alone must be allowed—indeed, the therapeutic relationship is clearly one (no matter how much it is claimed that this, through the process of transference, simply replicates the infantile family experience: it clearly cannot do so isomorphically).

Thus the focus of psychoanalysis is no longer simply the internal mechanism whereby psychic states or conditions are generated; it is also the effect of externality in both sustaining and disintegrating the construction of a personal life. Psychoanalysis has returned, in other words, to an acceptance of the possible effect of the reality of objects as encountered, even when those objects have been mentally constructed into a replication of earlier experience. It follows that it would be impossible on psychoanalytic grounds alone to exclude the possibility that God is a source of the sense of God: however much a sense of God may be constructed through, and as a consequence of, the replication of infantile experience, and however much the characterization of God may replicate parental relationships, the possibility cannot be excluded that there may be x in reality which has in the past sustained those replications and which has reinforced the continuity of such terms as 'god'.

The point will perhaps be a little clearer if we consider, as an example, the case of marriage—or more particularly, the case of the Yonghy-Bonghy-Bò.[44] He lived, it will be remembered,

On the coast of Coromandel
Where the early pumpkins blow

and his circumstances were somewhat deprived:

Two old chairs, and half a candle,
One old jug without a handle,—
These were all his worldly goods:
In the middle of the woods . . .

Then he comes across the lady Jingly Jones:

'Lady Jingly! Lady Jingly!
Sitting where the pumpkins blow,
Will you come and be my wife?'
Said the Yonghy-Bonghy-Bò.
'I am tired of living singly,—
On this coast so wild and shingly,—
I'm a-weary of my life;
If you'll come and be my wife,
Quite serene would be my life!'—
Said the Yonghy-Bonghy-Bò,
Said the Yonghy-Bonghy-Bò.

This is a good example, in miniature, of compensatory replication and projection. The Lady Jingly Jones is created in the imagination of the Yonghy-Bonghy-Bò as the means through which his misery will somehow dissolve. It is entirely possible to regard approaches to marriage as projective in that way, as attempts to find in another person the response to one's own needs. In that sense, the other person is created in the image of what she or he is needed to be; and that 'need' is constructed to a very great extent out of the experience of relationship—or the lack of adequate relationship—in infancy.

From this projective standpoint, the partner in a marriage is always an illusory construction, fulfilling, or failing to fulfil, roles which exist only in the psyche of the other person. The partner, or would-be partner, is thus created as the object of belief, a belief that he or she will lead to certain consequences:

> "If you'll come and be my wife,
> Quite serene would be my life!"

The real truth in this analysis is indispensable if one is going to have any understanding of achievement in marriage or equally of marital breakdown. Yet one knows immediately that it is a wholly inadequate account: what it fails to include is the rather obvious fact that there is a reality in the object of belief, a reality in existence of the other person which has its own contribution and effect. There is, in other words, a feedback from the reality of the object into the mental construct, which has to be assimilated in some way.

Freud took the point perfectly well in the case of love. On the one hand, love, according to Freud, represents desire and frustration in the ego, as in this passage: 'Being in love is based on the simultaneous presence of directly sexual tendencies and of sexual tendencies that are inhibited in their aims, so that the object draws a part of the narcissistic ego–libido to itself. It is a condition in which there is only room for the ego and the object.'[43] But there is in this case a responsive object which, by its response, enables the transcendence of the need, the point of departure: 'Love in itself, in the form of longing and deprivation, lowers the self-regard; whereas to be loved, to have love returned, and to possess the beloved object, exalts it again.'[46]

There is, in other words, according to Freud, a sequence of instinctual libidinal energy seeking an object, of the object responding in effect, and of the consequent relationship wholly transcending the desire/frustration point of departure. But this sequence

Freud could not allow in the case of the religious emotion of worship. Taking it as certain that worship has an instinctual point of departure, the desire for the continuity of life in a hostile universe and its frustrations (so that an object is created in relation to which continuity can be ensured), Freud could not allow an analogous sequence: he could not allow that there might be a response from the object of worship in effect, or that consequently there might emerge a relationship wholly transcending the desire/frustration point of departure.

The point, to Freud, was obvious: there could not be a reality in the object of religious belief, not least because there is not *one* object of belief but many, and some of the beliefs in question are incompatible; nevertheless, they continue to be held. Yet the impossibility of the reality of the object of religious belief would have to be established on other grounds than psychoanalytic alone. Granted that the motives for belief, or the reasons why people believe, may well be, in Freud's sense, abject (they lower, as he said of love, the self-regard, once they are understood); granted also that the uses to which belief in God are put are frequently terrifying in their cruelty and cynicism; the fact remains that in the experience of believing, as in the experience of loving, the points of departure can be transcended: the self in relation to the other is, as Freud put it, exalted once more. If this were not so, it would be difficult to understand how, within the realm of religious discourse itself, utterances, ritual as well as verbal, come to be judged as appropriate or inappropriate, and how, even in the Vatican, those judgements do not remain identical. By concentrating its focus on the ways in which individuals form a personal construct of life, psychoanalysis necessarily returns to an interest in the possible reality of the objects of belief. It does *not* say that all objects of belief therefore have a reality in existence; but it no longer excludes the possibility of a reality of objects of belief in effect, and hence perhaps, in some instances, of a reality in existence as a sufficient ground for the effect. The question obviously then arises where such an effect, in the possible case of God, can be discerned. Can it, for example, be discerned somewhere in the vast confusion popularly referred to as 'religious experience'? Is it the case that what is vaguely referred to as 'religious experience' is the proper court of appeal for those who wish to specify an effect of God, or is it the case that the 'sense of God' in so-called 'religious' experience is nothing but dramatic chemical activity in the brain, which can now be induced by such hallucinogenic drugs as LSD, and which consequently has nothing to do with a supposed reality in existence, to which the term 'God' might refer? To reflect on these questions, we will need to look first at certain features of experimental psychology, in so far as these throw light on conceptual and religious behaviour.

VII

THE PHYSIOLOGY OF THE BRAIN AND CLAIMS TO RELIGIOUS EXPERIENCE

OF all areas of research which might throw light on how human beings come to form a sense of God, experimental psychology might seem to be the most promising—in particular, in three areas: the psychology of concept formation, the physiology of emotional behaviour, and the relation of experience-inducing drugs, such as LSD, to claims to experience of God. There is, however, a very immediate problem: very little indeed is known about the neurophysiology of the brain, or even (except in descriptions of effect) of 'the global action' of neuropsychopharmacological agents.[1] This is true, despite the revolutionary advances in understanding which have taken place in this century. If one thinks, for example, of the psychology of conceptual behaviour, it is clear that despite the power of recent research in particular areas—sometimes in literal areas of the brain—the understanding of conceptual behaviour has scarcely begun. Lyle Bourne began a survey of the field, which appeared in 1966, with this forthright statement: 'Not many years ago, there was no experimental psychology of conceptual behaviour.'[2] Certainly, he continued by pointing out that progress is being made,[3] but, even so, these are early days.

Or again, to take another example which could be equally relevant to the sense of God, the psychometric approach to creativity: after the paper and researches of Guilford in the early fifties, the topic of creativity became, as Hudson put it, 'a bandwaggon, one which all of us sufficiently hale and healthy have leapt athletically aboard'.[4] A major concern of these intellectual athletes was to establish criteria of measurement, by means of which the elusive notion 'creativity' might be discerned. Then—and then only—would the dominance of IQ testing, which frequently misses 'creative' individuals, be challenged. Thus Wallach and Kogan suggested, as a criterion of measurement, cognitive association, a criterion which in degrees of correlation with intelligence testing led to the formation of behavioural predictions in relation to school behaviour.[5] Along these lines, it would then be necessary to establish sets of correlation with other criteria of creativity, in the hope that eventually the correlation of criteria will approach unity in linear terms, so that a sufficient definition of creativity will have been attained—sufficient, that is, for the educational consequences which follow in recognizing and encouraging creativity.

But although one has real sympathy with any attempt to rescue children from being labelled by inadequate measures, as though IQ testing is the single indicator of worth, the fact remains that the initial enthusiasm has had to pause and realize that it will be a very long and very complicated business to unravel the functioning of creative behaviour and establish criteria of measurement.[6] Certainly it is far too early to draw conclusions about the imaginative conceptualizations of God, or about the mechanisms or conditions of that function.

These opening remarks must seem very negative. Yet in fact they are designed simply to point out that in comparison with the understanding which is already coming within reach (or, perhaps better, into vision), our present knowledge is still minute. Perhaps for this reason many of the current debates about brain behaviour—particularly the debates about Skinnerian behaviourism—have not advanced much further than the level of the cheese-mites and the cheese:

> The cheese-mites asked how the cheese got there,
> And warmly debated the matter:
> The orthodox said it came from the air,
> And the heretics said from the platter.

Granted, then, that these are early days, and that much must be provisional, what *is* the contribution, at this time, of an experimental or a psychometric approach to an understanding of the human senses of God?

Part of the answer lies in the way in which it helps to establish the parameters of individual behaviour: it helps to establish the boundaries within which individuals are likely to move in constructing their own personal route from birth to death. It helps to establish, to put the same point slightly differently, the boundaries of the available routes which are possible, or likely, or even in some instances predictable, in individual cases. For example, it can establish relations between contexts and beliefs, in both directions: the contexts, say, of family or of village, which are likely to encourage particular beliefs, but also the contexts which are likely to disrupt existing beliefs—the consonant and dissonant contexts: these clearly establish parameters of probable action.[7] Similarly, if one links this up with the example of creativity, one can tentatively establish correlations between religious affiliation and certain sorts of non-religious conceptual behaviour. The work of Datta on the hypothesis that 'achievement in the area of science varies with religious background' (because 'values congruent with and supportive of scientific development may not be found equally in all major religions'[8]) is an interesting example of this, because there were already in the field three hypothetical explanations (not based so strictly on measurement techniques) which could be tested by the experimental approach of Datta.

Those are examples of attempts to establish parameters through correlative function. But manipulative function is equally relevant,[9] even if in practice it is difficult to operate in relation to religious behaviour and beliefs. Nevertheless, it can at least specify, for example, some of the reinforcements which sustain, or extinguish, particulars of religious behaviour and/or belief. But even when the parameters have been drawn in, with increasing precision, we are still left with the question whether they specify the only possibilities where a sense of God is concerned—whether, to put it in reverse, the sense of God is a dependent variable, dependent on specific conditions which have run together and focused in the brain behaviour of a particular individual. In that case, there would be no room (indeed, there could be no room) for a contributory effect of that to which the term 'god' has attempted (but mistakenly attempted, from the point of view of this argument) to refer.

According to this strictly behavioural analysis, the reference of the term 'god' would be to certain events in the internal environment—or rather to a mosaic of events, through which experience is interpreted, which is then conceptualized extensively, so that the term 'god' becomes culturally available. But if this behaviourist argument is to be established, it would have one very ironic implication: it would mean that a strict Skinnerian behaviourism would have to be abandoned. It is fundamental to a Skinnerian approach that the inner environment should be able to be discounted in the modification and control of human behaviour. This must be so, because otherwise 'cultural engineering', to use Skinner's famous phrase, would not be possible. An inner-determining agent might resist or disrupt cultural direction. Thus Michael and Meyerson, who are self-confessedly Skinnerian,[10] attempted to establish a behavioural system 'without reference to unobservable, hypothetical inner-determining agents'.[11] Once again, it is possible to have sympathy for at least one of the motives behind this argument: interference in the brain, particularly surgical interference (for example, frontal lobectomy) for the modification of behaviour, is by no means a closed issue, particularly in America. The Skinnerian argument is that cultural engineering, by changing conditions which might otherwise lead to breakdown or to so-called anti-social behaviour, should make such interference unnecessary. 'The consequences of this orientation should be made explicit: inherited genetic and constitutional determiners are not under the control of, or subject to, direct experimentation by behavioural scientists. This means that the only channel open . . . for influencing human behaviour is through changes in the environment.'[12]

But here again, laudable though that desire may be, the understanding of brain-behaviour which it implies is far too impoverished to do even remote justice to the facts, particularly where the sense of God is concerned. At the heart of the problem lies the fact that the brain itself appears to function *as* an inner-determining agent. At the very least, a mediated SR (stimulus-response) theory looks more probable—meaning by this an attempt to include in explanation the internal (and frequently symbolic in representation) activities which intervene between external stimulus and overt response, and which evidently contribute to those responses. A difficulty here lies in the fact that it is still extremely uncertain what, in all cases, initiates particular thinking (one thought, for example, rather than another) within the mechanism of the brain. One aspect of this difficulty can be illustrated by the example of a lecture: almost anyone at a lecture spends at least a part of the time 'miles away', no longer responding to the most immediate external stimuli, the vibrations in the air, but engaged far more happily in other thoughts. No doubt Sherlock Holmes would rapidly retrace the sequence of those thoughts back to the point of departure; but the fact remains that it is possible to abstract oneself from immediate—or even mediated—stimuli, and rely on the internal environment for the continuity of brain process. No human being can do this for long; experiments in sensory deprivation have shown this clearly enough.[13] But the fact that we are able to do it at all means that the internal environment cannot be excised, even in designs for cultural engineering.

What seems clear is that internal response mechanisms (muscles, glands, or nerves) and internal sensing mechanisms (nerves, specialized receptor cells) are constantly alert and active—as alive to the internal environment as external receptors are alive to the external environment, though we know, at present, very little about it. Could one, then, apply *this* argument to the sense of God, and suggest that the furthest possible specifiable 'sense of God' is the condition obtained by deliberate and (so far as possible) complete abstraction from external stimuli, and that the true sense of God (the sense that God is, and nothing else besides) is only fleetingly possible in that state of abstraction? Could this be the, so to speak, 'event' in the internal environment which suggests to interpretation that God is?

This obviously *does* represent the mechanism of many procedures and states to which the term 'mystical' has been applied. In most, if not all, religious traditions it is possible to find techniques and procedures whose effect is to abstract the mental process of an individual from the pressure of external stimuli and so far as possible from the intervention of the internal environment: examples (among many) are the repetition of a sacred name or syllable, ascetic restraint, physical isolation, even to the extent of Stylites on his pillar, concentration on one image as a means to the exclusion of all others, the Bodhisattva vow in its Chinese form: 'I vow to conquer the thieves of the mind'. There are almost innumerable examples, often in unexpected quarters:

A kind of waking trance I have frequently had, quite up from boyhood, when I have been all alone. This has generally come upon me thro' repeating my own name two or three times to myself silently, till all at once, as it were out of the intensity of the consciousness of individuality, the individuality itself seemed to dissolve and fade away into boundless being, and this not a confused state, but the clearest of the clearest, the surest of the surest, the weirdest of the weirdest, utterly beyond words, where death was an almost laughable impossibility, the loss of personality (if so it were) seeming no extinction but the only true life.[14]

Some of these techniques (for example, the constant repetition of a name or syllable) are probably related to group techniques which also induce response in brain-behaviour by the pressure of a single repeated stimulus—or, perhaps better, complex of stimuli: the pressure, for example, of drums and dancing. These, too, induce dramatic effects; but they are not necessarily the *same* effects as those induced in the way of abstraction. Nevertheless, they also lay claim to making one sensible of God.

If West's theory of the origin of hallucinations were correct,[15] all this would assimilate the sense of God very closely to hallucinatory experience. West suggested that hallucinations are close in this respect to the effects of LSD and certain other hallucinogenic drugs, in the sense that there appears to be an impairment of sensory threshold combined with a state of high arousal in the brain. West therefore suggested that hallucinations are caused by the partial blocking of sensory input which then allows a release into the perceptual experience of material stored behind immediate conscious awareness. Neatly though this would fit, it appears not to be wholly true. As Jarvik points out, a good deal of research now establishes that, under the influence of hallucinogens, sensitivity to external stimuli is heightened, not impaired, but that *other* inhibitions are caused within brain connections by the drug.[16] Certainly, one of the few generalities of LSD experience is precisely this reported sensitivity, which suggests that the pathways to the visual cortex are themselves profoundly affected. Jarvik offered a different solution, that what *is* impaired by hallucinogenic drugs (and in hallucinatory behaviour) is short-term memory retrieval: this allows increased retrieval of long-term memory traces which are so 'out of context' that bizarre neural relations are established: 'We propose that hallucinations are a memory defect characterized by uninhibited retrieval and that one of the ways hallucinogenic drugs work is by impairing short term memory and inducing vicarious retrieval.'[17] What seems clear is that hallucinatory experiences of God, whether of seeing God or of being God, are not *caused* by abstraction from stimuli alone. On the contrary, in so far as they involve memory retrieval of a bizarre kind, the necessary traces must already be available for the brain-behaviour in question. What first establishes those traces, from which the God-labelling of the experience is derived (supposing it is), is another matter, and one which we will shortly explore further. But certainly it is the reliance on personal memory retrieval of a bizarre kind which makes it almost impossible to disconfirm hallucinatory claims, as Rokeach found in the case of the three Christs of Ypsilanti.[18] The resource of interpretation lies in the personal authority of the individual concerned, because it lies in the memory which is uniquely his own.

Obviously, these mechanisms of experience are highly important in the human senses of God. They have led to experiences which have seemed, or which have been claimed, to be literal sensings of God; and those claims have been utilized in the history of religions in many different directions. But one would still want to know (particularly if bizarre memory retrieval is involved) why senses of *God*? Why have some of these experiences received the cognitive label of God? Obviously, they have not all done so: experiences induced or approached by similar techniques have been 'labelled' as experiences of a very wide range of claimed realities. It follows, therefore, that the warrant for a particular label does not lie in the experience itself, but in the conceptual background, the conceptual foundations, which create particular expectations and supply particular symbols to *any* experience. This does not mean that we are *necessarily* talking about undifferentiated 'experience' which is then diversely labelled. That is certainly a possibility, as we shall see when we come to discuss the physiology of emotional behaviour. But it may be the case, at the very least, that the conceptual structure itself is affective, and that the 'experience' is by no means as undifferentiated as enthusiasts for the perennial philosophy suppose. But this is virtually impossible to establish either way so long as the argument has to depend on reported behaviour. In either case, one will still have to probe very much deeper into the background of conceptual formation in order to know why in some instances certain experiences become labelled as senses of God.

This point becomes critically important when we come to consider some of the claims which are made about hallucinogenic drugs and religious experience. Might it not be the case that 'experience is all'? The argument here would be that the issue of whether 'experience' is undifferentiated is irrelevant: the intensities of brain experience under the influence of hallucinogenic substances are so dramatic and so unlike the world of everyday reality, that in times gone by they have seemed to demand, as a cause of them, a super-natural, super-everyday reality, which men have called by many names. In that case, the whole question of external grounds of belief becomes essentially unimportant.[19] Whether or not there are such grounds makes no difference to the essential core-reality of experiencing in a dramatic mode. It is the dramatic nature of the experience which seems to demand such terms as 'God'.

Here, at last, we come to the one area where it seems possible to some to identify the origin of the sense of God with as much assurance as anyone in the nineteenth century. The sense of God originates in the experience which is so dramatically 'out of this world' that it demands 'God' as its explanation, an experience which works, as Gary Snyder put it, 'in terms of forms, devotions, personal deities, appearances of Bodhisattvas, Buddhas, and gods to your eyes: it doesn't work in terms of non-forms, emptiness'. But that actually is his description of the experience induced, or released, by LSD: so why not make the connection—to borrow a phrase—and regard the psychedelic drugs as initiating precisely that brain-behaviour which is also operative in experiences which traditionally have been regarded as religious? Snyder made exactly this connection.[20]

Hallucinogenic drugs thus offer the one area of confidence in the contemporary scene, in identifying the origin of the sense of God. Here at last we arrive at apparent certitude that the origins of the sense of God can be identified: God, to put it in its briefest possible form, grew in a flower-pot. This is almost exactly the title of an article by Mary Barnard—'The God in the Flowerpot':

When we consider the origin of the mythologies and cults related to drug plants, we should surely ask ourselves which, after all, was more likely to happen first: the spontaneously generated idea of an afterlife in which the disembodied soul, liberated from the restrictions of time and space, experiences eternal bliss, or the accidental discovery of hallucinogenic plants that give a sense of euphoria, dislocate the centre of consciousness, and distort time and space, making them balloon outwardly in greatly expanded vistas. Perhaps the old theories are right, but we have to remember that the drug plants were there, waiting to give men a new idea based on a new experience. The experience might have had, I should think, an almost explosive effect on the largely dormant minds of men causing them to think of things they had never thought of before. This, if you like, is divine revelation ... Looking at the matter coldly, unintoxicated and unentranced, I am willing to prophesy that fifty theo-botanists working for fifty years would make the current theories concerning the origins of much mythology and theology as out of date as pre-Copernican astrology.[21]

A similar line of argument (though extended to include derivative factors) has been developed in recent years by Weston La Barre, whose book on the origins of religion represents a thoroughgoing nineteenth-century approach to explanation, almost to the point of caricature, in its treatment of evidence.[22] Other attempts to apply this line of explanation to particular religions, as in the case of Wasson or of Allegro, are probably even more familiar. The argument, in general terms, was summarized by Aaronson and Osmond:

The technology of drugs is one of the oldest technologies and probably began when our ancestors browsed their way through the forests and found that, among the foods they sampled, some produced interesting changes in how they felt, how they perceived, and how they could accommodate themselves to the world. Substances that alter consciousness are found in use among probably all the people of the world.[23] In particular, substances containing alcohol and caffeine seem to be used nearly everywhere, and hemp and its derivatives also seem widely used.[24]

What, then, are we to make of the claim that experiences which have traditionally occurred in religious contexts and experiences which are induced by hallucinogenic substances (particularly LSD) are identical; and that the discovery of some of these substances by early man is the origin of the sense of God? There appear to be four matters of fact in the present situation: first, that hallucinogenic substances initiate and inhibit activity in the brain which, in the case of the subject concerned, would not otherwise be occurring; the consequences of this activity are introspectively noticeable and in some aspects are externally observable. Second, that reports of the experiences use religious terms and refer to religious components in the experience, such as seeing God, being at peace with God, seeing the Virgin Mary, entering nirvana. Third, that the memory traces of the experience may continue to affect the religious behaviour of *some* participant subjects. Fourth, that claims are made that hallucinogenic experience and something referred to as 'religious experience' are identical; the point is put about as briefly as it can be put by Stace: 'It is not a matter of its being *similar* to mystical experience; it *is* mystical experience.'[25]

Taking the first fact first, it is clear, and not in the least surprising, that there is an effect in brain-behaviour, as a consequence of chemical intrusion, which can receive a generalized description. Thus, in the case of LSD, for example, there are certain general effects which frequently recur, and which have almost equally frequently been described.[26] The fact that some of these generalities of experience interlock with those which are generated by other hallucinogenic substances suggests that the chemical structures involved may also interlock—or rather, more accurately, that they may in part be superimposed on each other when redrawn with spatial aspects; and this is exactly what the research of Keup on structure–activity relationship among hallucinogenic agents suggests.[27] What Keup attempted was a classification of the empirical relations existing in the molecular structure of known hallucinogenic substances, of which about 150 are known. What is of interest is that although some substances fell outside in terms of chemical classification and analysis (for example, Sernyl, which is phencyclidine, an anaesthetic with hallucinogenic properties), the structural similarities were sufficient to suggest 'the existence of a single receptor site for psychotomimetic compounds; superpositioning of the features of active molecules, as compared to inactive congeners, yields a number of spatial characteristics of that assumed binding site.'[28]

This is way out on the edges of research—in fact, it is in part beyond them. But the one certain result of these descriptive and analytic generalities is that one cannot label them *as* 'religious experience' or *as* anything. On the contrary, we are precipitated into a very familiar problem, the problem of the cognitive labelling of experience, particularly of emotions. What, then, is this problem, and why is it important? The point will perhaps become more obvious if we look first at the relatively neutral ground of emotions—joy, fear, anger, and so on. Let us take the most extreme statement possible, that emotions represent a general pattern of sympathetic discharge in neural activity, which is then labelled contextually. In other words, in its most extreme form, the physioneurological base of emotions is undifferentiated: the differentiations occur by matching, so far as possible, the present situation with past experience. If that is so, it should then be possible experimentally to affect emotional feeling by manipulating the context; and this is exactly what has already been done. A familiar example is the work of Schachter and Singer,[29] in which groups of students were injected with epinephrine, having been told that they were testing a vitamin compound; some, of course, were injected with a saline solution as a placebo. The groups were put in contexts suggestive in one case of euphoria, in the other of anger. Some of each group were well informed to expect side-effects, others were not warned at all, and in the case of the euphoric situation some were *mis*informed (i.e. were told to expect symptoms which do not in fact occur as a consequence of epinephrine). The results support Schachter's three basic propositions.[30] Schachter's conclusion is this: 'Given precisely the same state of epinephrine-induced sympathetic activation, we have, by means of cognitive manipulations, been able to produce in our subjects the very disparate states of euphoria, anger, and amusement at a movie.[31] It may, indeed, be the case that cognitive factors are major determiners of the emotional "labels" we apply to a common state of sympathetic arousal.'[32]

To some extent one can test this oneself: a 'horror' film, or a film in which danger is represented, is a context in which various devices, both visual and auditory, are used in order to evoke the 'emotion' of fear, by identification with the participant in the suggested action. But it is in fact easy to disengage that emotion. It can be done, for example, by imagining a director shouting 'Cut!', or by visualizing microphones and lights hanging just above the actors' heads. In that case, the manipulated emotion simply disappears. It can even be converted into sudden laughter, when one realizes how absurd the pretence is. A more subtle example, in which this switch is manipulated by the director, is a film like *The Cat and the Canary*, a straightforward melodrama in origin, converted to be a vehicle for Bob Hope, in which fear and humour were therefore alternated.[33]

This, then, is a clear statement of a theory of emotions as a general state of arousal, which is then labelled cognitively according to context; the suggestiveness of context can be experimentally demonstrated. This basic statement may have to be modified, at least in the direction proposed by Pribram:[34] it may be the case that the learning of diverse situations and of appropriate labels for them may engage different resources of neural activity; this would be suggested by the steady mapping-out of different receptor sites which are sensitive to a variety of chemical agents. It is possible, therefore, that *meaning* (the already integrated recognition of component elements) could serve to initiate one emotionally labelled state rather than another, and that consequently the activity is not a wholly undifferentiated general release. The point is made by Pribram in quantitative terms, that it is no longer adequate to think that the *amount* of arousal determines its outcome (this is what Pribram refers to as the classical answer), important though that is:

The evidence for this view[35] has been marshalled so repeatedly that it need not be mentioned here. What can be added is that, on the evidence obtained in the studies of the orienting reaction, 'amount' is shown to be dependent on experiential organization, on the configuration of the expectancies challenged by the novel input. 'Amount' is thus viewed as amount of match and mismatch between configurations, not as an amount of excitation or energy available to the neuro-behavioral system. It is the *distribution* of excitation which is altered—and further; the amount of change can be measured as information.[36]

And later, returning to the same point:

The suggestion is, therefore, that motivation and emotion occur when the organism attempts to extend his control to the limits of what he perceives. To the extent that this attempt is appraised as feasible at any moment, the organism is motivated; to the extent that the attempt is appraised infeasible at any moment, the organism—unless he is to 'give up'—becomes of necessity emotional, i.e. he relies on self-regulatory mechanisms; either to participate in the uncontrollable or to prepare for another attempt.[37]

This leads us, yet again, to the principle of the compound of limitation as the necessary context of explanation, here as elsewhere. What is implied here is that appropriate labelling depends in part on the degree and manner in which particular situations are resolved—or as yet have failed to be resolved. To put it crudely, 'fear' is an appropriate label, not simply because the immediate situation is threatening and past experience informs one that that is so but also because the situation is as yet unresolved; whereas humour, 'amusement', is an appropriate label because a situation *is* resolved—frequently in ways which are unexpected, bizarre, or inappropriate so far as past experience and senses of ordered behaviour are concerned. In other words, meaning is a highly important component element in the labelling of emotional states.

This accords very well indeed with the theory of limitation which was proposed earlier as the correct general context in which to examine religious behaviour. If we take Pribram's suggestion, 'that motivation and emotion occur when the organism attempts to extend his control to the limits of what he perceives', and if further we bear in mind the contribution of resolution and irresolution, then it is clear that the labelling of physiological arousal as 'religious' will be appropriate in relation to particular compounds of limitation—for example, at the furthest extreme, those relating to the continuity of one's own existence, the discernment of intelligent purpose in the universe, or the worth of one's own feelings and actions. The state of arousal evoked, for example, in recognizing the problem of resolving the epistemic gap between God and one's own self is appropriately labelled 'religious' even though the means of resolving the situation (or of leaving it unresolved) vary enormously in different 'religious' developments: one might, for example, believe that one had achieved absolute union with God; or that God was a conceptual stepping-stone to a state of being beyond time and symbol; or that the resolution takes place after death, when the gap may be perpetuated or resolved for ever; or that *God* resolves the situation himself by invading human life, or natural objects, or sacral persons. Equally, the label may itself be *extinguished* by 'giving up' (by ceasing to set oneself at those particular limits), much as one can extinguish the label 'fear' in relation to a horror film by saying 'It is only a film': one is no longer engaged in the irresolution of the situation.

If this extreme account of the emotions is at all correct, even if only in outline, it follows that contexts will occur and will be developed in which states of arousal can be initiated and can be appropriately labelled as 'religious'—ceremonies at birth and death, architecture, dances, chants, sermons, the list is almost endless: the religions of the world exemplify this point *ad libitum*. The point of interconnection is the labelling of the state of arousal in relation to the compounds of limitation with which religions have to do, and on which they are focally concentrated. This means that one simply cannot isolate 'religious experience' as though it were an identifiable 'thing', any more than one can isolate 'fearing experience' as though it were a 'thing'. On the contrary, it is the context, matched, or mismatched, to past experience, which suggests appropriate labelling.

The attempts, therefore, to define 'religious experience' as an entity are mistaken, and to some extent the multiplicity of rival definitions bears this out. Even more radically mistaken are attempts to work on the basis of a surface content definition and to argue that religions exist to realize that content in the case of participant believers; or that this 'content-experience' is the unity at the heart of all religions, towards which religions should be aspiring. The most that can be attempted, in the immediate future, is the mapping-out of those contexts in which the state of arousal seems to be appropriately labelled as religious. Even if this had been achieved, it would *not* mean that 'content' was undifferentiated, as though one could argue that there is no real difference between joy and fear; they happen to be different labels for undifferentiated states of arousal. On the contrary, the labels become appropriate for the experiencing subject by their relation to the realities (or supposed realities) of particular situations. It follows, therefore, that far from this theory of the emotions dissolving the importance of what may in reality be the case, the question of what is in reality the case becomes absolutely vital. One may extinguish the label by realizing that it is, after all, 'only a film'; or the label may be powerfully reinforced by realizing that one is *not* in a dream or in a film, but in a situation which cannot be extinguished by manipulation of labels. So far as the labelling of theistic experience is concerned, this theory of the emotions by no means lets us off the hook of the possible reality of the object of belief, and of the importance of the reality or the unreality in effect in extinguishing or reinforcing the appropriateness of the labelling where particular contexts of arousal are concerned. This is exactly why *some* contexts of arousal have become suspect in developed theistic traditions, and why 'experience as an end in itself' is equally suspect in, for example, some parts of the Christian tradition. Too simple an appeal to experience obscures the problem of wrestling with the reality, or the unreality, of the object of belief, because it involves prematurely labelling states of arousal as warrant evidence of God. In fact, the most those states supply are *sustenance* arguments, and even these may collapse when the mechanism of particular arousal is clarified. (This also explains why theistic traditions contain an uneasy partnership between those for whom the sustenance arguments of experience remain valid and those for whom the clarification of the mechanism involved empties the experience of even sustaining significance—an uneasy partnership between emotion and intellect, the evasion of which as a problem is all too apparent in the religious programmes which appear on British television.)

It now becomes clear that we cannot identify experiences induced by LSD with an entity 'religious experience' defined by content alone. On the contrary, the most that could be attempted would be to claim that the state of arousal chemically induced is appropriately labelled as 'religious'. But this depends on cognitive cues in the immediate situation: in other words, it depends, to use the language which has emerged, on the 'set'. If there is a connection between LSD and 'religious experience', it lies, not in there being an entity 'religious experience' which can then be equated with LSD experience, but in the fact that sufficient cues are provided in the settings in which LSD is ingested to suggest the term 'religious' as an appropriate label. This in itself has no bearing whatsoever on the validity of experiences labelled as religious in other contexts, still less on the possibility of the reality of the objects of belief: for, what is obvious is that LSD experience depends on highly specific backgrounds of context recognition from which to draw the label 'religious'. The very most that could be hoped for, therefore, would be reinforcement arguments: that because the label 'religious' seems appropriate, an on-going commitment to certain sorts of beliefs and behaviour might also seem appropriate.

All these points, about the importance of the 'set' in drug-induced experience, are well attested. Nevertheless, the dramatic nature of the experiences as such has led many to draw exactly the opposite conclusion, that there *is* a single entity, 'religious experience', which LSD induces. Hence we arrive at a typical statement, like that of van Dusen:

There is a central human experience which alters all other experiences. It has been called satori in Japanese Zen, moksha in Hinduism, religious enlightenment or cosmic consciousness in the West . . . It is not just an experience among others, but rather the very heart of human experience . . . Once found, life is altered because the very root of human identity has been deepened ... The drug LSD appears to facilitate the discovery of this apparently ancient and universal experience.[38]

This is exactly the identification and conclusion which cannot be justified. A far more judicious form is offered by Clark, commenting on Zaehner's argument that mescaline may approximate to pantheistic or monistic experience, but not to an experience of relation to God personally conceived:

It is true that the religious experience of many of the drug users seems to them to fit more readily into pantheistic and Eastern religious patterns. But the experience itself is essentially non-rational and indescribable. In order that it may be described, one is forced to use concepts of one type or another, none of which seems to do justice to the experience. Consequently these are of great variety, and while some will agree with the Zaehner theological typology, others have no more trouble seeing their experiences as essentially Christian than did St. Theresa when she described one of her mystical visions as revealing to her the secrets of the Trinity.[39]

If anything like the labelling theory of emotions is correct, it seems clear that Clark's observations are valid. Without commenting on the issue with Zaehner, the point to be emphasized lies in the phrases, 'one is forced to use concepts', and 'others have no . . . trouble seeing their experiences as . . .' In a wholly unintended way, this is emphasizing the fundamental point, that LSD does not induce 'religious experience' but that it initiates a state of excitation and arousal which is labelled and interpreted by available cues. The general point is made very clearly by Nevitt Sanford, in a foreword to the composite survey, edited by Richard Blum, *Utopiates; The Use and Users of LSD 25*.[40] The point made there, about the context of psychological, social, and cultural factors, can equally be put in reverse, that the administration of psychedelics in conditions of sensory deprivation is able to extinguish the effects usually attributed to the psychedelic agent in question. This is, for example, what the research of Pollard, Uhr, and Stern on the effects of LSD, psilocybin, and Sernyl on college students suggests.[41] Once again, it must be emphasized that this point, about the importance of the set, is not controversial: even the most extreme enthusiasts for identifying LSD *as* religious experience accept it. This is so well attested that it scarcely needs illustrating; it is what Leary has called 'the engineering of ecstasy'.[42]

The set, therefore, can be manipulated and made deliberately suggestive of the appropriateness of religious labelling. In one institution, for example, the subject is prepared by preliminary sessions of CO_2, which break up—or confirm—apprehension in advance; the first administration of LSD may take place with a dark cloth over the eyes; when the cloth is suddenly removed, it is not difficult to suggest that the shock of sunlight *is* the vision of God.

The most familiar example of the influence of the set is probably the Good Friday experiment of Pahnke—more popularly referred to as 'the miracle of Marsh chapel'.[43] Here the subjects, in a very carefully contrived religious setting of a Good Friday Service, received either psilocybin or a partial placebo, nicotinic acid (partial, because the placebo had to produce sufficient effects for the subjects who received it to believe that they might have received the hallucinogen). The results showed that those who received the hallucinogen labelled their experiences in religious categories to a significantly greater extent than those who had received the partial placebo, and who were, of course, experiencing *some* arousal (because of the religious setting), but not (probably) the same degree of arousal. The results, needless to say, are usually quite differently reported, to the effect that those who received psilocybin had, or reported, significantly more religious or mystical experiences than the controls—for example, Leary: '. . . The results clearly support the hypothesis that, with adequate preparation and in an environment which is supportive and religiously meaningful, subjects report mystical experiences significantly more than placebo controls'.[44] It is significant how many of the popular accounts of this experiment—including Pahnke's own[45]— omit all reference to the one subject who deliberately set out to extinguish the religious or mystical labelling, and succeeded (much as one is able to extinguish 'fear' by saying 'It's only a film'), as this account summarizes: 'The only experimental subject in the Good Friday experiment who failed to report a mystical experience was one who did not believe it possible and deliberately set out to demonstrate this belief, partly by omitting the religious preparation engaged in by the other subjects.'[46] One can, of course, justify this omission by saying that 'one' is worthless statistically. But from the point of view of understanding the relation between physiological arousal and the nature of religious experiencing the single instance is highly important: it points yet again to the inappropriateness of attempting to abstract an entity, 'religious experience', which is the product of hallucinogenic substances; it suggests, instead, that states of arousal will be labelled according to available cues.

This point about the 'set', or the contextual expectation brought by an individual to a 'seeing-through' or 'seeing-other' experience, is by no means confined to dramatic incursions into brain-behaviour, as in the case of drugs. It appears to apply also, for example, to psychotic delusions. There is an interesting example of this in a comparative study of American and South Italian patients suffering from paranoid delusions, made by Anne Parsons.[47]

What now becomes clear is that the suggestion from which we started, of Mary Barnard ('The God in the Flowerpot'), that the origin of the sense of God is more likely to have occurred in the discovery of hallucinogenic plant substances than in conceptual construction, needs as a matter of fact to be exactly reversed. It is in fact much more likely that senses of a reality or realities which might appropriately be labelled as 'God' or 'gods' have reference to what would seem necessarily to have to be the case if particular limitations are to be penetrated or resolved. It is foolish to underestimate the abilities of chronologically early mentality. One may put this more precisely by suggesting that the characterization of the nature of a supposed reality which falls within the range of theistic description will be related to whatever is perceived as a limitation and to what is conceived to be necessary for its penetration or resolution, and that this *may* be conceptually arrived at. No doubt it remains true that early men would not have understood Ramanuja on the Gita or Marx on economics. But this is simply to accept the point of Bernard of Chartres, that we see further than other men, because we stand on the shoulders of giants. It is not a comment on the alertness of consciousness in early men as they scanned the limitations which circumscribed the continuity of their lives and of their life-ways. In fact, their achievements, which depended on a high conceptualizing ability, were prodigious.

The point about limitation and characterization has already been made at length. But if, for example, an illness is perceived as a limitation which cannot be resolved without the intervention

of realities in addition to the application of techniques and substances (for example, herbs or poultices), then the nature of the
reality in question will necessarily be characterized as able to intervene. If continuity through the limitations of death cannot be
plausibly conceived without the replication of personal relations
no longer terminated by death (because of the existence in reality
of one term of the relation being beyond the limitation of death),
then the nature of the supposed reality must necessarily be characterized as itself personal and eternal—or at least untouched by
death.

In these circumstances, hallucinogenic substances are likely to
act, not as innovatory of concepts in abstraction but as reinforcement or confirmation of concepts already formed, or in the process
of formation. This would certainly fit much better with straightforward considerations in the field of psychopharmacology—the
principle, as Seymour Kety referred to it, 'that no drug ever
introduces a new function into an organism; it merely accentuates
or inhibits or otherwise modifies a function which already exists.
We cannot expect drugs to introduce anything new into the mind
or into behaviour, but merely to accentuate or to suppress functions in behaviour which are already present.'[48]
Kety emphasized the same point in his conclusion:

Drug effects are not likely to establish new behaviour. The reason is
that human behaviour is so largely determined by the information itself
which is stored and present in the sensory input. I know of no way in
which a drug can modify the stored information in any meaningful
way. Of course, it can erase it, it can suppress it, it can, perhaps, help to
accentuate certain parts of it, but it is not likely that a drug will be discovered that will affect the stored information in a discriminatory and
meaningful manner.[49]

The main implication of all this is that, far from hallucinogenic
experience dissolving the possible reality of the objects of belief,
it reopens inquiry into precisely that problem and that possibility.
It does so, because the labelling of the induced state of arousal
depends on concepts already established, some with reference to
that possible reality; and what will become abundantly clear in the
subsequent lectures in this series, focused on the theistic traditions, is that the grounds for supposing that there may be reality
in existence which is appropriately labelled 'God' have been far

more extensive than an appeal to states of high arousal in brain-behaviour. In fact, in some of the major theistic traditions such states have been regarded with extreme circumspection. Even Eckhart (who is a good example because he became suspect in parts of the Christian tradition precisely for the intensity of his description of what the experience of union with God may be like, even to the extent of nondifferentiation),[50] even Eckhart constantly insists that this is not the object or the necessary consequence of the exercise: 'As I have often said, if a person were in such a rapturous state as St. Paul once entered, and he knew of a sick man who wanted a cup of soup, it would be far better to withdraw from the rapture for love's sake and serve him who is in need.'[51]

This is not in the least to deny the corresponding importance of religious groups or practices which *do* exist to induce or release 'experience', from transcendental meditation to orgiastic release, nor to deny the extent to which the two may interpenetrate—as, for example, in what Downing and Wygant referred to as 'periods of unrestrained, orgiastic release through festivals and carnivals ("flesh days") such as the pre-Lenten celebrations or the Oktoberfest of contemporary Bavaria.'[52] They continued:

In the past, the salvation and revival sects of the United States included even the presently staid middle-class Methodists and Baptists. One observer of the great nineteenth-century Methodist camp-meeting revivals observed drily, 'It was hard to know whether more souls were saved or conceived.' The Foursquare Gospel Church founded by Aimée Semple McPherson, many Negro churches, and the Pentecostal sects still provide ecstatic religious group experiences of a nonerotic type.[53]

It was obviously this kind of experience-orientated group-religion which provided William Sargant with the base material for his book *Battle for the Mind*. There is not the slightest doubt that this is important, for particular senses of God, in the history of religions. But all that this means is that one simply cannot generalize about 'religious experience' as an entity, as a 'thing-in-itself', nor can one conclude that experience is the sole object of all religions—an objective which can now be reached more rapidly by LSD. There may be real issues between Eckhart and Snyder, despite the fact that Eckhart recognized the intensity of experiencing which can occur in religious contexts. For Eckhart would not have regarded, as do Talbott and Snyder (in the conversation on

LSD, already referred to on p. 142), 'the everyday mind of a secretary in an industrial office' as 'the most awful thing imaginable'.[54] Eckhart would have insisted that the realization of what is otherwise a notion of God is only possible in the whole construction of unevaded life, in the actual realities of the *civis*, of civilization, with all its discontents, not in a flight from the predicament of the office typist in order to experience one's own release.[55] Perhaps Eckhart was wrong. But this does not alter the fact that there is an issue between Eckhart and Snyder, between incarnation and transcendental release.

The most, then, that can be said for LSD or for other hallucinogenic substances in this connection is that they confirm or reinforce concepts already available in religious universes of meaning. They cannot comment on the validity, truth, or reality of the objects of belief within those universes of meaning, because they are derivative from, and dependent on, those universes of meaning for the interpretation of their effect; and this is so, even when those objects are believed to be the ground of certain manifest experiences. Reality or unreality has to be established or argued on a much wider range of issues. The grounds of perception, on which all interpretation ultimately depends, cannot be eliminated as contributory *to* interpretation. It is true that so far as the mapping of brain-function is concerned, it is conceivable that external stimulus and internal image are equally of effect, and that in some instances, by involving sensory pathways, they are observationally and operationally indistinguishable. If this seems extreme, it is in fact the conclusion reached by Segal on the basis of experimental research into judgement-forming on the basis of ambiguous cues. In *some* circumstances, he even suggests, the percept and the image do not really differ at all.[56] But here, yet again, we have to notice the importance of the 'set', only this time, the diachronic 'set' (not simply the synchronic context), the unique accumulation and 'cross-referencing' of data in each individual brain, which itself may have its own structural idiosyncrasies; and this, too, may throw light on hallucinatory behaviour.[57] But the fact that we are talking about the accumulation of data means that the ground of a percept, even though it can be wrongly signified, is unquestionably indispensable, at some stage, to the image. Questions of ontology remain alive. This was the critical point (expressed, of course, in quite other terms), which made phenomenology, as Husserl conceived it, an unremitting commitment to ontology, paradoxical though that is. Phenomenology, therefore, may be an important comment on this issue. But before we come to phenomenology, what have we achieved, so far, in looking at disciplines or activities which take the individual as their focus and subject, so far as human senses of God are concerned?

Psychoanalysis supplies intuitive mythologies through which some individuals can learn what is involved in the construction of their behaviour, and can modify that behaviour through the insights gained; experimental psychology maps both how the brain behaves and also the parameters within which behaviour, or personal construction, is likely to occur—the 'parametric windows', for example, as Scheibel put it in the case of sensory channels;[58] chemical incursion into the brain makes possible the study of excitation, both its arousal and its suppression, in two main areas, one therapeutic, the other 'going on a trip'. In all these different approaches, claims have been made that 'god' is an internally generated symbol which is organizationally useful (pathological though it may also be) which has no reference to any external reality for which the term 'god' is an appropriate label.

But, in fact, what is now happening is that the question of the reality or the unreality underlying the formation of concepts or of beliefs, or even of behaviour itself, is far less prejudged than it was, and that the question of the grounding of the cues of perceptual or imaging behaviour has become an important part of the study of the internal environment in itself. Is it of any importance to the formation of personal constructs whether a supposed object has any reality in existence or not? There are some areas, such as habituation, in which it is clear that the importance is fundamental. It is clear, in the shift in psychoanalysis to object-relations theory, that the reality or unreality of the object makes a very profound difference indeed. The simplest example is the mother–child relationship, which has to do, not with an abstraction about the formation of personality but with the real effect in actual psychological formations of the absence or the presence of that relationship, and its consequent quality. In this example, the reality or the unreality of the object is precisely what makes so radical a difference.

But it is one thing to take a relatively straightforward example, the reality of the object with whom an infant first experiences (or fails to experience) relationship. Can similar considerations be applied to the reality or the unreality, in their effect, of the objects of conceptual belief? In the case of God, one would certainly then have to identify or specify the nature of the effect. But the question, nevertheless, would then become whether the sense of God is simply built up from an extensive patterning of stable, consensual cues which then receive (but do not actually demand) theistic interpretation, or whether some of the cues, so to speak, arrive from that reality in existence to which a term such as 'god' is appropriately applied, so that those cues arriving from the external universe demand (but do not always receive) a response of faith? The latter may seem unlikely, but it cannot be ruled out within the procedures of psychoanalysis, psychobiology, or hallucino-genesis alone. On the contrary, they return us to a real concern with the question, how *does* a sense of God appear in consciousness in a sufficiently general way for it also to appear in hallucinatory or drug-induced episodes? Is there any other way, or procedure, through which we could attack that question? An answer is, of course, contained within the words of the question itself—how does a sense of God *appear in consciousness*? It is precisely to that question that phenomenology addresses itself: how does a sense of anything appear in consciousness? It is appropriate, therefore, to turn at this point to phenomenology and to Husserl, the founder of modern phenomenology as a method.

VIII

PHENOMENOLOGY AND THE APPEARANCE OF GOD

AT the end of the previous chapter it seemed appropriate to turn to Husserl, and to phenomenology, in order to know whether the phenomenological method might have any light to throw on human senses of God. However, it is one thing to say that one will turn to phenomenology; it is quite another thing to do so. Indeed, it is quite difficult to know what to turn to. When Passmore surveyed and described some of the many works which have been written to explain 'what Husserl meant', he added the comment: 'But for all this explanation, to say nothing of innumerable articles in *Philosophy and Phenomenological Research*, many philosophers have been wont to complain that what Husserl taught is even more obscure than it was before his disciples began to explain him.'[1] Certainly, in a 'Philosophers into Europe' conference, held in 1969,[2] the divergence in recent years between philosophy focused on linguistic analysis (so strong on this side of the Channel) and philosophy conceived as phenomenological method (equally strong in Europe) was taken as a point of departure: 'The encounter between the Anglo-Saxon and French philosophers at Royaumont in the late 1950s . . . seems to have ended in mutual incomprehension.'[3] Similarly, the problematic nature of phenomenological method led Schmitt to the conclusion that he had shown an essential feature of Husserl's method to be either a muddle or alternatively a complete mystery.[4] Yet when one considers the influence of phenomenology on what is loosely referred to as 'existentialism', and when one considers its influence on such deeply diverse lives as those of Heidegger, Jaspers, Edith Stein, Schutz, Sartre (however much some of them may later have broken away from phenomenology as Husserl conceived it), it is clear that phenomenology cannot be dismissed as a negligible aberration—or at least, should not be so dismissed until its critique of other ways of reflecting philosophically has been assessed.

The radical divergence about phenomenology, with all its

attendant consequences in misunderstanding and even in hostility, is not in the least surprising: it is exactly what Husserl foresaw, and perhaps even intended. When he was alive (1859–1938) the two prevailing extremes of philosophy which he encountered, idealism and empiricism, seemed to him to be philosophy lost in the world. To establish knowledge on an unshakeable foundation one would need, in Husserl's view, to break radically from the dominance of those two tendencies—and by radical he meant literally going down to the roots, to the one thing of which we can be certain. This obviously sounds like a reiteration of Descartes: he too had attempted to pare away assumptions until he came to the one and only conclusion of which he could be certain, *cogito, ergo sum*. This reiteration of Descartes, in the case of Husserl, is exactly right: Husserl specifically adopted from Descartes the method of radical doubt, and he entitled one of his last major works (a developed version of some lectures given in Paris) *Cartesian Meditations*.

But Husserl believed that Descartes had not employed radical doubt with sufficient rigour: there is only *one* certainty: *cogito*. The conclusion, *ergo sum*, is not entailed. Consciousness, without any further necessary conclusions, is the only fact of which consciousness can be absolutely certain. No other conclusions necessarily follow. That there are also 'appearances in consciousness', *cogitationes*, is no doubt the case; but one must not start with any prior, *a priori*, assumptions about the *nature* of these appearances, or of the realities or unrealities underlying them, or of the nature of the cause which has brought them into effect. No prior, *a priori*, assumptions: back to the only certainty, *cogito*, consciousness; this was Husserl's programme. Where did it lead him? And what comment does phenomenology itself make on the appearance of God in consciousness? And is this comment useful, illuminating, or true? These are the questions to which we can now turn.

But to find a way into phenomenology, and to understand why Husserl felt it imperative to break up the Western philosophical traditions, it is necessary first to go back a little in time. In order to understand the point of phenomenology, it is necessary to understand at least a little of the situation in which Husserl found himself, and in particular the extraordinarily wide gap in Western philosophy between idealism and empiricism. The issue which seemed to Husserl to have precipitated the crisis was the notion of necessity, and in particular the post-Newtonian sense that perhaps the actions of men are constrained by natural law as much as a stone is constrained by gravity when it falls. Why had this become problematic, and how had this problem been handled? The answer to this, which is indispensable for understanding Husserl, can best be approached by recognizing that we have now come round, in full circle, to the opening chapter, where brief reference was made to the acuteness, in the nineteenth century, of the dilemma of individual meaning, the dilemma that if the actions of men are wholly constrained by the mechanism of cause and effect, then how can one attribute to individual actions any worth or value or merit?

> And, spite of Pride, in erring Reason's spite,
> One truth is clear, Whatever is, is right.[5]

Pope thus summarized one possible eighteenth-century understanding of necessity. One might, of course, attempt to consecrate necessity, much as one can consecrate a pile of stones as a cathedral, by saying that whatever is, is, because it falls into place as a part of God's providence or plan. This was the defence, in several quite different ways, of Deism. It is also the defence put forward by the angel Jezrad who comes down to debate with Voltaire's Zadig the reason why misfortune befalls the virtuous:

'All that you see on this little atom where you were born must be fixed in its place and time according to the immutable decrees of him who encompasses all ... There is no such thing as accident. All is either trial or punishment, reward or foresight ... You [Zadig] are a weak mortal, and have no business to argue about what you must adore.'
'But—' said Zadig.
As he said the word, the Angel took flight towards the Empyrean. Zadig fell on his knees, worshipping Providence in true submissiveness.[6]

'But', said Zadig; and men have been saying it ever since—indeed, they were undoubtedly saying it long before. *Zadig* appeared in 1747: it by no means took the Lisbon earthquake to destroy a belief in Providence, although the earthquake powerfully focused the debate. But Voltaire was sceptical of men's ability to discern Providence long before All Saints' Day, 1755. Voltaire drew from this situation, in which the constraint of natural law seemed to disclose neither purpose nor providence, moderately agnostic, decently civilized conclusions: 'Il faut cul-

tiver notre jardin', the famous concluding words of *Candide*; or, again, the equally succinct conclusion of his entry on Toleration (Tolérance) in the Philosophical Dictionary: 'Would a reed laid into the mud by the wind say to a neighbouring reed bent in the opposite direction: "Creep in my fashion, wretch, or I shall petition to have you torn up and burned"?'[7]
But this implies that Pope can be corrected. He had concluded, 'Whatever is, is right'. But why not simply conclude, 'Whatever is, is necessary', and thus dispense with value judgements of right or wrong? This is exactly the conclusion of de Sade: "And so whatever is in this world, is necessary':[8] not 'right', but 'necessary'. That sentence comes from *A Dialogue Between a Priest and a Dying Man*, which de Sade completed in 1782. The dying man draws out the implications of the natural nature of necessity in human actions:

By Nature created, created with very keen appetites, with very strong passions; placed on this earth for the sole purpose of yielding to them and satisfying them, and these effects of my creation being nothing but necessities directly relating to Nature's fundamental designs or, if you prefer, nothing but essential derivatives proceeding from her intentions in my regard, all in accordance with her laws, I repent not having acknowledged her omnipotence as fully as I might have done, I am only sorry for the modest use I made of the faculties (criminal in your view, perfectly ordinary in mine) she gave me to serve her; I did sometimes resist her, I repent it ... I only plucked an occasional flower when I might have gathered an ample harvest of fruit.[9]

If whatever is, is necessary, then the only advisable course is to go with the tide, to lie down and enjoy it. It follows that life and so-called morality are reduced in de Sade to a prolonged game of 'Opportunity Knocks'. In this situation, of going, so far as opportunity allows, with the tide of natural necessity, so-called morality can be summarized in a single sentence; and de Sade did so summarize it: 'The entirety of human morals is contained in this one phrase: *Render others as happy as one desires oneself to be*, and never inflict more pain upon them than one would like to receive at their hands.'[10]
But this, of course, is dramatically close to that other great summarizing principle of de Sade's almost exact contemporary, Bentham: "The right and proper end of government in every political community, is the greatest happiness of all the individuals of which it is composed, say, in other words, the greatest happiness .

of the greatest number.'[11] This, for Bentham, was 'the basis on which all legislation and all morality rests'.[12] The principle is no more original to Bentham than it is to de Sade.[13] But the fact that it occurs in both as the only apparently defensible foundation on which human actions can be constructed indicates to what extent both were caught in the dilemma of individual meaning— the dilemma (except, of course, that to de Sade in his writings it was not particularly a dilemma) of knowing how, if at all, one can attribute worth or praise or merit to actions governed by necessity. And just as one can legitimately say that de Sade is the Bentham of sexuality, so also one can say that Bentham is the de Sade of economics, as one can see in this compression by Bentham of Adam Smith's *laissez-faire*: 'The requests which agriculture, manufactures and commerce, present to governments is as modest and reasonable as that which Diogenes made to Alexander: "Stand out of my sunshine".'

de Sade and Bentham are extreme examples of how deep the crisis posed by necessity had gone in the eighteenth century. What is in some ways ironic is that a naïve notion of necessity had already received a severe jolt from David Hume. Hume had actually attacked the very citadel of cause and effect, and had shown that that concept is by no means as simple as it had seemed. What Hume argued was that where we suppose that we see a necessary causal connection between one event and its successor, as when a billiard ball strikes another and the second moves (and we see a cause-and-effect relation between the two), Hume insisted, in strict empiricist fashion, that we *see* nothing of the sort: we see, in sense phenomena, successive events. Because of their extensive consistency—what Hume called 'constant conjunction'[14]—we suppose that there is a necessary connection. But this is something we impose on the accumulation of our sense impressions. The connection itself is not perceived, no matter how, apparently inevitably, we may imagine it. The constant conjunction or consistency of certain observations makes our attribution of cause and effect psychologically intelligible, and thus justifiable; but we do not *perceive* cause and effect.

Hume's achievement was extraordinary, because it was an attack on the very centre of what had appeared to be established in the emergent empiricist tradition (the necessity of natural law), within the terms of the empirical tradition itself. But this meant that Hume could not easily be deployed against the extreme deductions exemplified in de Sade and Bentham. Hume could scarcely suffer the fate of Andrew Lang, and be hailed as a new defender of the faith.[15] Hume may have leapt out of the fire of necessity but had he not landed in the pan of chance associations? Clearly, moral judgements and religious beliefs are even less capable of being ultimately justified than is natural necessity: natural necessity is at least psychologically intelligible, since it arises from the extensive observation of consistency. But where is the comparable 'constant conjunction' in the case of the putative truth-claims of religion? The conflicts of religious, and of moral, judgements suggest that a basis of extensive consistency does not exist to be found. But this leads us to a rather odd problem: the human mind, in its actual activity, *does* arrive at those conjunctions, beliefs, and judgements, which a strict empiricism reveals to be unjustified—unjustified, that is, unless one can specify the conditions (constant conjunction in the case of cause and effect, and of other scientific judgements), which produce the 'imagination' in question. What, then, are the conditions which produce the moral or the aesthetic or the religious imagination? Men arrive at these judgements as undoubtedly as they arrive at scientific judgements. No doubt they are frequently mistaken in all cases. But the question, in strict empiricist terms, cannot be evaded: what must be the case for the different modes or categories of human thinking to occur at all? How *do* men arrive at moral or at aesthetic judgements?

It was to these questions that a man addressed himself, whose regularity of life was such that the citizens of Königsberg, where he lived, were able to set their watches by the time of his afternoon walk. The man, of course, was Kant; and with Kant we arrive at many points of new initiative in Western thought. Yet when Heine recorded that famous anecdote, of the man more regular in daily life than the great clock of the cathedral, he went on to describe Kant, not as a point of new initiative or of new construction but of savage destruction and of the death of God. The anecdote is familiar, but it bears repeating, all the same, if we are to understand the exact nature of Husserl's radical doubt:

In very truth, if the citizens of Königsberg had dreamed of the real meaning of his thought, they would have experienced at his sight a greater horror than they would on beholding an executioner who only kills men. But the good people saw nothing in him but a professor of philosophy, and when he at the regular hour passed by, they greeted him as a friend, and regulated their watches by him. But if Kant, the great destroyer in the world of thought, went far beyond Robespierre in terrorism, he had many points of resemblance to him which challenge comparison between the two . . . There was manifested in both, to the very highest degree, the type of *bourgeoisie* [der Typus des Spießbürgertums]. Nature meant them to weigh out coffee and sugar but destiny determined that they should weigh other things; so the one placed a king, and the other a god in the scales—and they both give exact weight [das richtige Gewicht].[16]

Kant could thus seem as radically destructive as any eighteenth-century sceptic. Yet within the nineteenth century, countless writers, musicians, artists—not to mention philosophers and religious believers—believed that Kant's 'revolution', to retain Heine's metaphor, had cleared the ground for new opportunities of expression and of feeling, and that he had validated the worthwhileness of feeling and of judgement over against the extreme deductions of necessity which we saw were possible in the case of de Sade. Goethe, Schiller, Beethoven: for them, Kant was a great (though not uncriticized) ally in the laying of new foundations on which, once more, the worthwhileness of emotion and of the expression of feeling could be established.[17]

How was it possible for Kant to produce such very different reactions? And in so far as Kant was developed in the nineteenth century as offering a new foundation for the worthwhileness of ideas, beliefs, and feelings, what effect did this have on the continuing empiricist tradition?

Let us look first at the question why Kant evoked such different reactions. In general terms, it is not difficult to see why this happened. The reason lies, obviously, in the fact that both destructive and constructive themes seemed manifest in his work. On the one hand, on the destructive side, once Hume had awakened Kant from his dogmatic slumber,[18] Kant accepted as correct the negative implications of Hume's observation, that from observed phenomena it is not possible to infer the necessary presence of any other existence not in itself observable. But this at once raises the question which Kant posed to himself; can, then, any *meta*physical argument be justified? Is metaphysics possible?[19]

Clearly metaphysical propositions are not analytic, in Kant's sense (that is to say, they are not true in the sense that a proposition in which the predicate is part of the subject must be true, as in the analytic proposition, a small room is a room; to deny that a small room is a room is to fall into self-contradiction). Metaphysical propositions are not like analytic propositions of that sort, because whereas analytic propositions do not extend our knowledge ('a small room is a room' does not extend our knowledge), metaphysical propositions certainly purport to extend our knowledge. They must, therefore, be synthetic. Yet in fact metaphysical propositions are full of contradiction and confusion, and do not appear to be able to justify their claim to extend knowledge at all. They cannot, for example, point to consistency, or to Hume's constant conjunction, which serves to justify physics. So is *meta*physics possible? If one answers no, then clearly Kant is as sceptically destructive in this area as Hume.[20] By the time Kant had finished with the traditional proofs of God's existence in this destructive vein, the death of God certainly seemed to be at hand, and perhaps even effectively accomplished.

But, moving to the constructive side, Kant did *not*, like Hume, in the famous passage later quoted with approval by Huxley, commit metaphysics to the flames as sophistry and illusion, or as, in Huxley's case, questions of lunar politics.[21] Far more judiciously, Kant observed that however true it may be that all knowledge begins with experience, it does not necessarily arise directly out of experience. There are some 'uses of reason', of 'pure' reason, which are not directly tied to sense-experience, and which in consequence, although they cannot constitute knowledge in a scientific sense, have their *sui generis* and necessary part to play. They can, for example, regulate inquiry by clarifying the necessary presuppositions which make certain sorts of inquiry worthwhile and rewarding. But the uses and advantages which Kant saw in 'pure reason' have to be paid for, and the price is high: if there is nothing in sense-experience which directly corresponds to the transcendental ideas of pure reason (the psychological idea, or soul; the cosmological idea, or world; the theological idea, or God), then there cannot be any control in that quarter over their speculative use. The dilemma occurs because the use of reason in metaphysics (occurring in the same brain which is so successful in physics or in mathematics) is not sufficient to remove the inherent contradictions which arise. Even worse, reason can in some cases actually support each of two mutually contradictory propositions; hence arise the familiar antinomies of reason. These are problematic because the thesis and the contradictory antithesis can both be 'proved', so far as reason is concerned, 'by equally clear, evident, and irresistible proofs, . . .' as Kant put it, 'a state at which the sceptic rejoices, but which must make the critical philosopher pause and feel ill at ease'.[22]

The critical philosopher has to pause because the human thinking process actually, as a matter of fact, does operate in modes or categories of thinking which transcend strict deductions from phenomena. Human beings do arrive at moral judgements, at aesthetic judgements—indeed, they arrive at scientific judgements. There must, Kant came to argue, be certain a priori conditions which make the different kinds of judging (including scientific judgement) possible, and which allow synthetic a priori propositions to occur—a proposition which may indeed be elicited from experience, but once it is discerned, it can be seen to have a ground other than experience alone. A child may learn from experience that one mum plus one dad makes two people, and thus that one plus one makes two, but he soon grasps that this is a general truth which does not require each time to be confirmed from experience. Yet where does this general certainty come from? Certainly not inductively from all known instances. There must, therefore, be an a priori condition which enables that judgement to be made, and to be a general truth. Thus a truth of pure mathematics, which at first sight seems to be analytic (one plus one makes two: does that add more to our knowledge than 'a small room is a room'?), turns out, in Kant's view, to be synthetic, but to depend on an a priori condition of 'the way things happen to be'; in other words, it is a synthetic a priori proposition.

Could it, then, be the case that moral and aesthetic judgements require a priori conditions, if such judgements are to be made? The discernment, for example, of order in nature cannot possibly be inductively arrived at, because we have no knowledge of nature as a whole, nor even of all its parts. Yet we do discern order in nature, or at least in those parts of it which we observe; and the order, both the orderliness and the teleological process apparent in nature, is suggestive of beauty. What this implied, to Kant, is that there must be a 'givenness' of certain correspondent structures which exist *before* an aesthetic response or judgement is made, since otherwise the judgement itself would not be possible. There must, in other words, be *a priori* conditions of aesthetic judgement: a sufficient structure in nature to be suggestive of order (though we can never conclude that there is order *in* nature, as a proposition), and a sufficient correspondent structure in the mind to be able to discern it.

This is vastly to over-simplify the lines along which Kant moved; indeed, in some respects, particularly with regard to teleology, it is to misrepresent him.[23] But it is sufficient to help us understand how Kant was understood by his successors (whether rightly or wrongly) to have arrived at two suggestions which seemed to unlock new opportunities for them: first, that there must be *a priori* conditions which enable the different categories of human judgement, since otherwise those judgements could not occur, *a priori* categories of scientific, or of moral, or of aesthetic judgement; and second, that these judgements must necessarily be partial discernments of what is really the case, but only partial. It seemed clear that unless one discerned something of what is actually the case no valid judgement could ever occur, with which others would be able to agree, or which they would be able to understand. Yet equally clearly, men do not discern the totality of what is actually the case, otherwise, presumably, they would have arrived at a knowledge of all knowledge.

Kant summarized this distinction in the terms *noumena* and *phenomena*, meaning by *noumena*, roughly, that which is what it is in itself and which gives rise to sensation (to what we perceive) but is never wholly captured in perception; and meaning by *phenomena*, what appears in perception. There are thus two parts in *phenomena*, in what appears in sensation: the part arising from the object, sensation, and the part contributed subjectively by the mind, in organizing the multiplicity of sensation into certain relationships. These, roughly, are the correspondent *a priori* structures, the subjective as much as the objective, without whose prior existence, independent of experience, no experiencing and no judgement could occur.

This summary is undoubtedly too compressed, but it is, perhaps, enough to make clear why a situation in Western philosophy developed which seemed hopelessly problematic to Husserl, and which led to the radical break-away of phenomenology. For, far from seeming destructive, as Heine had supposed, Kant was believed by many to have unlocked them from the bondage of necessity, and to have re-established the validity of moral and aesthetic judgements. In other words, he appeared to have offered a way in which the dilemma of individual meaning could be solved, and in which the worthwhileness of feeling and of moral choice could be defended: judgements in these areas could apparently now be understood as *sui generis*, but legitimate, ways of experiencing the world. Kant was rapidly developed in many different directions. In some forms of idealism, for example, the 'thing-in-itself' understanding of *noumena* was dissolved. Why not simply say that our approximate understandings are not approximations to 'things-in-themselves', but to ideal postulates of reality, which draw us into certain sorts of action or of judgement? If this seemed to be solipsistic, doubting the reality of anything external to our perception, then so be it. So far as the sense of God is concerned, the most specific development of Kant lay in the suggestion that religious judgements are a *sui generis* category of judgement, depending, like aesthetic judgements, on sufficient *a priori* conditions. There is a religious way of experiencing the universe, just as there is a scientific, or a moral, or an aesthetic. They cannot be collapsed into each other. The religious way of experiencing as a basis of a Kantian category of judgement is already foreshadowed in Schleiermacher, but it received its most thoroughgoing and culminating expression in Rudolph Otto's *The Idea of the Holy*.[24] When one considers the impact of that book when it appeared in 1917, and its subsequent influence for a time, one can see how effectively Kant could be deployed for the defence of religious belief over against the empiricists who had insisted that worthwhile knowledge must be built up from sense experience without appeal to anything *a priori*.

What effect, then, did this kind of deployment of Kant have on empiricists? The answer is, virtually none. That is to say, empiricists were perfectly aware that post-Kantian developments were taking place, but that did not in the least deter them from pursuing their own programme, or from continuing to insist that ideas *are* built up from experience, and that all superstructures must finally be evaluated in relation to their foundations in experience. We have just seen this in the case of Huxley;[25] we saw it in the first chapter in the case of Helmholtz, and in the oath of

Brücke and du Bois-Reymond;[26] and it was emphasized then how pervasive the empiricist ambition, on the basis of scientific positivism, had become. Indeed, if this were not so, it would be hard to account for the origin of *logical* positivism itself. The power of the empiricist argument came to a culminating assurance in the much-quoted statement of Schlick. 'After so-called "rational knowledge" is accounted for, empiricism now has the right and the power to claim the whole field of knowledge. We know nothing except by experience, and experience is the only criterion of the truth or falsity of any real proposition.'[27]

It was into this situation of confusions and conflict, in which idealists and realists, transcendentalists and empiricists, pursued their lives in isolation from each other, that Husserl arrived. He came from a mathematical background, and as he looked at the philosophical scene, he observed that after centuries of effort to resolve such ancient problems as the relation between essences and universals, all that had happened was that the labels 'idealist' and 'realist' had been reversed: what would be referred to as idealism in the classical philosophy of the Middle Ages was now called realism, and what would be referred to as realism was now idealism: 'The philosophers meet but, unfortunately, not the philosophies.'[28] The sudden flash of illumination which occurred to Husserl was this: not only had this issue and other issues—notably, solipsism (whether the world is 'really' there apart from my perceiving it)—remained unresolved, despite the life-hours devoted to them, but actually, even if the issue of solipsism *was* resolved, it would make virtually no difference to the way in which human beings live their lives. This, to Husserl, was 'the greatest and most magnificent of all facts: I and my life remain—in my sense of reality—untouched by whichever way we decide the issue of whether the world is or is not.'[29] What has gone wrong with philosophy that it makes so little difference to, and has apparently so little connection with, the living of life? And where should philosophy begin if it is to re-establish that connection? It can only begin with the Delphic expression, *gnothi seauton*: know yourself:

In other words, the necessary path to knowledge which can be ultimately justified in the highest sense—or, what is the same, knowledge that is philosophical—is the path of *universal self-knowledge* ... The Delphic expression *gnothi seauton* has acquired new meaning . . . *Noli foras ire*, said St. Augustine, *in te redi, in interiore homine habitat veritas* ('Do not wish to go outside; go back into yourself. Truth dwells in the inner man').[30]

With those words, Husserl concluded the Paris Lectures, in 1929 (the lectures which he re-worked into *Cartesian Meditations*), and in those words one can find the foundation of modern phenomenology: *gnothi seauton*: Know yourself. But how? What could it mean to 'know oneself'? What is the 'self' that one is setting out to know?

There seemed, to Husserl, to be only one possible answer: there is only the stream of consciousness, 'the flowing conscious life',[31] which represents my 'I-ness' at any particular moment. The only fundamental fact of which I can be sure is that I experience my own consciousness. *What* I experience is less immediately certain. Our access, therefore, to the only certain foundation of *all* knowledge must lie in a much clearer attention to what consciousness is. Although much (perhaps most) human activity ignores (or rather circumvents) this fact (most people walk down the street without great agonies of introspection), it remains, in Husserl's view, the one fact which lies at the foundation of all else which we come to regard as factual. For, although the positive sciences (as Husserl called them) have achieved 'a brilliant development',[32] they have done so in the attitude of Dr. Johnson, by kicking a stone and regarding it as 'there'. This is necessary, in terms of evidence, as Husserl frequently made clear.[33] Yet the more fundamental fact is that there is a Dr. Johnson who hurts his foot. It is consciousness which lies at the foundation of *knowledge*, not the stone. Consciousness is the one fact of which we can be really sure, since without being conscious, how could we know that the stone is 'there'?

It is at this point that Husserl's connections with Descartes are obvious and self-confessed. But Husserl believed that Descartes's 'Cartesian' doubt was not radical enough. In particular he rejected a Cartesian 'move', whereby the consciousness of a 'clear and distinct idea' can be taken to prove the necessary existence of the ground of that idea in reality. Still less did he accept that the idea of God is unaccountable except on the assumption that God exists. The one fatal mistake is to suppose that having isolated the one fact of which I can be certain, *cogito*, I can then draw from this fact substantial conclusions: *ergo sum*, therefore *I* am; and, if *I* can be deduced as a *substantia cogitans*, a thinking substance, that it is then reasonable to deduce other substances, including the *substantia* of God, as objective reality. Yet in fact *true* Cartesian doubt arrives at only one conclusion: *cogito, ergo cogito.* So Husserl commented:

We must under no circumstances take for granted that, with our apodictic and pure ego, we have salvaged a small corner of the world as the single indubitable fact about the world which can be utilized by the philosophizing ego. It is not true that all that now remains to be done is to infer the rest of the world through correct deductive procedures according to principles that are innate in the ego. Unfortunately Descartes commits this error, in the apparently insignificant yet fateful transformation of the ego to a *substantia cogitans*, to an independent human *animus*, which then becomes the point of departure for conclusions by means of the principle of causality. In short, this is the transformation which made Descartes the father of the rather absurd transcendental realism.[34]

It follows that the basic phenomenological procedure is to exclude everything (all presuppositions, all existing interpretations, *everything*), in order to isolate the one fact, *ego cogito*. Only if one understands *what* consciousness is can one then put in a proper, and uniform, perspective the consequences of consciousness, whether in art, or science, or religion, or in kicking Dr. Johnson's stone. The basic method is to bracket off everything from the awareness itself. For this bracketing, Husserl revived the Greek word *epochē*: 'We must regard nothing as veridical except the pure immediacy and givenness in the field of the *ego cogito* which the *epochē* has opened up to us.'[35] Only by this suspension, this *epochē*, can it really come home to me, that nothing is, apart from my consciousness of it. Note that Husserl was not prejudging the question whether the external world 'really exists'; he was simply saying, let us bracket that question out, in order to concentrate on the pure act of consciousness.[36]

At once, as soon as one makes this fundamental *epochē*, wholly new perspectives open up. For one thing, phenomenology itself is initiated, because one wants to know how things come to appear to be. Phenomenology is, in the Greek sense of the component words, the discussion of appearances. It is in this sense that phenomenology is constituted as reflection on the only certain fact, the foundation of all other knowledge, the experience of consciousness: 'Phenomenological experience as reflection must avoid any interpretative constructions. Its descriptions must reflect accurately the concrete contents of experience, precisely as these are experienced.'[37]

This leads to one apparently indispensable hypothesis in Husserl's strategy, that the 'I' can survey the 'I'—in other words, that within consciousness there can be an awareness of what is going on in the activity of consciousness: 'The phenomenological Ego establishes himself as *"disinterested onlooker"*, above the naïvely interested Ego.'[38] It was this which led Husserl to posit the transcendental ego, a term which points to the fact of introspection, to the very fact that 'I' am an observer of 'myself', even though, as Husserl accepted, this implies that 'the phenomenological reduction thus tends to split the ego'.[39] Or again, 'I have become a pure observer of myself.'[40] Husserl's conclusion, at this point, is as follows:

The phenomenological attitude, with its *epochē*, consists in that *I reach the ultimate experiential and cognitive perspective thinkable.* In it I become the disinterested spectator of my natural and worldly ego and its life . . . I am detached in as much as I 'suspend' all worldly interests (which I nonetheless possess), and to the degree that I—the philosophizing one— place myself above them and observe them, and take these as themes for description, as being my transcendental ego.[41]

How, then, do we proceed from this point to the building-up of knowledge? In fact, quite simply, by realizing that it is consciousness which allows reality to become a phenomenon. Here at once an advantage can be seen in the breaking of the Kantian distinction between *noumena* and *phenomena* (*noumena* being 'the thing in itself', to which we have no absolute access, and *phenomena* being the perceived appearance). By bracketing the question out, the issue becomes wholly unimportant as a primary puzzle or problem: what men know is that consciousness creates reality *so far as consciousness is concerned*, by moving out towards the objects of itself. In other words, as Husserl put it, every *cogito* has its *cogitatum*: 'The *epochē* changes nothing in the world. All experience is still his experience, all consciousness still his consciousness. The expression *ego cogito* must be expanded by one term. Every *cogito* contains a meaning: its *cogitatum*.'[42]

This leads on to another of Husserl's fundamental concepts, intentionality. What he meant by 'intentionality' was an observable fact about consciousness (as much a given fact as consciousness itself) that consciousness is directional.[43] Intentionality is the interrelation between the subject itself and the constituted object (constituted in consciousness) which makes consciousness what it is at any particular moment. This means that intentionality is the movement from the subject which constitutes the object, and the movement from the *apparent* object which constitutes the subject as a conscious being. From this point of view it is obvious that 'intentionality' is an unfortunate word, because it suggests acts of will and decision. Certainly, it may be these, but far more often it is 'passive genesis'. It is simply the interaction of subject and object without anything specifically 'intentional' in mind. But with that *caveat*, it is clear that what Husserl wanted to convey by intentionality was the way in which consciousness is the movement between the subject and the appearing or the apparent object. I move out to designate the world, but the appearing world moves in to give my consciousness particularity and being:

We take intentional relation, understood in purely descriptive fashion as an inward peculiarity of certain experiences, to be the essential feature of 'psychical phenomena' or 'acts', seeing in Brentano's definition of them as 'phenomena intentionally containing objects in themselves' a circumscription of essence, whose 'reality' (in the traditional sense) is of course ensured by examples. Differently put in terms of pure phenomenology: Ideation performed in exemplary cases of such experiences—and so performed as to leave empirical-psychological conception and existential affirmation of being out of account, and to deal only with the real phenomenological content of these experiences—yields us the pure, phenomenological generic Idea of *intentional experience* or *act*, and of its various pure species. That not all experiences are intentional is proved by sensations and sensational complexes. Any piece of a sensed visual field, full as it is of visual contents, is an experience containing many part-contents, which are neither referred to, nor intentionally objective in the whole.[44]

Thus, intentionality is what distinguishes human beings from all else: '*The essence of consciousness, in which I live as my own self,* is the so-called intentionality. Consciousness is always consciousness of something.'[45]

This means that the building-up of knowledge is the creation within consciousness of the kind of meanings that appear to bear the weight one wants to put on them: 'The tremendous task placed on description is to expound the universal structure of transcendental consciousness in its reference to and creation of meanings.'[46]

But does this mean that 'knowledge' is arbitrary, the private property of individual consciousness? The answer must be both yes and no. Yes, in the fullest existentialist sense. What one man in his own consciousness accepts from the appearing world is uniquely and inalienably his own, even if it appears madness to others. The criterion is not sanity, which would introduce presupposition and mean a betrayal of phenomenological reduction or *epochē*. The criterion is authenticity, adherence to the absolute givenness of experiencing as it occurs in and to oneself. The implications for existentialism are at once obvious: 'Truth here coincides with sincerity.'[47]

But the answer can also be no; knowledge is not wholly private, because the construction of some meanings can bear considerable public weight. The construction of such meaning comes from the synthesis of perceptions, particularly when they recur, or are of the same type. Husserl argued that there cannot be consciousness without apparent constitutive objects of consciousness (and this is a fact, *not* about the reality or otherwise of the object, since that is a 'bracketed-out' problem, but about the nature of consciousness), and he therefore concluded: '*It follows that the stream of consciousness is permeated by the fact that consciousness relates itself to objects.* This relation is an essential characteristic of every act of consciousness. It is the ability to pass over—through synthesis—from perennially new and greatly disparate forms of consciousness to an awareness of their unity.'[48] So knowledge may indeed be constituted by 'constant conjunction' as Hume had argued. But that is not the *only* way in which it is constituted. Consciousness is, therefore, both protentive and retentive: it recovers from past experiencing the means of synthetic consciousness, but it organizes its retention into the penetration of the future. It belongs to the universal structure of the ego that it can be what Husserl called 'a progressing object index',[49] and that there can be an appearance of other people in my consciousness because they appear as 'walking object indices'. This underlines both the success and the limitations of human knowledge and achievements. If, then, intentionality expresses the relation between subject and appearing object, between consciousness and what it is consciousness of, then the extension of knowledge is 'the search for correlations'[50] in the obtained relations, which are held in the retentive power of consciousness, albeit assisted by other means of retention, such as printing or the computer. But none of this extension of knowledge, from given relation to intelligible correlation, remotely affects the fact that even the most complex extension of knowledge has its existence, not 'out there', but in the consciousness of some particular conscious being: '*True being, therefore, whether real or ideal, has significance only as a particular correlate of my own intentionality*, actual or potential.'[51]

From this point of view, it is entirely proper to speak, as Leibniz spoke and as Husserl borrowed the term, of the ego as a monad, whose consciousness is all:

The ego is ... the permanent and enduring subject of persisting convictions and habits through whose alterations *the unity of the personal ego and its personal character is* first *constituted*. From this we must dissociate the ego in its full concretion, because the ego is concrete only in the flowing multiplicity of its intentional existence and with the objects that are meant and constituted for it therein. The ego may thus also be viewed as a concrete monad.[52]

But does not this lead, wholly, completely, and absolutely, into solipsism? Husserl was well aware of the question; it was his one 'truly disturbing thought'.[53] *Prima facie*, the answer is yes: 'I am, thus, at least *prima facie*, in a certain sense *solus ipse*, but not in the ordinary sense, in which one might say that a man survived a universal holocaust in a world which itself remained unaffected.'[54]

Here at once one sees the way through the apparent dilemma: provided one starts, not from solipsism as a primary philosophical puzzle but from *epochē*, bracketing off all else but the givenness of consciousness, it becomes clear that among the constituents of consciousness (that which comes into appearance) is the manifestation of the *alter ego*. This has the same initial *phenomenological* status as other constituents of consciousness: 'In the ego, the *alter ego* manifests and confirms itself as an experienced presentation ... I experience the world not as my own private world but as an intersubjective world, one that is given to all human beings and which contains objects accessible to all.'[55]

It follows that one can, in the end, retain a notion of reality, since the appearances of things and what Husserl called 'the consistency of their indices' have exactly the truth of their appearances. It is the consistency and the apparent co-experience of *some* appearances which allow particular constructions to be built upon them in the mosaic of apparent intersubjectivity. This is obvious in the positive sciences, and this even suggests a fundamental ontological structure, because, for consistency to appear in the indices, it must occur also in the interactive process of intentionality, in each appearing *alter ego*. But this does not constitute the positive sciences as the only paradigm of worthwhile knowledge. They are simply one way of being conscious. Positive science which abstracts itself from consciousness, and which thus monopolizes both epistemology and also ontological possibilities (because they become bound exclusively to it), is science which has lost its way. In particular, it has lost all possibility of control over itself, because it no longer has any serious means to see that it is only *one* procedure among many in intentional consciousness, and that it is *not* the only valid or worthwhile way of being human, or of arriving at 'knowledge'. So at last we come full circle, and we can fill in the gaps in the paragraph from which (pp. 169f.) we began:

The path to knowledge which can be ultimately justified in the highest sense—or, what is the same, knowledge that is philosophical—is the path of *universal self-knowledge*, first in a monadic and then in an intermonadic sense. The Delphic expression *gnothi seauton* has acquired new meaning . . . Positive science is science lost in the world. One must first lose the world through *epochē* so as to regain it in universal self-examination. *Noli foras ire* . . .56

From this, it follows that the 'phenomenology of religion' is the search for the ways in which appearances in consciousness are religiously suggestive, and for the locus of intentionality in those *cogitata* which are suggestive, for example, of God. Obviously, if one starts from the point of phenomenological reduction, all questions of the existence or nature of God are 'bracketed out'—initially. One simply concentrates reflectively on those appearances in consciousness which give rise to the sense of God, and which must ultimately underlie theological language if that language is not to be wholly vacuous. But the question which was never adequately faced by Husserl is whether those appearances in consciousness are simply *giving rise* to the sense of God, or whether they are the sense of *God*. So far as the positive sciences are concerned, phenomenological reduction opens the way to a returning of reality to the world, not as a contribution to the debate about solipsism but because, no matter which way that debate is solved, the intersubjectivity and cross-indexing of appearances enable scientific procedures, and return that degree of necessary reality to the world.[57] But in that case, what of the appearances of *God* in consciousness? If one examines these and finds that there are 'essential structures of these experiences'[58] which enable intersubjectivity and cross-indexing, must one not examine the possibility that a comparable kind of reality must be returned to God, as was returned to the world, not as a contribution to scholastic debates or metaphysical arguments but as a fact demanded by particular modes of consciousness itself? But Husserl arrived at this possibility too late, according to reports of his views: 'We may recall that at the end of his life Husserl was assessing the difficulties and possible failure of his religious philosophy. He said that his mistake had been to seek God without God. That is the temptation of idealism.'[59]

To avoid that temptation, one would have to ask, phenomenologically: what must be the case for there to be the appearances of God in consciousness which do in fact obtain? This may seem a very Kantian question—as indeed it is; but it does not necessarily lead in the direction of *a priori* arguments. It requires first a very careful 'mapping' of the exact nature of those appearances, so far as they can be expressed or observed externally; and this is exactly the task to which phenomenologists of religion, such as van der Leeuw, have in part committed themselves. This procedure may well support the view that the sense of God is constructed in consciousness as a defence against what appears, otherwise, to be the case—oblivion at death, undeserved suffering, and the various other factors which made Freud believe that religion is projection. But phenomenological attention to what actually happens in consciousness as a consequence of the appearance of God makes it crystal clear that the account of Freud is far too restricted and limited. When God is constituted in consciousness the complexity of consequence is such that one cannot any longer exclude the possibility that the term 'God' represents a way of being, in relation to the universe, which is not wholly disclosed in immediate terms (far from it) but which gives sufficient indication of its possibility for men to move their intentionality towards it, and to receive into consciousness constructive possibilities. One can still 'bracket out' the 'problem' of God's existence: but the phenomenological facts of consciousness in this area remain as they are. The metaphysical issue, or the issue ultimately of truth, in relation to the existence of God, would then be posed by asking whether that way of being in relation to the universe is itself independent of the consciousness which constitutes it as real and which embodies the consequences into the construction of life. It is not at issue that the term 'god' refers, in historical terms, to a conceptual resource of interpretation from which theistic meaning is continuously constructed. Nor is it at issue that men, from that resource of meaning, have constructed in their own case ways of being related to the universe and to their fellow men which clearly would not occur without that resource of meaning or interpretation. The issue is whether they have been mistaken in hypostasizing that resource of meaning, and in believing that it must be prior to, and independent of, their own consciousness if it is to have the effects which do in fact appear in consciousness. The phenomenological issue is whether the term God requires hypostasis in order adequately to account for the constitutive appearances in consciousness—a way of Being, in other words, in relation to the universe, not identical with it, but manifest through it, disclosing itself sufficiently for it to become that *sui generis* resource of meaning in the construction of human life-ways: 'God', as Andrew Young once put it, 'in a point', whereby 'infused with grace' we are enabled to

> cry with Meister Eckhart,
> 'Up, valiant soul, put on thy jumping-shoes
> Of love and understanding.' Soon I should learn;
> The ghost must go; the cocoon spun by the worm,
> The butterfly would burst. New eyes would see
> The invisible world into which my brother vanished.[60]

A phenomenological argument of that kind could only be defended provided it took seriously the distinction drawn by Ayer about the nature of unobservable entities—of 'invisible worlds':

I see no objection to the postulation of unobservable entities, so long as the hypotheses into which they enter have consequences which can be empirically tested, and it is quite customary to speak of such entities as causes of the phenomena which they are invoked to explain ... What I do find objectionable, on the other hand, is the notion that these unobservable entities are located in an unobservable space. I cannot see that we have any justification for the inference that there is such a thing as unobservable space; and indeed I am not at all sure that I find the idea of it intelligible.[61]

Yet that is exactly what such a phrse as 'infused with grace' is accepting, that if no effect of any kind can ever be specified, the problem of God's existence is already dissolved. Yet from a phenomenological point of view, this leaves open the intriguing possibility that perhaps it is in relation to the sense of God that the purest of the pure acts of consciousness are possible, in an intentionality towards that which does *not* appear as other appearances (varied and different as *they* are in themselves), but which is nevertheless constitutive of distinct, and publicly recognizable, sequences of existential construction. This would result, as was also the case in the consideration of information and structure, in an indefinitely regressing horizon of approximations, which nevertheless allows of intersubjectivity and cross-indices in the long sequences of life and time; and it is this, in part (within the context of the various precipitating factors, sociological, economic, epistemological), which has kept *some* theistic universes of meaning in movement. This *sui generis* mode of appearance is constituted in the intentionality of faith which in turn is suggested as worthwhile by certain focal qualities or persons—the person of Christ, for example, and the consequent quality of life in the case of Christians; Torah and the consequent quality of life in the case of Jews. But faith can only be distinguished and rescued from credulity—or indeed from becoming a matter simply of words or complexly of hypocrisy—by the *inter*active intentionality towards the object of itself—in other words, by intentionality towards God, or towards whatever *in constituted reality* is represented in or through that term. Faith thus controlled becomes constitutive of further publicly intelligible appearances in consciousness. It is in this way that intentionality becomes the fundamental meaning and practice of prayer; and here as elsewhere it is essential to bear in mind that 'intentionality' is not necessarily a matter, in Husserl's sense, of wilful acts of initiative: it may be passive genesis.

Thus even phenomenology, the most subjective of all possible modes of human inquiry, even phenomenology cannot dispense with the possible reality of the object of belief in the case of God. This does not mean that all beliefs therefore become true. On the contrary, it has been emphasized that the controls of intersubjectivity are by no means wholly absent, even here. But the real phenomenological conclusion is that one will never know from theology in abstraction anything about the nature of God. It is necessary first to 'bracket off' theology, and learn the intentionality of consciousness which issues in prayer. It may be the case that 'prayer' in this sense bears very little relation to what is encouraged as that activity in religious systems or institutions. But this is because, just as Husserl regarded positive science as science lost in the world because it abstracted itself from the one fact of consciousness (as though scientific knowledge can be detached from consciousness), so he regarded systematic theology as theology lost in the world, if it regards itself as independent of men, who alone constitute it in their consciousness. Theology is not thereby emptied of significance. Exactly the reverse, it remains one of the deeply rewarding and necessary modes of human reflection, so long as human consciousness retains its integrity (and is politically and socially allowed its integrity) in seeking to understand what *is*, in the nature of this case. Theology does not always work in this way, as Husserl observed; but it can do so.

What, then, does prayer mean in relation to the sense of God? This is indeed something that bears much reflection; but not in lectures, nor in a public context, nor in any context which suggests that it is primarily a matter for discussion: for, what, as Phil Fuller asked, is really there?

Lucy finished cutting the bread.
'Lucy, do give me that hunchy bit,' said Nina.
'Hunchy is not in the dictionary,' said Cecilia.
'I want it in my plate, and not in the dictionary,' said Nina.[62]

IX

CONCLUSION

THERE is no conclusion. Or to put it more accurately, it would be foolish to press for general conclusions before looking, with the insights gained from this survey, at the theistic traditions themselves. But some interim conclusions emerge. What has been suggested here is a new context in which we can organize our approach to the understanding of religions, by seeing them as route-finding activities, homeostatic and conservative, focused on particular compounds of limitation, but rapidly extending, because of their plausibility, to become whole contexts of life, and whole universes of meaning. It has then been suggested that we must look very carefully at what happens when those routes or those meanings come into crisis, into crises of implausibility. This is *not* something which is necessarily imposed from without. Far more frequently, in historical terms, it has occurred *within* traditions, as men, in their own existence, have wrestled with God.

This observation leads at least to one, more than interim, conclusion, which has been a recurrent theme in this survey (a theme, incidentally, not in the least foreseen at the outset of the work involved): what has emerged quite separately in each of the various disciplines surveyed is an entirely new concern with the differentiating consequences of the responsive objects of encounter. It is this which represents so important a revolution in recent years, because it implies a reversal of the nineteenth-century ambition. It now becomes clear that we are not studying massive mechanisms of social process, or of individuation, alone, in which it is virtually irrelevant what objects are or are not encountered—as though the mechanism will in any case run on. It is the contributory effect of the actual objects of encounter which is returning into the analysis of behaviour in all these different disciplines.

Does this point extend to the supposed objects of belief? It no longer seems so possible to assume, as it was usually assumed until very recently, that the claimed objects of belief are irrelevant to the analysis of believing behaviour. Far from the disciplines we

have been surveying dissolving the possible reality of reference in
the term 'God', they actually seem to demand a return to that
possibility if sense is to be made of their own evidence. This does
not in the least imply that, because someone reports something, it
therefore has a reality in existence external to the belief and independent of it. In that case everything conceivable would exist.
But the task of theologies in relation to behavioural sciences is
crystal clear (they may, of course, have much else to do, but in
this respect their task is clear): they must endeavour to specify
what would count as an effect of the claimed object of belief in
their own case, and where such an effect can be discerned. Then,
and only then, can we proceed to the issue, as Quine put it, of
ontology, and to the question of whether indeed God contributes
to the sense of God. But for that discussion we undoubtedly need
the theistic traditions and their own account of the struggle with
the godness of God—the struggle, that is, with what God must be
if God *is* to be God.

The struggle is by no means over; and this is what makes
theology so lively a subject. But what the issue of the struggle in
any person's life will be is beyond external prediction. When
George Eliot set out, in *Middlemarch*, to explore 'the history of
man, and how that mysterious mixture behaves under the varying
experiments of Time',[1] she was drawing attention to the fact that
human lives can be diversely constructed in vastly different directions as a consequence of the symbols which are allowed to be
effective within them (in her case, particularly the symbolized
nature of 'womanhood'). The question of rationality is the question,
first, of where those symbols are ultimately grounded (what, in
other words, are the resources which contribute to their meaning
and their availability), and second, whether an individual allows
that that question must be asked. As Freud frequently observed,
there is no limit to the absurdity of possible, as-if, beliefs. It is
possible for men to believe that the earth is flat, that advertisements
are extensively accurate descriptions, that politicians tell the truth
in public. The question of rationality resists the creation of (to
take an extreme example) a Nazi Aryan mythology, by constantly
asking where it is grounded and where it is directed. More posi-
tively, it probes and explores the way in which words and other
symbols stretch out the construction of individual and social lives
at the limits of both tragedy and joy, and of the way in which the

words surrounding the possible effect of God within those constructions are realized in life:

> I will make treasure of words,
> Each one secured as it occurs
> Sills, tables, cupboards, half-forgotten spaces,
> Shelves piled so high
> That even spiders are scarce.
>
> I will travel the world for a rarity:
> Kamavacara-somanassa,
> That was worth a journey.
> Even meliorisationsgenossenschaft
> Shall not be alien,
> Nor even jargon.
>
> All mine; all for my own uses:
> Each morning shall be the first day of creation.
> I will build structures unacquainted of the world,
> 'Colorless green ideas sleeping furiously'
> Shall not be the only innovation in language:
> I will build Eve from Adam for delight.
>
> All mine: but yours as well
> A common substance for a common dream of truth:
> Let us shipwreck ourselves in a sea of words
> Plunge and cascade each other
> Until the sun sinks
> And the hand is silent and the voice still
> And the word alone lives on.

REFERENCES

I. EXPLAINING HUMAN BEHAVIOUR

1. Baines, pp. 293 f.; Aubry, i, p. 295.
2. Conrad, p. 312.
3. Ibid., p. 313.
4. Mill, vi. 1. 2 (pp. 419 f.).
5. So, for example, Buckle (i. 1): 'Statistical evidence and the regularity of the moral world: the most comprehensive inferences respecting the actions of men, which are admitted by all parties as incontestable truths, are derived from this or analogous sources; they rest on statistical evidence, and are expressed in mathematical language . . . Of all offences, it might well be supposed that the crime of murder is one of the most arbitrary and irregular. For when we consider that this, though generally the crowning act of a long career of vice, is often the immediate result of what seems a sudden impulse; that when premeditated, its committal, even with the least chance of impunity, requires a rare combination of favourable circumstances for which the criminal will frequently wait; that he has thus to bide his time, and look for opportunities he cannot control; that when the time has come, his heart may fail him; that the question whether or not he shall commit the crime may depend on a balance of conflicting motives, such as fear of the law, a dread of the penalties held out by religion, the prickings of his own conscience, the apprehension of future remorse, the love of gain, jealousy, revenge, desperation; when we put all these things together, there arises such a complication of causes, that we might reasonably despair of detecting any order or method in the result of those subtle and shifting agencies by which murder is either caused or prevented. But now, how stands the fact? The fact is, that murder is committed with as much regularity and bears as uniform a relation to certain known circumstances, as do the movements of the tides, and the rotations of the seasons. M. Quételet, who has spent his life in collecting and methodising the statistics of different countries, states, as the result of his laborious researches, that "in every thing which concerns crime, the same numbers re-occur with a constancy which cannot be mistaken; and that this is the case even with those crimes which seem quite independent of human foresight, such, for instance, as murders, which are generally committed after quarrels arising from circumstances apparently casual. Nevertheless, we know from experience every year there not only take place nearly the same number of murders, but that even the instruments by which they are committed are employed in the same proportion." This was the language used in 1835 by confessedly the first statistician in Europe, and every subsequent investigation has confirmed his accuracy.'
   It was this break-through which made possible Durkheim's landmark in the development of sociology, *Suicide, a Study in Sociology*, even though in the course of that book he rejected emphatically many of Quételet's actual conclusions and methods.
6. Runciman, 'Explanation', particularly, p. 81.
7. There is an inconsistency over the actual date. *Coningsby* begins in the

spring of 1832, with the resignation of Lord Grey: this is referred to as 'some twelve years ago' (I. i), i.e. the date of writing is 1844 (the actual year of first publication). Coningsby is about 14 in 1832 (I. i), and he leaves Eton in 1835 (II. vii), 'eager for fancied emancipation and passionate for a novel existence'. He meets Sidonia (who tells him that 'the age of ruins is past') in the forest 'some six or seven years ago' (III. 1), i.e. 1837 or 8. But Coningsby inscribes the visitor's book at Mr. Millbank's mill: 'Harry Coningsby, Sept. 2, 1836'.

8. Disraeli, pp. 170 f.
9. Ibid., pp. 171, 173.
10. *Proceedings*, 1920, p. 314.
11. *Proceedings*, 1894, p. 210.
12. 'Speaking of the variations in the earth's field, physicists are practically certain that this field is not due to any magnetism like that of hard steel, but almost entirely to electric currents conducted by the molten metal which forms the earth's core. This molten metal flows, slowly but restlessly. So the magnetic map, changing from century to century, somewhat as a weather map changes from day to day, reflects a sort of slow, ponderous, subterranean weather.' Webster, p. 158.
13. There is a hint of this in Wilde's own 'Wilde' lecture, in the series he established in Manchester, in 1902. He entitled it: 'On the Evolution of the Mental Faculties in Relation to some Fundamental Principles of Motion'.
14. 'One evening in the late eighteenth century an Italian woman stood in her kitchen watching the frogs' legs which she was preparing for the evening meal. "Look at those muscles move," she said to her husband. "They always seem to come alive when I hang them on the copper wire." Her husband looked. He was the Professor of Surgery in the University of Bologna, but he is known to us as the discoverer of electricity—Luigi Galvani. Here was the beginning of it all two hundred years ago. The cut end of the frog's nerve was in contact with the copper wire, and electric current produced by the contact was passing along the nerve to the muscle; as a result, the muscle was twitching and contracting.' Penfield, p. 3.
15. Jones, *Freud*, i, p. 45.
16. E.g. Guntrip, pp. 30 f., 75–81; Shands, p. 10: 'In striking contrast to the inappropriateness of the scientific model used by Freud, the *method* prescribed by him in working with psychiatric patients appears to be a stroke of genius ... Where Freud's elaborate theoretical system now seems obsolete because so concrete in its formulation (borrowing from a physical theoretical model which became demonstrably outmoded around the time of Freud's first important psychoanalytic book was published), the method of free association remains vigorously alive and effective. The technique of free association allows the therapist to participate in what would otherwise be purely interior conversations with the self.'
17. Pribram, 'Foundation', esp. pp. 395 ff.; 'Proposal', esp. pp. 499 ff.: 'Only within the past decade has it become generally known that Freud indeed relied heavily on a model of the way in which experience leaves its mark on the nervous system. As a rule Freud's contributions to basic neurology have been ignored except to point out that he left them behind to go on to endeavours felt to be really "important" or "misguided" according to whether the viewer came from a "soft" or "hard" science background. Careful examination of Freud's "Project for a Scientific Psychology" [see Bibl.] and perusal of later works ... shows that despite protestations to the contrary,

Freud repeatedly turned to neurology for his model—that indeed his model, though altered in detail and emphasis, remained in most essentials the model first conceived as "The Project".' The 'scientific' status of Freudian theory, and the empirical testing of Freudian hypotheses, will be discussed in greater detail in ch. VI.

18. *First Supplement*, ad. loc.

19. See Bowker, *Suffering*, p. 190.

20.   '1. Idea is the object of thinking: every man being conscious to himself that he thinks and that which his mind is applied about whilst thinking being the ideas that are there, it is past doubt that men have in their mind several ideas, such as those expressed by the words "whiteness", "hardness", "sweetness", "thinking", "motion", "man", "elephant", "army", "drunkenness", and others. It is in the first place then to be inquired, how he comes by them. I know it is a received doctrine that men have native [i.e. innate] ideas and original characters stamped upon their minds in their very first being. This opinion I have at large examined already [and rejected]; and I suppose what I have said in the foregoing book will be much more easily admitted, when I have shown whence the understanding may get all the ideas it has, and by what ways and degrees they may come into the mind; for which I shall appeal to every one's own observation and experience.

2. All ideas come from sensation or reflection: let us, then suppose the mind to be, as we say, white paper, void of all characters, without any ideas; how comes it to be furnished? Whence comes it by that vast store which the busy and boundless fancy of man has painted on it with an almost endless variety? Whence has it all the materials of reason and knowledge? To this I answer, in one word, from experience; in that all our knowledge is founded, and from that it ultimately derives itself. Our observation, employed either about external sensible objects, or about the internal operations of our minds, perceived and reflected on by ourselves, is that which supplies our understandings with all the materials of thinking. These two are the fountains of knowledge, from whence all the ideas we have or can naturally have, do spring.' (*Essay*, II. i.)

21. In addition to Skinner, *Verbal Behaviour*, there is a clear summary of behavioural explanations of language acquisition and development via reinforcement in Staats, 1963. The most immediate of Chomsky's criticisms of Skinner occur in 'A Review . . .': 'The preceding discussion covers all the major notions that Skinner introduces in his descriptive system. My purpose in discussing the concepts one by one was to show that in each case, if we take his terms in their literal meaning, the description covers almost no aspect of verbal behaviour, and if we take them metaphorically, the description offers no improvement over various traditional formulations.' (p. 54.)

22. 'A serious investigation of generative grammars quickly shows that the rules that determine the form of sentences and their interpretations are not only intricate but also quite abstract, in the sense that the structures they manipulate are related to physical fact only in a remote way, by a long chain of interpretative rules [How, for example, does even a child recognize that of the following two sentences the first is ambiguous, the second not? I heard the shooting of the hunters; I heard the growling of the lions]. This is as true on the level of phonology as it is on the level of syntax and semantics, and it is this fact that has led to the questioning both of structuralist principles and to the tacitly assumed psychological theory that underlies them. It is because of the abstractness of linguistic representations that one

is forced, in my opinion, to reject not only the analytic procedures of modern linguistics . . ., but also principles of association and generalization that have been discussed and studied in empiricist psychology. Although such phenomena as association and generalization, in the sense of psychological theory and philosophical speculation, may indeed exist, it is difficult to see how they have any bearing on the acquisition or use of language. If our current conceptions of generative grammar are at all accurate, then the structures manipulated and the principles operating in these grammars are not related to given sensory phenomena in any way describable in the terms that empiricist psychology offers, and what principles it suggests simply have no relation to the facts that demand explanation.' Chomsky, 'Linguistic Theory', p. 57.

23. 'The existence of innate mental structure is, obviously, not a matter of controversy. What we may question is just what it is and to what extent it is specific to language.' Chomsky, 'The Formal Nature . . .', p. 439.

24. Chomsky's definition is: 'A grammar of the sort described previously ["A grammar generates a certain set of pairs (s, I) where s is a phonetic representation and I its associated semantic interpretation" (p. 398), operating "under constraints of memory, time, and organization of perceptual strategies that are not matters of grammar" (p. 399)], which attempts to characterize in an explicit way the intrinsic association of phonetic form and semantic content in a particular language, might be called a *generative grammar*.' ('Formal Nature', p. 407.) This is then more precisely articulated: 'In general, a set of rules that recursively define an infinite set of objects may be said to *generate* this set. Thus a set of axioms and rules of inference for arithmetic may be said to generate a set of proofs and a set of theorems of arithmetic (last lines of proofs). Similarly, a (generative) grammar may be said to generate a set of structural descriptions, each of which, ideally, incorporates a deep structure, a surface structure, a semantic interpretation (of the deep structure) and a phonetic interpretation (of the surface structure).' Ibid , pp. 439 f.

25. *First Supplement*, ad loc.

26. Durkheim, 'Review', p. 650. For the whole passage, see further p. 22.

27. Durkheim, *Elementary Forms*, pp. 228 f.: 'Collective representations very frequently attribute to the things to which they are attached qualities which do not exist under any form or to any degree. Out of the commonest object, they can make a most powerful sacred being. Yet the powers which are thus conferred, though purely ideal, act as though they were real; they determine the conduct of men with the same degree of necessity as physical forces. The Arunta who has been rubbed with his churinga feels himself stronger; he is stronger . . . Surely the soldier who falls while defending his flag does not believe that he sacrifices himself for a bit of cloth. This is all because social thought, owing to the imperative authority that is in it, has an efficacy that individual thought could never have . . . Thus there is one division of nature where the formula of idealism is applicable almost to the letter: this is the social kingdom. Here, more than anywhere else, the idea is the reality . . . The ideas thus objectified are well founded, not in the nature of the material things upon which they settle themselves but in the nature of society. We are now able to understand how the totemic principle, and, in general, every religious force, comes to be outside of the object in which it resides. It is because the idea of it is in no way made up of the impressions directly produced by this thing upon our senses or minds. Religious force is only the sentiment inspired by the group in its members,

but projected outside of the consciousnesses that experience them, and objectified. To be objectified, they are fixed upon some object which thus becomes sacred; but any object might fulfil this function.'

28. 'Animism is, in fact, the groundwork of the Philosophy of Religion, from that of savages up to that of civilized men. And although it may at first sight seem to afford but a bare and meagre definition of a minimum of religion, it will be found practically sufficient; for where the root is, the branches will generally be produced. It is habitually found that the theory of Animism divides into two great dogmas, forming parts of one consistent doctrine; first, concerning souls of individual creatures, capable of continued existence after the death or destruction of the body; second, concerning other spirits, upward to the rank of powerful deities.' Tylor, *Primitive Culture*, i, p. 426.

29. See. e.g., von Görres, *Mythengeschichte*, 1810. For Müller on language as 'the earliest work of art wrought by the human mind', see *Chips*, ii, p. 7.

30. 'Mythology, which was the bane of the ancient world, is in truth a disease of language.' *Lectures*, p. 11.

31. Ibid., p. 537.

32. For Preuss, see, e.g., 'Der Ursprung . . .'; there are bibliographical references to his own field-work in his contribution to the Oxford Congress, p. 41.

33. 'The theorist who believes in ancestor-worship as the key of all the creeds will see in Jehovah a developed ancestral ghost, or a kind of fetish god . . . The exclusive admirer of the hypothesis of Totemism will find evidence for his belief in worship of the golden calf and the bulls. The partisan of nature-worship will insist on Jehovah's connection with storm, thunder, and the fire of Sinai.' Lang, *Making of Religion*, p. 294.

34. 'Dear Robertson. Wellhausen seems to think there was a stone of a worshipful sort in the ark [of the Covenant], and Kuenen, that "probably" Jehovah lived in a stone in the ark, although he was also a young bull. Renan thinks the Ark was a museum of "objects of general interest". What a crew, and how easily a Voltairean assault on those learned gentry might be made, if only the orthodox possessed a humourist! Can't they *hire* one? *Moi chétif*, I could get the laugh on the orthodox side, I think. The fact is that they know nothing about it: and Martez Kuenen seems [   ] all of the old mythological fudge of 1857–70. However, I do admit that Wellhausen is another pair of Reeves, and not like a Homeric critic, that is an ex officer ass . . . Yours very truly, A. Lang.' (Cambr. U.L. Add. MS. 7449, D 384.)

Lang in fact changed his mind on totemism (two further letters to Robertson Smith exemplify this, Add. 7449, D 388, 389), and came round to the view that the root 'origin' of the idea of God lay in a supreme being, in original monotheism from which subsequent varieties degenerated—the argument later so elaborately developed by Schmidt. Lang's 'monotheistic heresy', as some of his contemporaries called it, led to two disagreeable consequences: first, he was attacked by his former friends and colleagues; but second, he was hailed by orthodox believers as a new defender of the faith. Lang was never sure which of the two fates was the worse.

35. See bibl. under Gaidoz.

36. 'You will find Epiphanius a mine of folklore. That is the true way to regard him and not him alone.' Conybeare, MS. letter to Frazer, 26 Oct. 1899.

37. 'I will empty out some of my notes higgledy-piggledy on the chance of this serving your purpose.' Frazer, MS. letter to Robertson Smith, 22 July 1889.
38. 'Is there any good book on basketwork which being largely unchanged savagery interests me. The basket-makers in England have some curious name for the different plications, which are called "hurdles" or something of the kind.' Tylor, MS. letter to Jenkinson, 12 Nov. 1903.
39. Marshall, 'The Old Generation', p. 121. The paragraph in full makes the contrast even clearer: "Social science or the reasoned history of man, for the two things are the same, is working its way towards a fundamental unity; just as is being done by physical science, or which is the same thing, by the reasoned history of natural phenomena. Physical science is seeking her hidden unity in the forces that govern molecular movement; social science is seeking her unity in the forces of human character. To that all history tends; from that proceeds all prediction, all guidance for the future.'
40. Conrad, p. 10.
41. Ibid.
42. 'I suppose I must have fallen into a sentimental mood; I only know that I stood there long enough for the sense of utter solitude to get hold of me so completely that all I had lately seen, all I had heard, and the very human speech itself, seemed to have passed away out of existence, living only for a while longer in my memory, as though I had been the last of mankind. It was a strange and melancholy illusion, evolved half-consciously like all our illusions, which I suspect only to be visions of remote unattainable truth, seen dimly. This was, indeed, one of the lost, forgotten, unknown places of the earth; I had looked under its obscure surface; and I felt that when tomorrow I had left it for ever, it would slip out of existence, to live only in my memory till I myself passed into oblivion. I have that feeling about me now; perhaps it is that feeling which has incited me to tell you the story, to try to hand over to you, as it were, its very existence, its reality—the truth disclosed in a moment of illusion.' Ibid., p. 243.
43. Quine, From a Logical Point of View, p. 1.
44. Harré and Secord, Explanation, p. 7.
45. e.g. Leach, Lévi-Strauss, p. 42; but note ibid., The Structural Study, p. xvii.
46. Conrad, p. 313.
47. Shakespeare, Julius Caesar, II. ii. 61–4, 72.
48. Ibid., 27 f.
49. See, e.g., Lashley 'Serial Order', esp. pp. 113 and 121 f.
50. Kitzinger, 'An Anatomy', p. 231.
51. Ibid., p. 233.
52. Conrad, p. 8.

II. SOCIOLOGY AND THE SOCIAL CONSTRUCTION OF REALITY

1. Durkheim, 'Review', p. 648.
2. See particularly Marx and Engels, German Ideology, ch. 1.
3. Durkheim, 'Review', p. 650.
4. Marx, 'Contribution', Introduction.
5. Bell, Art, esp. pp. 6–8.
6. See Fishman, p. 85.

7. Armstrong, *The Affecting Presence*, p. 191: 'If the anthropologist is concerned not with human *being* but only with extrapolations and models, then these observations will have little meaning for him . . . In any event, the anthropologist can no longer regard "the arts" as merely decorative, or the decorative as being of negligible or only ancillary importance. Rather he must see both as being in their own right, as existing in the universe of affects and thus of the greatest importance in studying human *being* in culture.' The objections of Lévi-Strauss to 'affectivity' as explanatory are considered further on pp. 99f.

8. Swanson, p. vii.

9. Ibid., p. 29: 'Both the primordial and the constitutional structures in which human life is immersed have properties which are also those that define the supernatural.'

10. Ibid., p. 22.

11. Ibid., pp. 20f: 'To summarize, the characteristics of spirits suggest that we identify them with specific groups which persist over time and have distinctive purposes. What groups meet these specifications? Our next step is to propose an answer to this question.

'There is a term in law and political science which seems to catch the qualities we seek. It is "sovereignty". A group has sovereignty to the extent that it has original and independent jurisdiction 'over some sphere of life—that its power to make decisions in this sphere is not delegated from outside but originates within it, and that its exercise of this power cannot legitimately be abrogated by another group . . .

'In these studies, we shall assume that in so far as a group has sovereignty, it is likely to provide the conditions from which a concept of spirit originates. The purposes of sovereign groups, like their special spheres of influence, tend to be distinctive and clear. By contrast, the purposes of non-sovereign groups are more likely to be seen as coming from a source other than themselves. The identity of the sovereign group is especially clear-cut just because its areas of control, and hence its purposes, are readily located. All we need add is the requirement that such a group shall persist over time. This will almost certainly be the case for many groups in any stable and enduring society.'

12. See Swanson, pp. 55–7.

13. Ibid., p. 65.

14. Ibid., p. 73.

15. Ibid.

16. The book opens with this generalization: 'Most men at most times have lived in two environments, one natural, the other supernatural. The distinction between these worlds is sometimes sharp, sometimes vague. It has even been declared an illusion. For the atheist, there are no gods—for the pantheist, all of nature is also supernatural.'

17. 'Some years since, a question which brings out this point was put to me by a great historian—"How can a statement as to customs, myths, beliefs, etc., of a savage tribe be treated as evidence where it depends on the testimony of some traveller or missionary, who may be a superficial observer, more or less ignorant of the native language, a careless retailer of unsifted talk, a man prejudiced or even wilfully deceitful?" . . . If two independent visitors to different countries . . . agree in describing some analogous art or rite or myth among the people they have visited, it becomes difficult or impossible to set down such correspondence to accident or wilful fraud . . . So strong, indeed, is this means of authentication, that the ethnographer in

his library may sometimes presume to decide, not only whether a particular explorer is a shrewd, honest observer but also whether what he reports is conformable to the general rules of civilization. "Non quis, sed quid".' Tylor, *Primitive Culture*, i, pp. 9 f.

18. Annandale to Frazer, MS. letter, 1 June 1904.
19. See p. 12.
20. Frazer was very well aware of the doubtful nature of his theories, but hoped that the facts which he had accumulated would stand. In the volume in which he made his final additions to *The Golden Bough*, he wrote:

> 'In that work [*The Golden Bough*], as in all my other writings, I have sought to base my conclusions by strict induction on a broad and solid foundation of well-authenticated facts . . . Now, as always, I hold all my theories very lightly, and am ever ready to modify or abandon them in the light of new evidence. If my writings should survive the writer, they will do so, I believe, less for the sake of the theories which they propound than for the sake of the facts which they record. They will live, if they live at all, as a picture or moving panorama of the vanished life of primitive man all over the world, from the Tropics to the Poles, groping and stumbling through the mists of ignorance and superstition in the eternal search after goodness and truth.' (*Aftermath*, p. 5.)

And yet, despite this very clear intention, the work is pervaded by an instinctive dislike of what is being recorded. Almost subconsciously, Frazer was prepared to believe the worst; 'facts' were by no means so well-authenticated as he claimed, and in any case his accounts were frequently organized in order to emphasize the absurd. In this respect, Frazer can be described, with some justice, as the Gibbon of primitive religion, and this at least makes *The Golden Bough* highly readable—even his style of writing is similar, but so also are his attitudes. In his additional volume, he reflected on his life's activity:

> 'I was beguiled, as by some subtle enchanter, into inditing what I cannot but regard as a dark, a tragic chronicle of human error and folly, of fruitless endeavour, wasted time, and blighted hopes. At the best the chronicle may serve as a warning, as a sort of Ariadne's thread, to help the forlorn wayfarer to shun some of the snares and pitfalls into which his fellows have fallen before him in the labyrinth of life.' (*Aftermath*, p. vi.)

21. See Zelditch, 'Role Differentiation', p. 317.
22. Swanson, p. 38.
23. Swanson, p. 71 f. Schmidt (in *Der Ursprung*) had attempted to reverse the Tylorean argument (cf. Lang in ch. I, ref. 33, above): instead of concluding that God evolved from animistic beliefs in spirits, Schmidt reviewed all the evidence available to him in order to argue that the prevalent primitive belief is belief in one supreme high-god, which necessitates belief in other gods in order to establish contact with the world of men. Swanson has here rejected the evidence of one of Schmidt's researchers, on the grounds that it will be biased towards the proof of this monotheistic hypothesis; but, according to the 'Zelditch principle', 'to question one is to question all'.
24. 'Now so bad are we that the world is stripped of love and of terror. Here came the other night an Aurora so wonderful, a curtain of red and blue and silver glory, that in any other age or nation it would have moved the awe and wonder of men and mingled with the profoundest sentiments of religion and love, and we all saw it with cold, arithmetical eyes, we knew how many

colours shone, how many degrees it extended, how many hours it lasted, and of this heavenly flower we beheld nothing more: a primrose by the brim of the river of time. Shall we not wish back again the Seven Whistlers, the Flying Dutchmen, the lucky and unlucky days, and the terrors of the Day of Doom?' Emerson, p. 137.

25. Berger, *Social Reality*, p. 3.

26. Ibid., p. 3.

27. *Self-Help* begins by arguing exactly this point, that the individual has it within him to change, by his own 'free and independent action', his own or other social conditions. The opening chapter is prefaced with two quotations, the first from J. S. Mill, the other from Disraeli: ' "The worth of a State, in the long run, is the worth of the individuals composing it"; "We put too much faith in systems, and look too little to men." '

28. 'Perhaps some will be surprised to see us connect the most elevated forms of thought with society; the cause appears quite humble, in consideration of the value which we attribute to the effect. Between the world of the senses and appetites on the one hand, and that of reason and morals on the other, the distance is so considerable that the second would seem to have been able to add itself to the first only by a creative act. But attributing to society this preponderating role in the genesis of our nature is not denying this creation; for society has a creative power which no other observable being can equal. In fact, all creation, if not a mystical operation which escapes science and knowledge, is the product of a synthesis. Now if the syntheses of particular conceptions which take place in each individual consciousness are already and of themselves productive of novelties, how much more efficacious these vast syntheses of complete consciousnesses which make society must be! A society is the most powerful combination of physical and moral forces of which nature offers us an example. Nowhere else is an equal richness of different materials, carried to such a degree of concentration, to be found. Then it is not surprising that a higher life disengages itself which, by reacting upon the elements of which it is the product, raises them to a higher plane of existence and transforms them.

'Thus sociology appears destined to open a new way to the science of man. Up to the present, thinkers were placed before this double alternative: either explain the superior and specific faculties of men by connecting them to the inferior forms of his being, the reason to the senses, or the mind to matter, which is equivalent to denying their uniqueness; or else attach them to some super-experimental reality which was postulated, but whose existence could be established by no observation. What put them in this difficulty was the fact that the individual passed as being the *finis naturae*—the ultimate creation of nature; it seemed that there was nothing beyond him, or at least nothing that science could touch. But from the moment when it is recognized that above the individual there is society, and that this is not a nominal being created by reason, but a system of active forces, a new manner of explaining men becomes possible. To conserve his distinctive traits it is no longer necessary to put them outside experience. At least, before going to this last extremity, it would be well to see if that which surpasses the individual, though it is within him, does not come from this super-individual reality which we experience in society. To be sure, it cannot be said at present to what point these explanations may be able to reach, and whether or not they are of a nature to resolve all the problems. But it is equally impossible to mark in advance a limit beyond which they cannot go. What must be done is to try the hypothesis and submit it as methodically as possible to the control of facts. This is what we have tried to do.'

29. See esp. pp. 159 ff.
30. Berger, *Social Reality*, p. 16.
31. See ref. 24, above.
32. Berger, *Social Reality*, p. 28.
33. Ibid., p. 17.
34. Ibid., p. 24.
35. Berger's projective view of religion is clear in the following passage: 'It can thus be said that religion has played a strategic part in the human enterprise of world-building. Religion implies the farthest reach of man's self-externalization, of his infusion of reality with his own meanings. Religion implies that human order is projected into the totality of being. Put differently, religion is the audacious attempt to conceive of the entire universe as humanly significant.' (*Social Reality*, p. 88.)
36. Ibid., p. 26.
37. Ibid., p. 10.
38. Berger's general statement of the theory appears in the book he wrote with Luckmann, *The Social Construction of Reality*.
39. See ref. 32, above.
40. See ref. 33, above.
41. Hacker, p. 308.
42. Quine, 'Speaking of Objects', in *Ontological Relativity*, pp. 16 f.: 'By finding out roughly which non-verbal stimulations tend to prompt assent to a given existential statement, we settle, to some degree, what is to count as empirical evidence for or against the existence of the objects in question . . . Statements, however, existential and otherwise, vary in the directness with which they are conditioned to non-verbal stimulation. Commonly a stimulation will trigger our verdict on a statement only because the statement is a strand in the verbal network of some elaborate theory, other strands of which are more directly conditioned to that stimulation. Most of our statements respond thus to reverberations across the fabric of intralinguistic associations, even when also directly conditioned to some degree. Highly theoretical statements are statements whose connection with extralinguistic stimulation consists pretty exclusively in the reverberations across the fabric. Statements of the existence of various sorts of subvisible particles tend to be theoretical, in this sense; and, even more so, statements of the existence of certain abstract objects. Commonly such statements are scarcely to be judged otherwise than by coherence, or by considerations of overall simplicity of a theory whose ultimate contacts with experience are remote as can be from the statements in question. Yet, remarkably enough, there are abstract existence statements that do succumb to such considerations. We have had the wit to posit an ontology massive enough to crumble of its own weight.' Quine then gave as an example the paradoxes of classes, and concluded: 'The moral to draw from the paradoxes is not necessarily nominalism, but certainly that we must tighten our ontological belts a few holes.'
43. I have discussed this concept briefly in my article, 'Can Differences Make a Difference?'
44. Berger, *Rumour*, p. 50.
45. Ibid.
46. Ibid., p. 63.
47. Ibid., p. 64.

48. Berger, *Rumour*, p. 57.
49. Ibid., p. 44.
50. Ibid., p. 70.
51. 'Quantum mechanics represents the latest great step in our efforts to throw off the shackles of that limited experience termed "everyday life".' Frisch, *Nature of Matter*, p. 16.
52. 'It is ultimately the function of art, in imposing a credible order upon ordinary reality, and thereby eliciting some perception of an order *in* reality, to bring us to a condition of serenity, stillness, and reconciliation; and then leave us, as Vergil left Dante, to proceed toward a region where that guide can avail us no farther.' Eliot, *On Poetry*, p. 87.
53. 'If there are genuine cases of the discovery of religious truth, we must come to grips with their history, for the very word "discovery" implies a historical process. This is even more clearly the case if we repudiate the idea of "progress". If all history were a steady progression, there might be a certain logic to ignoring the past. By definition, every past situation would in its approach to truth be inferior to the present. One would concern oneself with the past, if at all, simply for self-satisfied edification, in about the same mood as that of some early ethnologists' studies of "savages". But if, on the other hand, each age is seen in its "immediacy to God", each age must be carefully looked at for whatever signals of transcendence might be uniquely its own.' Berger, *Rumour*, p. 100.
54. Ibid., p. 111.
55. 'It seems, then, that the form of the earthly no less than of the heavenly Christ is for the most part hidden from us. For all the inestimable value of the gospels, they yield us little more than a whisper of his voice; we trace in them but the outskirt of his ways. Only when we see him hereafter in his fullness shall we know him also as he was on earth. And perhaps the more we ponder the matter, the more clearly we shall understand the reason for it, and therefore shall not wish it otherwise. For probably we are at present as little prepared for the one as for the other.' Lightfoot, *History*, p. 225.
56. Berger, *Rumour*, pp. 104, 116.
57. Ibid., pp. 104 f.
58. See ref. 7, above.

III. ANTHROPOLOGY AND THE EXPLANATION OF RELIGION

1. Quine, *Ontological Relativity*, p. 41.
2. Quine, *From a Logical Point of View*; the phrases used occur on pp. 4 and 5.
3. 'To summarize, the aim of this paper is to indicate that discussion about God is incoherent, confusing, and frustrating unless the God-concept to be discussed is clearly defined; that there are thousands of logically possible God-concepts; that since these God-concepts are different, and for the most part mutually incompatible, it is logically impossible to arrive at a universally acceptable quintessential definition of God; and that God-concepts have a family-resemblance (in Wittgenstein's sense of the phrase) and not an essential or core meaning.' Gastwirth, p. 152.
4. Nadel, p. 661.
5. Fürer-Haimendorf, p. 131. Cf. also the similar (and extreme) emphasis in Firth's studies of the religion of the Tikopia, summarized in 'Problem and Assumption', p. 145. On variability in the Himalayas, see Berreman.

6. This point is discussed by Firth, 'Problem and Assumption', pp. 134 ff.

7. ' "One event is always the son of another, and we must never forget the parentage" ', a remark made by a Bechuanaland chief to the missionary Casalis, and quoted with approval by Tylor, *Primitive Culture*, i, p. 5.

8. Tylor, *Primitive Culture*, i, p. 3.

9. Lienhardt, 'Religion', p. 310.

10. Goode, *Religion*, p. 22.

11. 'Authors with varying competence have suggested that dinosaurs disappeared because the climate deteriorated (became suddenly or slowly too hot or cold or dry or wet), or that the diet did (with too much food or not enough of such substances as fern oil; from poisons in water or plants or ingested minerals; by bankruptcy of calcium or other necessary elements). Other writers have put the blame on disease, parasites, wars, anatomical or metabolic disorders (slipped vertebral discs, malfunction or imbalance of hormone or endocrine systems, dwindling brain and consequent stupidity, heat sterilization), racial old age, evolutionary drift into senescent overspecialization, changes in the pressure or composition of the atmosphere, poison gases, volcanic dust, excessive oxygen from plants, meteorites, comets, gene pool drainage by little mammalian egg eaters, overkill capacity by predators, fluctuation of gravitational constants, development of psychotic suicidal factors, entropy, cosmic radiation, shift of the Earth's rotational poles, floods, extraction of the moon from the Pacific basin, drainage of swamp and lake environments, sunspots, God's will, mountain building, raids by little green hunters in flying saucers, lack of even standing room in Noah's Ark, and palaeoweltschmerz.' Jepsen, 'Terrible Lizards', p. 7; Goin, p. 446.

12. Cannon, p. 24 (but note p. viii for his earlier uses of the term).

13. Cannon refers to Bernard in op. cit., pp. 37 f.: ' "No more pregnant sentence, in the opinion of J. S. Haldane, was ever framed by a physiologist" ' (p. 38).

14. For an introduction to the issues involved here, see particularly Murray, *Genetic Diversity*.

15. Hockett and Ascher, p. 23.

16. Dobzhansky, ibid., p. 77; note the reply to Dobzhansky on p. 95.

17. 'Many features in the anatomy of the early amphibians point definitely to the lobe-finned fish as the ancestors of all land forms . . . A primitive amphibian was, in essence, only a lobe-finned fish in which limbs capable of progression on land had been developed.

'Why land life? The most primitive of known amphibians were, as we have said, inhabitants of fresh-water pools and streams in Carboniferous and Devonian times. Alongside them lived representatives of the ancestral crossopterygians, forms similar to them in food habits and in many structural features and differing mainly in the lesser developments of the paired limbs. Why should the amphibians have developed these limbs and become potential land dwellers? Not to breathe air, for that could be done by merely coming to the surface of the pool. Not because they were driven out in search of food, for they were fish-eating types for which there was little food to be had on land. Not to escape enemies, for they were among the largest animals of the streams and pools of that day.

'The development of limbs and the consequent ability to live on land seem, paradoxically, to have been adaptations for remaining in the water, and true land life seems to have been, so to speak, only the result of a happy accident.

'Let us consider the situation of these two types —lobe-finned fishes and amphibians living in the streams and pools of the late Paleozoic. As long as the water supply was adequate, the crossopterygian was probably the better off of the two, for he was obviously the better swimmer; legs were in the way. The Devonian, the period in which the amphibians originated, was a time of seasonal droughts. At times the streams would cease to flow, and the water in the remaining pools into which the fish and ancestral amphibians were crowded must have been foul and stagnant. Even so, the lobe-finned fish, since he possessed lungs, was at no disadvantage, for a short time at any rate, for he could come to the surface and breathe air as well as the amphibians.

'If, however, crowded conditions continued for a period of time, the local food supplies would be exhausted, and the situation would be a desperate one. Still worse, the water might dry up completely. Under such circumstances the crossopterygian would be helpless and must die. But the amphibian, with his newly-developed land limbs, could crawl out of the shrunken or dried-up pool, walk up or down the stream bed or overland, and reach another pool where he might take up his aquatic existence again. Land limbs were developed to reach the water, not to leave it.

'Once this development of limbs had taken place, however, it is not hard to imagine how true land life eventually resulted. Instead of immediately taking to the water again, the amphibian might have learned to linger about the drying pools and devour stranded fish. Insects were present by coal-swamp days and would have afforded the beginnings of a diet for a land form. Later, plants were taken up as a source of food supply, while (as is usually the case) the larger forms on land probably took to eating their smaller or more harmless relatives. Finally, through these various developments, a land fauna would have been established.' Romer, pp. 93 f.

18. Romer, p. 95.
19. 'In the long run, the trees would be held by the more powerful, while the less powerful would repeatedly have to get along as best they could in the fringes of the forest or in open country. Here is a double selective process. The trees went to the more powerful, provided only that they maintained a minimum ability to traverse open country when necessary: some of these successful ones were ancestral to the great apes of today. Our own ancestors were the failures. We did not abandon the trees because we wanted to, but because we were pushed out . . . It is no joke to be thrown out of one's ancestral home.' Hockett and Ascher, p. 30.
20. Lehrman, p. 155.
21. Ibid., p. 132.
22. For the finds at Shanidar, see bibl. under Solecki. The arguments suggesting that the right arm of Shanidar I had been amputated during life, just above the elbow, will be found in Stewart.
23. See, e.g. Beck, p. 89: 'Hence it may be expected that when a plethora of facts is elaborated in hypotheses of low generality, the broad outlines of an overarching theory may be subtly adumbrated. But in view of the complexity of subject matter, the looseness of theoretical structure, and the uncontrolled character of many of the observations of society, it is too soon to expect—indeed, it is too soon to be impatient for—a Newton of the social sciences.'
24. See ref. 7, above.
25. Tylor, *Primitive Culture*, i, p. 3.
26. Ibid., p. vii.
27. MacRae, p. 304.

28. For the details of this, and for a critical assessment of this kind of argument, see M. Bowker, in R. F. Bennett, ed., *First Class Answers in History*, due to be published in 1974.
29. See M. Bowker, op. cit.

IV. DEATH, BURIAL, AND CREMATION

1. Mandelbaum, p. 338.
2. Ibid.
3. 'There are great variations in the manner of bringing about . . . integrative results. As we examine the range of variation we find that among some peoples funeral ceremonies are great public events; in other societies they are conducted swiftly, quietly, almost furtively. The whole of a social order may be represented at the funeral, or only a small section of it.' Ibid., pp. 345 f.
4. Ibid., p. 346.
5. 'The emphasis in the funeral ceremony is quite different from other motifs in Hopi practice. Most life-cycle and calendrical rites are conducted with very elaborate ceremony, in contrast to the quick and meagre ritual of the funeral occasion. Hopi society is an elaborate structure of interlocking organizations. In most ceremonies members of different socio-religious organizations take part or attend at some stage. But the funeral ceremony is restricted mainly to the immediate household; there is little provision to show the multiple roles which the deceased may have occupied in the social network. The sovereign desire is to dismiss the body and the event. The urge is to despatch the spirit to another realm where it will not challenge the Hopi ideals of good, harmonious, happy existence in *this* world and where, as a being of another and well-known kind, it can be methodically controlled by the ritual apparatus of Hopi culture.' Ibid., p. 349.
6. Ibid.
7. Ibid., p. 346.
8. 'Kelly gives his impression that ". . . this action symbolized a desire to be free of the dead, and that the ceremony served, in part, to bring lurking spirits into the open, and, in dramatic fashion, to rid the earth of them by banning them again in the physical form of the costumes worn by the impersonators." ' Ibid., pp. 346 f.; Kelly, p. 161.
9. Firth, *Elements*, p. 64.
10. 1 Cor. 15: 35 ff.; cf. Katha Upanishad, i. 1. 6.
11. e.g. Katha Upanishad, ii. 2. 9 ff.; cf. the explanation of the fire-sacrifice in i. 1. 14 ff.
12. e.g. Brihadaranyaka Upanishad, iv. 5. 13 f.
13. Obviously some groups and some societies may contain many more than one projected way through the limitation of death. This, for example, was the conclusion of Ellis (p. 61), looking at the multiplicity of Norse burial customs:
    'Surveying the evidence as a whole, there is nothing to justify us in connecting any one custom rigidly to any one belief; one cannot say that ship-funeral is evidence of one belief in the future life, cremation another, and so on. It is clear that in Scandinavia different customs and beliefs have intermingled, and it is very unlikely that any consistent and definite body of beliefs was ever held at any one time about the disposal of the dead and the meaning of it.'

That may well be the case; but *some* beliefs were held; and the hypothesis is certainly worth testing that the more stable, detailed, and confident the characterizations are, in a particular society, of the nature of projected ways through death, the more uniform the burial customs will be—not only through time but also through society: much the same rites will attend both rich and poor, though there may well be great differences of degree according to status and wealth. Conversely, where the projected ways through are shadowy or diverse, there will be more noticeable differences in burial customs. This distinction appears to hold, for example, for Egypt, where beliefs were relatively detailed and stable, in comparison with Mesopotamia. For a general description of the two situations, see bibl. under Giedion.

14. See my *Problems of Suffering*, pp. 241 f.
15. The third wish of Naciketas is as follows:
 ' "There is this doubt concerning a man who has departed: some say he exists, others that he does not. I would know the answer to this from your instruction: this is the third of my wishes."
 [Yama]: "Even the gods of old had doubts on this. It is by no means easy to understand: elusively subtle is the underlying point [*aṇur eṣa dharmaḥ*]. Choose another wish, Naciketas—release me from this one." ' Katha (Upanishad, i. 1. 20 f.)
 But Naciketas persists:
 ' "Tell us, Death, about this matter of which they are so doubtful: this wish, which penetrates the hidden, this alone does Naciketas choose." ' (Ibid., i. 2. 29.)
 On the modes of Yama, see my *Problems of Suffering*, pp. 203, 205 f.
16. 'I remember how at Cambridge, I walked with her once in the Fellows' Garden at Trinity, on an evening of rainy May: and she, stirred somewhat beyond her wont, and taking as her text the three words which have been used so often as the inspiring trumpet-calls of men—the words God, Immortality, Duty—pronounced, with terrible earnestness, how inconceivable was the *first*, how unbelievable the *second*, and yet how peremptory and absolute the *third* . . . I listened; her grave, majestic countenance turned toward me like a Sibyl's in the gloom; it was as though she withdrew from my grasp, one by one, the two scrolls of promise, and left me the third scroll only, awful with inevitable fates.' F. W. H. Myers, quoted by John Morley in his review of J. W. Cross, *George Eliot's Life*, London, 1885.
17. Edgcumbe, pp. 80 f.
18. Ch. I, ref. 46.
19. Sonnets i–xvi argue for survival in descendants:

> So thou, thyself outgoing in thy noon,
> Unlook'd on diest, unless thou get a son. (vii)

xvii marks the transition to survival in the verse of the poet; in xvii, both suggestions are combined:

> But were some child of yours alive that time,
> You should live twice,—in it and in my rime.

From that point, 'survival in verse' is predominant:

> So long as men can breathe, or eyes can see,
> So long lives this, and this gives life to thee. (xviii)

Note esp. xix, lv, lxv. Survival in the memory and consequent actions of men was George Eliot's own answer, as it was of many who shared with her the same crisis of plausibility:

> O, may I join the choir invisible
> Of those immortal dead who live again
> In minds made better by their presence: live
> In pulses stirred to generosity,
> In deeds of daring rectitude, in scorn
> For miserable aims that end with self,
> In thoughts sublime that pierce the night like stars,
> And with their mild persistence urge man's search
> To vaster issues.

20. See ref. 16, above.
21. *Macbeth*, v. iii. 27 f.
22. 'Dover Beach', 35, 37.
23. For Matthew Arnold's comparable doubt about the possibility of grasping the actual or real 'self', see particularly: 'The Buried Life' (note, in comparison with 'Dover Beach', the appeal to love in ll. 77 ff.) and 'Below the Surface Stream'.
24. 'Alaric': the futility of conquest in terms of immortality, xxix–xxxv; the glimpse of continuing substance, xxxv; taken away, xxxvi–end. 'Cromwell': the two aspects of conquest, 131–212; an enigmatic glimpse of clarity at the end, 213–18; taken away, 219–end.
25. *King Lear*, iv. vi. 21 f.
26. Ibid. v. ii. 9 ff.
27. Ll. 28–37.
28. *Poems*, p. viii.
29. 'Empedocles' in *Works*, p. 411.
30. Purvis, p. 65; the whole section on ceremonies (pp. 159 ff.) is relevant to this point.
31. See, e.g., bibl. under *Cremation Considered* . . .
32. In Italy, for example, the only specific condition which seemed applicable was that the conditions of religious ceremony should be fulfilled. Even so, the local authorities managed to delay the cremation of Alberto Keller for two years after his death, in Jan. 1874, despite the fact that he had expressed a wish to be cremated and had designed and built an apparatus for the purpose. The novelty of the occasion can be seen in the fact that, when the cremation eventually took place, it was attended by government officials, representatives of scientific institutes, priests, journalists, and members of the family. After a religious service, a Professor Clericetti gave a lecture on the scientific principles employed in the apparatus, and he in turn was followed by two other addresses, one on the history of cremation. In this way, the ninety minutes, which the cremation took, were passed, and the ashes were found to weigh six pounds. The proceedings were then recorded for the family in a private publication, *Atti della Cremazione di Alberto Keller*, from which the above account is derived.
33. The Cremation Society of England had come close to testing the legal issue in 1875, when they secured the approval of the proprietors of the Great Northern Cemetery to build a crematorium within the grounds of the cemetery. Since, however, the land was already consecrated, the Cremation Society felt that they ought to approach the Bishop of Rochester, in whose diocese the cemetery lay, in order to secure, if not his approval, at least his permission. The answer they received was peremptory and clear, and might

have come straight out of Trollope—or at least out of the mouth of Mrs. Proudie:

> Danbury Palace, Chelmsford.
> August 26th, 1875.
>
> Gentlemen,
> I beg to acknowledge your letter of the 16th inst., asking my consent as Bishop to the setting apart a portion of the Great Northern Cemetery, in my diocese, for the purpose of Cremation. I cannot consent—moreover, I have not the power to consent—to the introduction of such a mode of disposing of the bodies of the dead.
> I am, Gentlemen, your obedient Servant,
>
> T. L. Roffen:

The Society did not pursue the matter, though they noted that it was, at that date, legally uncertain whether anyone had power to prohibit cremation in a cemetery. The case of the Welsh Druid was clearly different, because a challenge to a coroner's order was involved.

34. *Transactions*, iv, p. 24.
35. F. G. Marshall, p. 146.
36. Ibid., p. 147.
37. Note especially Glasgow, Liverpool, Hull, Leicester, Golders Green, Birmingham, Leeds, Bradford, Sheffield, West Norwood, Hendon, Pontypridd, Ipswich, Brighton, Nottingham, Newcastle; Reading, Stockport, Northampton are good examples of the use of a dome. The dominance of the classical church style began to break down in the late 1930s. Cheltenham (1938) is one of the last to retain the full tradition.
38. 'One of the problems of the elevations will be the tall chimney. This may be in itself well designed, but its appearance can give an unfortunate impression to mourners and I think it much better to camouflage this feature in the form of a tower or campanile.' Dahl, p. 114; cf. Freeman, p. 117: 'The chimney . . . is usually built within a tower, to hide its true purpose . . .'
39. See bibl. under Jeffers.

V. STRUCTURAL ACCOUNTS OF RELIGION

1. Nauta, pp. 115 f.
2. 'Thus, learning is essentially *interiorization of environmental constraints*. As soon as an i-system [information-system or interpreter] has grown to informational maturity [Nauta has already (p. 116) made it clear that "maturity" does not mean "fully-informed": "When the overall features of 'objective' constraint have been learned by the i-system, *i.e.* when these are matched by the system's internal ('subjective') representation of constraint, then it has *grown to maturity* in the informational sense . . . A living i-system is never *fully-informed*. It has always to *learn* and to *unlearn* something."], it *anticipates* coming events on the basis of received information. The anticipated events constitute redundant information in relation to the information received. Because of this very redundancy, the received information is meaningful and refers to the anticipated events.

   'The discriminable forms arriving at the input carry potential information to the i-system. In case this i-system did not "know" anything of its environment, all these inputs would be equally important to the i-system and, moreover, all these important "pieces of news" would be completely disconnected. But unless the environmental inputs constitute only "meaningless noise", there must be some coherence, some interrelation or regularity, that is, the environment must be objectively constrained in the transcendent sense. Now, when an i-system has learned some of these "objective constraints" it has discovered "order and method" in the disconnected nonsense of indifferently important pieces of news, which means that not all information received by it has the same novelty or unexpectedness any more; useful information has a degree of *redundancy*, varying from o (meaningless noise) to I (meaning without news). In other words, the learning of constraints results in reduction of the amount of information processed by the i-system. This is called the *informational accommodation* of the i-system to the redundancy of its environment.' Nauta, pp. 116 f.

3. Ashby, p. 3.
4. Ibid., p. 130.
5. Ibid.
6. Ibid.
7. Shannon, *Mathematical Theory*.
8. Khinchin, p. 31.
9. Cf. Ch. I, refs. 22, 23, 24.
10. Šaumjan, p. 336.
11. 'As a designer of codes, man attains progressively more subtle stages in the process of cognitive organization, thus realizing the evolution of science. The design of mathematical models has a central place in this development. Mathematical code systems are easily manipulatable, and if they exhibit a well defined (partial) *isomorphism* with processes in the surroundings (the "originals"), then they act as models of these originals; symbolic operations in the model predict or reflect ideally the actual course of events in the original. From "thought-models", formulated in natural language, to mathematical and other scientific models is a great step forward . . .; the organization of knowledge is thus advanced from the *semiotic* plane to the *metasemiotic* plane. The design of scientific code systems and models opens up the avenue for *de jure* analysis of syntactic, semantic, and pragmatic *metarelations*. This leads eventually to *logistics*, the metatheoretical study of the artificial language systems of logic, within which the mathematical models of science may be formalized.

'How is the transformation of *de facto* organization of behaviour into *de jure* organization of knowledge possible? It is confusing to see this in the light of *innate ideas* . . . Modifying a quotation from Wiener ("[As for] man . . . the particular language used is a matter which has to be learned in each special case. It apparently is built into the brain itself, that we are to have a preoccupation with codes . . . However, there is not one fragment of these codes which is born into us as a pre-established ritual, like the courting dances of . . . birds . . . [We have] not the gift of speech, but the gift of the power of speech." *The Human Use of Human Beings*, London, 1968, p. 75), one might see it as follows: We have not the gift of logical grammar and "objective truth", but we have the gift of the power to construct logical grammars and to manipulate with models in such a way as to arrive at intersubjective metasemiotic analysis of "truth". The relevant "objective criteria" for truth and reliability are determined by the isomorphism, which in turn is defined by the convertible mapping of observable data into their symbolic representation model; this mapping provides the *de facto* "feedback from reality" which is necessary for the verification of *de jure* truth. The same might be said differently in Lenneberg's terminology: we have not an innate set of symbol categories, but an innate mode of modelling and manipulating symbol categories and of matching them to "reality". Or, briefly, in Chomsky's terminology: We have not the gift of innate logical *performance* but of 'innate ideas" for the realization of logical *competence*.' Nauta, pp. 248 ff.

12. 'Friend', quoth the razor man, 'I'm not a knave:
      As for the razors you have bought,
      Upon my soul, I never thought
    That they would *shave*.'
    'Not think they'd *shave*!' quoth Hodge, with wond'ring eyes,
      And voice not much unlike an Indian yell;
    'What were they made for, then, you dog?' he cries.
      'Made!' quoth the fellow with a smile—'to *sell*.'
      Wolcot, 'Farewell Odes for the Year 1786', no. 3, in *Works*, i, p. 104.

13. Wisdom in Fann, q.v., p. 46.
14. Wittgenstein, *Philosophical Investigations*, § 43.
15. Phillips, p. 2.
16. Ibid., pp. 2 f.
17. Nauta, p. 185. He is in fact commenting on a suggestion of Pitts and MacKay that 'amount-of-information (which should be read as one word) has nothing to do with information in a qualitative sense'. Nauta responds: 'This amounts to saying that electro-magnetic waves with a wave-length of 5890 Å have nothing to do with "the yellow light of sodium"!'
18. Polanyi, p. 231.
19. Ibid., pp. 233 f.
20. 'We are still confronted with a fundamental problem: most semiotic quantitative frames are not really fixed once and for all, but are involved in a dynamic process of development. The process of biological evolution, for instance, may be viewed as a combination of the two main components: the *selection* of the fittest framework and the *mutation* of the genetic preformation of frameworks. The cognitive development of an individual may be viewed as a similar combination, in which *learning* (informational accommodation) and *creativity* call the tune . . . Mutation, creative processes, and the like, are prototypes of what will be called the realization of *constitutive* information, i.e. prototypes of break-through of the existent informational frames.

    'Thus, next to *quantitative* information we have to distinguish *constitutive* information. The latter is qualitative information which is transcendental as regards quantification. It may be viewed as information that outgrows the existent universe of reference, information that does not participate in the framework under consideration, but that is constitutive indeed of a new repertory, an extended framework.' Nauta, pp. 185 f.

21. Lévi-Strauss, 'Structural Study', p. 429.
22. Id., *Totemism*, p. 175. The general method is described by Lévi-Strauss (p. 84) as follows:
    'The method we adopt, in this case [totemism] as in others, consists in the following operations:
      (1) define the phenomenon under study as a relation between two or more terms, real or supposed;
      (2) construct a table of possible permutations between these terms;
      (3) take this table as the general object of analysis which, at this level only, can yield necessary connections, the empirical phenomenon considered at the beginning being only one possible combination

among others, the complete system of which must be reconstructed beforehand.'

23. Leach, *Lévi-Strauss*, pp. 42, 53.

24. This is Lévi-Strauss's point of departure for 'The Structural Study of Myth': 'In order to understand what a myth really is, are we compelled to choose between platitude and sophism? Some claim that human societies merely express through their mythology, fundamental feelings common to the whole of mankind, such as love, hate, revenge; or that they try to provide some kind of explanations for phenomena which they cannot understand otherwise: astronomical, meteorological, and the like. But why should these societies do it in such elaborate and devious ways, since all of them are also acquainted with positive explanations? On the other hand, psychoanalysts and many anthropologists have shifted the problems to be explained away from the natural or cosmological towards the sociological and psychological fields. But then the interpretation becomes too easy: if a given mythology confers prominence to a certain character, let us say an evil grandmother, it will be claimed that in such a society grandmothers are actually evil and that mythology reflects the social structure and the social relations; but should the actual data be conflicting, it would be readily claimed that the purpose of mythology is to provide an outlet for repressed feelings. Whatever the situation may be, a clever dialectic will always find a way to pretend that a meaning has been unravelled.'

25. Lévi-Strauss, *Totemism*, p. 140. He responds (p. 141): 'We do not know, and never shall know, anything about the first origin of beliefs and customs the roots of which plunge into a distant past; but, as far as the present is concerned, it is certain that social behaviour is not produced spontaneously by each individual, under the influence of emotions of the moment.'

26. Lévi-Strauss, *Savage Mind*, p. 204.

27. Leach, *Lévi-Strauss*, p. 90.

28. Lévi-Strauss, *Savage Mind*, pp. 205 f.

29. Ibid., p. 206.

30. Ibid.

31. Ibid., p. 207.

32. Leach, *Lévi-Strauss*, p. 91.

33. Ibid., p. 90.

34. *Final Catalogue*, p. 1505.

35. Old Age Pensioner
$$\begin{cases} \text{Grandad} \begin{cases} \text{White Star} \\ \text{Texaco} \end{cases} \\ \text{Cash in Hand} \begin{cases} \text{Banker's Dream} \\ \text{Holdfast} \end{cases} \end{cases}$$

36. Maranda, *Mythology*, p. 13; the definition is then 'unpacked' as follows (the references to further literature are omitted): ' "Discourses" refer to the articulation of narrative units into a plot. "Stylistically definable" means features of formulation which are characteristic of culture areas. "Strong components" is to be understood according to Digraph Theory, i.e. the elementary structures of myth are terms so related that they have the properties of *cycles* which are either *sources* or *sinks*. Finally, "semantic systems" add to the concept of "collective representations" that these are structured cognitive guidelines as products of historical accretions and of mental processes.'

If directed graph analysis is unfamiliar, an introduction will be found in Harary *et al.*: on Sources and Sinks, see particularly pp. 98–108, with suggested applications, pp. 106 ff.

37. It is, of course, dangerous to talk of myth as a cultural *artefact*. Concepts may have in common with cups the fact that they are human products, but to lump them together for that reason alone is obviously misleading. In recognition of this, Maranda has come up with the even uglier jargon, in the case of folklore, that it is 'unrecorded mentifacts': 'In this paper, we have used a tentative definition which can, in a compact fashion, be stated thus: *folklore is unrecorded mentifacts*. One of the corollaries is that no text as such is a real folkloristic item: texts are only records of mentifacts (whereas an artefact always is its own record). This has practical bearing on the investigation of texts, because the structure of a folkloristic item may not become manifest in the recorded text, but its use, e.g. in the magician's action, may be part of the item.' *Structural Models*, p. 16.

38. Ch. I, ref. 14.

39. Piaget, p. 140.

40. Maranda, *Structural Models*, p. 30.

41. Ibid., p. 30.

42. Lévi-Strauss, 'Structural Study', p. 428.

43. e.g. Dobzhansky, pp. 192 ff.

44. Lévi-Strauss, 'Structural Study', p. 428.

45. See bibl. under Piaget.

46. 'Over and beyond the schemes of atomist association on the one hand and emergent totalities on the other, there is, however, a third, that of operational structuralism. It adopts from the start a relational perspective, according to which it is neither the elements nor a whole that comes about in a manner one knows not how, but the relations among elements that count. In other words, the logical procedures of rational processes by which the whole is formed are primary, not the whole, which is consequent on the system's laws of composition, or the elements.' Piaget, p. 9.

47. First, that 'the laws governing a structure's composition are not reducible to cumulative one-by-one association of its elements: they confer on the whole as such over-all properties distinct from the properties of its elements' (p. 7); second, that 'if the character of structured wholes depends on their laws of composition, these laws must of their very nature be *structuring*: it is the constant duality, or bipolarity, of always being simultaneously *structuring* and *structured* that accounts for the success of the notion of law or rule employed by structuralists ... A structure's laws of composition are defined "implicitly", i.e. as governing the transformations of the system which they structure' (p. 10); and third, that structures are consequently self-regulating.

48. Piaget, p. 14.

49. Slonimsky, p. 251.

50. For a summary, see, e.g., Simkins, pp. 27 f.; 15 cycles per second might now be more accurate.

51. Schoenberg, Letter, 25 May 1938, in Rufer, p. 141.

52. The point is even more clearly exemplified in Emerson's comment to his daughter, in explanation of his poem 'Brahma', which has obvious dependence on Bhagavadgita ii. 19 ff. Emerson's daughter told him that many people were puzzled by the poem. Emerson replied: 'If you tell them to say Jehovah instead of Brahma, they will not feel any perplexity.' Whether Elijah in the cleft of the mountain would have agreed with him, is doubtful. For Holst's interest in Sanskrit, and for an account of 'the Sanskrit works', see I. Holst, *Biography*, pp. 21 f.; *Music*, pp. 21–32. Holst himself recognized that his first 'Sanskrit' music was more Wagnerian than Indian.

53. See, e.g., Allberry, ii, pp. 49–96.
54. *'There is no structure apart from construction*, either abstract or genetic . . . Since Gödel, logicians and students of the foundations of mathematics distinguish between "stronger" and "weaker" structures, the stronger ones not being capable of elaboration until after the construction of the more elementary, that is, "weaker" systems yet, conversely, themselves necessary to the "completion" of the weaker ones. The idea of a formal system of abstract structures is thereby transformed into that of the construction of a never completed whole, the limits of formalization constituting the grounds for incompleteness, or, as we put it earlier, incompleteness being a necessary consequence of the fact that there is no "terminal" or "absolute" form because any content is form relative to some inferior content and any form the content for some higher form . . . Genesis is simply transition from one structure to another, nothing more; but this transition always leads from a "weaker" to a "stronger" structure; it is a "formative" transition. Structure is simply a system of transformations, but its roots are operational; it depends, therefore, on a prior formation of the instruments of transformation —transformation rules or laws.' Piaget, pp. 140 f.
55. Ibid., p. 142.
56. Ibid., p. 141.
57. See bibl. under Robinson, and (for more recent discussion) Lightstone. The symmetry is not exact, because Robinson, in 'Formalism 64', makes it clear that he accepts a bifurcation between set theory and number theory at the present time, and that since 'the Gödel sentence which asserts its own improvability at the same time affirms its own truth, to this extent the present situation in Number Theory favours the Platonist' (p. 233).
58. Davis and Hersh, pp. 85 f.
59. For this, see Hick, ch. VIII.
60. Reprinted in Flew and MacIntyre, pp. 170–86.
61. Ibid., p. 179.
62. Nielsen, p. 135.
63. Bowker, *Targums*, pp. 187 f.
64. Berlioz, Letter. Berlioz continued the letter by saying that this enigma 'has reduced me to the state of grim, despairing resignation which is the scorpion's when surrounded by burning coals. The most I can do is hold myself back from piercing myself with my own sting.'

VI. FREUDIAN THEORY AND THE PROJECTION OF GOD

1. See further, p. 123.
2. Freud, *Letters*, pp. 418 f.
3. Cf. also the 'charge of energy' (*Energiebesetzung*) in the libido, which must seek an outlet: *Introd. Lectures*, p. 301, *Werke*, xi, p. 373.
4. Freud, *Outline*, p. 2.
5. Id., *Moses*, p. 184.
6. Id., *Outline*, p. 4.
7. Id., *Problem*, ch. 3.
8. Id., *Illusion*, p. 45.
9. Id., 'Neurosis and Psychosis', in *Coll. Papers*, ii, pp. 250 f.
10. Id., 'Formulations', in *Coll. Papers*, iv, p. 13.
11. Id., *Outline*, p. 71.

12. Freud, *Moses*, p. 121.
13. Id., *Illusion*, p. 25.
14. Ibid.
15. Vaihinger, p. 290.
16. Sackville, 'Everyman'.
17. Freud, *Moses*, p. 133.
18. Jones, *Life*, iii, p. 400.
19. 'By my analysis, I have established that Freud's theories not only roughly correspond to human psychology, but that they follow closely the modification in human nature brought about by various constitutions of Society. In other words, I have established a deep correlation between the type of society and the nuclear complex found there. While this is a notable confirmation of the main tenet of Freudian psychology, it might compel us to modify certain of its details, or rather to make some of the formulae more elastic.' Malinowski, p. 321.
20. Jones referred to this as 'the genetic aspects of the problem'; 'Mother-Right', p. 169.
21. 'It would seem more probable, in my opinion, that the matrilineal system with its avunculate complex arose . . . as a mode of defence against the primordial Oedipus tendencies than that it arose for unknown sociological reasons with then the avunculate complex as a necessary consequence and the Oedipus complex appearing only when the patrilineal system was subsequently introduced. The forbidden and unconsciously loved sister is only a substitute for the mother, as the uncle plainly is for the father. On Malinowski's hypothesis the Oedipus complex would be a late product; for the psychoanalyst it was the *fons et origo*.' Jones, 'Mother-Right , pp. 169 f.
22. 'The point we are now making is that this impression of complete diversity of various human groups is largely created by the Oedipus complex, that is to say, the Oedipus complex of the anthropologist or psychiatrist or psychologist. He does not know what to do with his own Oedipus complex—he therefore *scotomizes* clear evidence for the Oedipus complex, even when his training ought to enable him to see it.' Roheim, p. 362.
23. Hammerton, p. 264.
24. Ibid.
25. Ibid.
26. Ibid.
27. 'During much of Darwin's long life, he suffered from a mysterious illness, characterized by heart palpitations and feelings of lethargy and gloom. His doctors could discern no physical cause, and—as he himself suspected and rather resented—he was widely believed to be a hypochondriac. Darwin's hypochondria was a gift to the post-mortem analysts; and how they spread themselves over it! Darwin, they explain, hated his father. How do they know? you will ask. Well, they say so; and besides he once wrote that his father was the kindest man he'd ever known, and that proves it, doesn t it? So he hated his father and felt guilty about it. Also, they say, he felt that his theories had "dethroned God", who was a sort of heavenly father: which made his life-work "symbolically equivalent" to killing or castrating his father, which he wanted to do anyway (Oedipus and all that) and felt guilty about. So, having a powerful conscience (superego is the word in their jargon), he proceeded to punish himself with psychosomatic illness and misery. I have to spoil this lovely fantasy by pointing out that none of it is called for. Because it now appears that Darwin had contracted Chargas [*sic*] disease during his stay in Argentina; and the symptoms of Chargas' disease

—which is a kind of parasitic infection—are palpitations, lethargy and gloom.'

28. Kline, p. ix.
29. 'The observations on which Freudian theory rests are made by psychoanalysts during therapy. The raw data of psychoanalytic theory consist of the free associations of the patient and the report of dreams to which further free associations are elicited. These raw data are not even recorded as spoken but are recalled later by the analyst. Thus there is no quantification, no control group, nor indeed any check on the reliability of the analyst's memory.' Kline, p. 1.
30. Hammerton, p. 264.
31. See Rogers, *Therapeutic Relationship*.
32. 'Psychoanalysis has, now I believe, uncovered the deepest and most awe-inspiring problem from which human beings can suffer; the secret core of total schizoid isolation. A recent suicide was reported to have left a tape-recorded message, "There comes a time when you feel there is no meaning in life, and there is no point in going on with it." Far more people than we know have this feeling deep within them, although not all to the same degree of intensity. We may well pause before this problem, which no psychiatric or behaviour therapy technique, or classic Oedipal analysis can solve. The only cure for an ultimate sense of isolation and therefore meaninglessness in life, in anybody, is that someone should be able to get him back into a relationship that will give life some point again. Can we be sure that the patient can stand its being uncovered, or dare we leave him alone with it lest it break out willy-nilly and destroy him? Can the patient be sure that we can stand it and support him until a new thrust and a new meaning in life begins to be born again in him? One cannot always know the answers to these questions, but where patient and therapist are prepared to stick it out together, then, at the risk of tragic failure, a profoundly rewarding success can, in my experience, in a significant number of cases be achieved. I do not know how this can be statistically validated by the hard pressed general practitioner or analytic therapist, but the patient knows when he is literally "born again".' Guntrip, pp. 195 f.
33. Wittgenstein, *Tractatus*, 6. 54.
34. Neurath, 'Protokollsätze,' p. 206.
35. 'In the literature of psychology and sociology the opinion is sometimes expressed or implied that when a term of conversational language—such as "manual dexterity", "introversion", "submissiveness", "intelligence", "social status", etc.—is taken over into the scientific vocabulary and given a more precise interpretation by reference to specified tests or similar criteria, then it is essential that the latter be *"valid"* in the sense of providing a correct characterization of the feature to which the term refers in ordinary usage. But if that term has so far been used solely in prescientific discourse, then the only way of ascertaining whether a proposed set of precise criteria affords a "valid" gauge of the characteristic in question is to determine to what extent the objects satisfying the criteria coincide with those to whom the characteristic in question would be assigned in pre-scientific usage. And, indeed, various authors have adopted, as an index of the validity of a proposed testing procedure for a psychological or social characteristic, the correlation between the test scores of a group of subjects and the ratings which those subjects were given, for the characteristic in question, by acquaintances who judged them "intuitively", i.e. who applied the term under consideration according to its prescientific usage. But the

"intuitive" use of those terms in conversational language lacks both determinacy and uniformity. It is therefore unwarranted to consider them as referring to clearly delimited and unambiguously specifiable characteristics and to seek "correct" or "valid" indicators or tests for the presence or absence of the latter.' Hempel, pp. 47 f.

36. Kline, p. 137.
37. See Kline, p. 3.
38. See particularly Farrell, 'Scientific Testing'.
39. 'Daughter: Daddy, what is an instinct?
    Father: An instinct, my dear, is an explanatory principle.
    Daughter: But what does it explain?
    Father: Anything—almost anything at all. Anything you want it to explain.
    Daughter: Don't be silly. It doesn't explain gravity.
    Father: No. But that is because nobody wants "instinct" to explain gravity. If they did, it would explain it. We could simply say that the moon has an instinct whose strength varies inversely as the square of the distance . . .
    Daughter: But that's nonsense, Daddy.
    Father: Yes, surely. But it was you who mentioned "instinct", not I.
    Daughter: All right—but then what does explain gravity?
    Father: Nothing, my dear, because gravity is an explanatory principle.
    Daughter: Oh.'
                                          Bateson, 'Metalogue', p. 11.
40. Kelly, *Personal Constructs*.
41. See particularly Fairbairn, *Object Relations Theory*.
42. e.g., Winnicott, *The Family*.
43. There is a good example of the replication of dependence in the visions of Padre Cicero, who became the foundation of a popular religious movement of great political importance in Brazil from the time of the 1889 miracle, down to the present. The visions which prompted Cicero into his particular 'route' through life appeared at critical junctures of choice and clearly represent the replication of dependence-figures: for example, his father, shortly after he had died, appeared, in order to tell him to continue his religious studies; subsequently Jesus appeared with similarly clear instructions. Della Cava comments (on the vision of Jesus at Joaseiro): 'This was neither the first nor last of the cleric's "visions" . . . In later years, other "visions" occurred and in each there was the same discernible pattern: figures of unquestionable authority appeared to him to decree and assure the devout cleric of his future course of action.' R. della Cava, *Miracle at Joaseiro*, p. 11.
44. Lear, 'Courtship'.
45. Freud, *Group Psychology*, ch. 12.
46. Id., 'On Narcissism', in *Coll. Papers*, iv, p. 57.

VII. THE PHYSIOLOGY OF THE BRAIN AND CLAIMS TO RELIGIOUS EXPERIENCE

1. Himwich, p. 4, where the reasons for that almost unbelievable jumbo jargon are given.
2. Bourne, p. v.
3. 'While I do not mean to minimize the importance of pioneering efforts of

Hull, Smoke, Heidbreder, and others, these were for the most part isolated bits of empiricism and speculation, lacking the coherence of an integrated area of research. In the late 1940s and early 1950s . . . experimental psychologists began to show serious interest in the conceptual abilities and processes of human beings. This interest has continued to grow and with it has developed an appreciable body of knowledge.' Ibid., p. v; cf. pp. 126 f.

4. Hudson, p. 100.

5. See Wallach and Kogan. An alternative approach would be to take identified creative individuals in a particular profession, and attempt to correlate characteristics among them, as, for example, in the work of MacKinnon on architects—though his conclusion is virtually a restating of the problem.

6. For Guilford's own summary, see bibl. ad loc.

7. See, e.g., Rosenberg.

8. Datta, p. 626.

9. For the distinctions involved here, if these are unfamiliar, see, e.g., Simkins, pp. 83–95.

10. The authors (Michael and Meyerson) state, in a preliminary footnote (p. 23): 'A more complete treatment of the material basic to this systematic presentation is available in Holland and Skinner [see bibl. ad loc.] and in Skinner's earlier work, *Science and Human Behaviour*'.

11. 'A behavioural approach to human control does not consist of a bag of tricks to be applied mechanically for the purpose of coercing unwilling people. It is part of a highly technical system, based on laboratory investigations of the phenomena of conditioning, for describing the behaviour and specifying the conditions under which it is acquired, maintained and eliminated . . . It is necessary to understand at the outset that the familiar characterization of behaviour as a function of the interaction of hereditary and environmental variables is accepted, not with the lip service that is sometimes given before fleeing to hypothetical constructs of inner behaviour determiners that are neither heredity nor environment but with utmost seriousness . . . A behavioural system attempts to specify, without reference to unobservable, hypothetical inner-determining agents, the conditions and the process by which the environment controls human behaviour . . . In the case of humans, the reinforcers of biological significance are apparently very similar to those of other mammals and are fairly well known. On the other hand, the specification of the events of acquired reinforcing value for an individual human requires either a contemporary investigation or considerable knowledge of his environmental history.' Michael and Meyerson, pp. 23, 24 f.

12. Ibid., p. 23.

13. For a summary, see Vernon.

14. Tennyson, i, p. 320.

15. See bibl. ad loc.

16. Jarvik, pp. 295 f.; Jarvik gives as supporting evidence Becker, *et al.*; Blough; Landis and Clausen; for details, see bibl. ad loc.

17. Jarvik, pp. 296 f.

18. Rokeach brought together three men, each of whom believed he was Jesus Christ, into the same hospital. This resulted in adjustment but not in disconfirmation: see bibl. ad loc.

19. There is a curious parallel to this argument in the approach of those experimental psychologists for whom 'mechanism is all'. In this approach, organisms are envisaged as being able to acquire and use concepts, in virtual abstraction from the environment, as though no differentiations

could ever occur within the mechanism as a consequence of what the environment is or is not. An example of the argument occurs in Bourne (pp. 2 f.)

'Psychologists are primarily interested in the ways in which organisms acquire and use concepts rather than in any deep philosophical analysis of the nature and meaning of particular concepts . . . Although the bases for a concept may exist in the environment, in the form of things which illustrate it, and although the organism may have the intellectual capacity to "understand" the concept, some learning process has to take place before the concept exists for the organism.'

It is, in this case, the learning process which is the focus of attention, not the base or ground of a concept in the external environment. This means that one could not seriously reflect on the question of whether any differences occur in the learning process which are dependent on the modes of occurrence or non-occurrence of the bases of particular concepts.

20. Snyder's account of experience working in forms, not in non-forms, occurs in his conversation with Graham (in bibl., under Graham, p. 71). The connection with 'basic religion' is made in the following (ibid., pp. 69 f.):

'Marijuana focuses the senses. The sensations it produces are in some curious way spiritual, and also natural. Even in the less profound LSD experiences, everyone reports that they have for the first time seen the clouds, felt the wind, been aware of the birds, that they have had this sense of the living quality of their cat or their dog, the consciousness of the intelligence in the eyes of the animal, that the old ancient powers of earth and sky become real, the *kami*! Now, this is what I'm trying to say: LSD is primitive religion. LSD is *the* basic religion before all the organized religions got started. That's the experience it presents—of natural powers, natural forces. From that and certain other experiences I've had I tend nowadays to look on Buddhism, Christianity, Hinduism, Islam, you name it, as being degenerations that come with complex, civilized social systems that are in themselves not really so good.'

21. Quoted in Stafford and Golightly, pp. 73 f.
22. See bibl. ad loc. La Barre's book opens with the forthright statement: 'Naturalistically approached, human religion turns out to be an *entirely* human phenomenon, and entirely derived from the nature of human nature' (p. xi). But that statement is vacuous unless adequate content (adequate, that is, to the evidence, not merely to parts of it) is given to the term 'nature', and unless one reflects much more profoundly and extensively on the question of the capacities of human nature, the possibilities of this 'architecture of atoms' (cf. pp. 40f.).
23. Aaronson and Osmond refer here to Taylor, *Narcotics*.
24. Aaronson and Osmond, pp. 4 f.
25. Quoted in Stafford and Golightly, p. 149.
26. 'The effects of LSD vary to some extent with dosage, the subject's personality, his initial mood, expectation and surroundings . . . *Subjective* effects begin around 20–30 minutes after swallowing LSD. The first symptom is numbness around the mouth, and this is followed by sensations of dizziness, nausea, palpitations or headache. Perceptual changes develop gradually. Spatial relationships alter and walls and ceilings tilt, recede or advance on the patient. Coloured patterns and pictures appear on the walls . . . Sounds change in quality and quantity, formerly dull or dark

colours become dazzling and beautiful, smell and taste become intensified. Synaesthetic reactions sometimes occur, stimulation of one sense organ giving the sensation of a different modality.' Dally, pp. 121 f. An example of synaesthetic interchange occurs in the following:

'O frail fine blue star
your faint fragile tonalities swoon triumphant rainbows
as the berserk fury of the thunder's roar fades into words on paper.'

Andrews, p. 61.

27. In Keup, pp. 345 ff.
28. Ibid., p. 369.
29. See bibl. under Schachter.
30. '1. Given a state of physiological arousal for which an individual has no immediate explanation, he will "label" this state and describe his feelings in terms of the cognitions available to him. To the extent that cognitive factors are potent determiners of emotional states, one might anticipate that precisely the same state of physiological arousal could be labelled "joy" or "fury" or any of a great number of emotional labels, depending on the cognitive aspects of the situation.

'2. Given a state of physiological arousal for which an individual has a completely appropriate explanation (e.g. "I feel this way because I have just received an injection of adrenalin"), no evaluative needs will arise and the individual is unlikely to label his feelings in terms of the alternative cognitions available . . .

'3. Given the same cognitive circumstances, the individual will react emotionally or describe his feelings as emotions only to the extent that he experiences a state of physiological arousal.' Schachter, 'Interaction', p. 142.

It will be obvious that this theory has its roots in the James–Lange theory of emotion; and Schachter in fact set himself to the task of meeting the criticisms of Cannon which destroyed that theory, by rehabilitating cognitive factors, while the physiology or arousal remains neutral.

31. This refers to Schachter and Wheeler; it is worth noting that amusement is *not* manipulated in this experiment to the extent that it is in the other experiments referred to, even though Schachter has here assimilated them.
32. Schachter, 'Interaction', p. 162.
33. Cf. the comments on film-making of Mike Hodges, the director of *Get Carter* and *Pulp*: 'The two things to remember in making films were both said by Hitchcock, The first is "It's all sleight of hand" and the second, "It's only a movie". That's my motto, too. Movies can be many things but they should always be fun. Unfortunately too many people, particularly young people, take them far too seriously.'
34. Pribram, 'New Neurology'.
35. Meaning by 'this view', the 'classical answer' of Hebb and of Lindsley (for details, see bibl.).
36. Pribram, 'New Neurology', pp. 456 f.
37. Ibid., p. 463.
38. In Stafford and Golightly, p. 145.
39. Clark, pp. 189 f.
40. 'There has been a tendency in psychopharmacological work to accent the power of the substance itself, to design experiments for showing that one drug will affect this function, another that, and to assume that varying effects are due to the strictly chemical actions of the substance itself rather than to expectations, beliefs, social facilitation, and so on. The present

work is a contribution to a growing body of literature which argues, from evidence, that drug effects cannot be considered apart from their context of psychological, social and cultural factors.' Sanford in Blum, p. xiv.

41. See bibl. under Pollard.

42. This phrase occurs in Leary's comment on the Mexican experiment: 'The rationale was based on our conception of the almost limitless potential of consciousness, and our actions were guided by the set-setting hypothesis . . . From the beginning of our research our attention was directed to the engineering of ecstasy, the preparation for, the setting for, the architecture of ecstasy. Like post-Einsteinian physicists we sought to release (harmoniously and peacefully) the neurological energy latent in the cortex. Preparation of the subject. Set and expectancy. Collaboration with the subject in arranging the sort of session he wished. Careful planning of the setting to be supportive, understanding, aesthetic, spiritually meaningful, close to nature, and so on. Leary, 'Rationale', pp. 180 f.

43. See bibl. under Pahnke.

44. Leary, 'Religious Experience', p. 193.

45. Pahnke, 'Drugs' in Aaronson and Osmond.

46. Clark, p. 191.

47. 'There seem to be very marked differences between delusional perceptions of patients in an American private hospital and one in Southern Italy. In American delusions there is a very strong tendency toward abstraction. Actors in these delusions include, in addition to concrete individuals, such abstract social entities as Communists, an advertising agency, or the hospital perceived as a unitary whole. This tendency to think of the enemy in ideological or institutional terms is almost completely lacking in the delusions of Southern Italian patients. These, in contrast, although showing plentiful evidence of projection and dissociation, are centred almost completely on concrete persons and events within the patient's immediate context of family and neighbourhood. Although one might say that there was far more "reason" for these patients to construct delusions about the hospital, given the close restrictions on patients' behaviour that were imposed by the locked ward system and by hospital personnel, I found that most patients merely considered the hospital as an external restrictive force that did not arouse enough concern to enter into their psychotic ideation. The lack of abstractness in the thought processes of Southern Italian patients no doubt reflects the fact that in their cultural setting primary group membership alone is socially meaningful, while for middle-class Americans secondary institutions are crucial to the formation of an individual's sense of identity.' Parsons, pp. 204 f.

48. Kety, p. 79.

49. Ibid., p. 90.

50. 'Indeed, the soul, too, may be led so near to God by the body of our Lord that all the angels, not excepting the Cherubim and Seraphim, shall not see any difference . . . There never was another such union, for the soul is nearer to God than it is to the body which makes us human. It is more intimate with him than a drop of water put into a vat of wine, for that would still be water and wine; but here one is changed into the other so that no creature could ever again detect a difference between them.' Eckhart, xx, pp. 28 f.

51. Ibid., xiv, p. 13.

52. Downing and Wygant, p. 196.

53. Ibid.

54. 'H.T.: Does it [LSD] alter the efficiency of the mind?
    G.S.: Which mind?
    H.T.: Let's say the everyday mind of a secretary in an industrial office—
    the most awful thing imaginable, but it gets the job done.
    G.S.: Oh definitely. It alters that efficiency, to begin with, by removing
    the interest in doing that kind of work at all.' Graham, p. 63.
    And later (pp. 67 f.) the contrast is made equally specific: 'The thing that's
    happening now is that all kinds of people are taking this stuff, and are
    having their minds opened up in many unpredictable directions. There's a
    statistical probability of one out of about five that somebody who takes this
    stuff is going to have an experience of blinding light, waves of ecstasy and
    bliss, is going to see the face of God in the centre of the sun or some place
    like that, and is going to feel communion and comradeship with all beings
    and all varieties of existence. Then he's going to say, "College can't teach
    me anything, who wants to work, the universe is community and bliss and
    love and knowledge, and, whatever comes, I will live by that." So now
    they're walking the streets with long hair and beads.'
55. 'I was asked this question: "Some people withdraw from society and prefer
    to be alone; their peace of mind depends on it; wouldn't it be better for
    them to be in the church?" I replied, No! And you shall see why.
        'Those who do well, do well wherever they are, and in whatever company,
    and those who do badly, do badly wherever they are and in whatever com-
    pany. But if a man does well, God is really in him, and with him every-
    where, on the streets and among people, just as much as in church, or a
    desert place, or a cell. If he really had God, and only God, then nothing
    disturbs him. Why?
        'Because he has *only* God and thinks only God and everything is nothing
    but God to him. He discloses God in every act, in every place. The whole
    business of his person adds up to God . . . Of what does this true possession
    of God consist, when one really has him? It depends on the heart and an
    inner, intellectual return to God and not on steady contemplation by a
    given method. It is impossible to keep such a method in mind, or at least
    difficult, and even then it is not best. We ought not to have or let ourselves
    be satisfied with the God we have thought of, for when the thought slips
    the mind, that god slips with it. What we want rather is the reality of God,
    exalted far above any human thought or creature. Then God will not vanish
    unless you turn away from him of your own accord . . . To be sure, this
    requires effort and love, a careful cultivation of the spiritual life, a watchful,
    honest, active oversight of all one's mental attitudes toward things and
    people. It is not to be learned by world-flight, running away from things,
    turning solitary and going apart from the world . . . So you must be per-
    meated with divine Presence, informed with the form of beloved God who is
    within you, so that you may radiate that presence without working at it.'
    Eckhart, vi, pp. 7–10.
56. 'Both the signal and the image involve the sensory pathways; both are
    similar sensory-cognitive events which cannot always be distinguished . . .
    Thus we all perceive, we all image, we all hallucinate; there is no difference
    in the cognitive experiences of the schizophrenic, the hallucinating drug
    addict, and the college student in this regard. What varies are the patterns
    of past experience, individual differences, contextual probabilities, expect-
    ancies and biases that each one brings to the task, a process that passes as
    judgement. Presumably, the judgement of the schizophrenic is different,
    a broader range of experiences may appear ambiguous to him, and his

actions in the face of this ambiguity are probably idiosyncratic. However, the visual hallucinations of an alcoholic or drug addict are phenomenally in the same class as images, dreams, and perceptions; and as we have found the same effects for audition as for the visual mode, it is probably also true that the "voices" of the schizophrenic and a melody imagined by a composer are similar events, and may be further equated to the normal sensory processing of physical sounds.' Segal, pp. 110 f.

57. It is this clue which Scheibel and Scheibel have followed up, in suggesting inapt mosaic relations in the reticular core:

> 'The reticular core is made up of a combination of nerve cells and fibres, thrown together in haphazard fashion, in contradistinction to the usually discrete neural patterns of cell aggregates or nuclei, and fibre bundles or tracts . . . This peculiar type of organization maximizes the opportunity for each cell to receive a heterogeneous array of synaptic inputs and goes far to establish the type of role the reticular formation is likely to play in the overall neural pattern . . .
>
> 'The unique relation of the reticular formation to the entire hierarchy of each sensory system, its demonstrated ability to set gain levels and establish parametric windows for these channels, together with its equally central role in pacing the level of interaction of the organism with its environment, all would appear to give it central importance in the complex task of experiencing and interpreting reality. It does not seem inappropriate to suggest that pathologic functioning of such a system could well lead to perceptual dysfunctions like hallucinations.' (Scheibel and Scheibel, pp. 60, 66.)

58. See ref. 57.

VIII. PHENOMENOLOGY AND THE APPEARANCE OF GOD

1. Passmore, p. 108.
2. See bibl., Mays and Brown.
3. Ibid., p. 2.
4. Schmitt, p. 144.
5. Pope, *An Essay on Man*, i. 283 f.
6. Voltaire, *Zadig*, pp. 98 f.
7. Id., *Dictionary*, p. 394.
8. de Sade, *Dialogue*, p. 169.
9. Ibid., pp. 165 f.
10. Ibid., p. 174.
11. Bentham, *Code*, p. 5.
12. Ibid.
13. For Bentham's own account of the background and origin of the principle, see *Memoirs*, pp. 79 f., and this summary in *Commonplace Book* (p. 142): 'Priestley was the first (unless it was Beccaria) who taught my lips to pronounce this sacred truth:—That the greatest happiness of the greatest number is the foundation of morals and legislation.'
14. Hume, *Treatise*, I. iii. 6.
15. See ch. 1, ref. 34.
16. Heine, *Zur Geschichte* . . ., pp. 260 f. The comparison was drawn by Heine elsewhere: see, e.g., 'Einleitung', p. 276, 'Kant war unser Robespierre'.

17. On Kant, Schiller, Goethe, see Vorländer; on Goethe and Kant, see Rabel; on Schiller and Kant, see Meakin, i, pp. 244–54, Kühnemann, *Schiller*, ii, pp. 85–91, *Kants und Schillers Begründung* . . ., esp. pp. 162 ff. The connections between Beethoven and Kant are less overt (see, e.g., Turner, pp. 103–5). Despite his well-known refusal to attend lectures on Kant in Vienna (the anecdote is in Thayer, i, pp. 182 f.), the insight Beethoven owed to Kant is summarized in the *Tagebuch* entry, Feb. 1820: 'The moral law in us, and the starry sky above us—Kant!', a passage derived from the *Critique of Practical Reason* (Thayer, iii, p. 25).

18. Kant, *Prolegomena*, Introduction.

19. This is the heading of *Prolegomena*, §4.

20. 'There is no single book to which you can point as you do to Euclid, and say: This is Metaphysics; here you may find the noblest objects of this science, the knowledge of a highest Being, and of a future existence, proved from principles of pure reason . . . In all ages one Metaphysics has contradicted another, either in its assertions, or their proofs, and thus has itself destroyed its own claim to lasting assent . . . Metaphysics floated to the surface, like foam, which dissolved the moment it was scooped off. But immediately there appeared a new supply on the surface, to be ever eagerly gathered up by some, while others, instead of seeking in the depths the cause of the phenomenon, thought they showed their wisdom by ridiculing the idle labour of their neighbours.' Kant, *Prolegomena*, §4.

21. 'If a man asks me what the politics of the inhabitants of the moon are, and I reply that I do not know; that neither I, nor anyone else, have any means of knowing; and that, under these circumstances, I decline to trouble myself about the subject at all, I do not think he has any right to call me a sceptic. On the contrary, in replying thus, I conceive that I am simply honest and truthful, and show a proper regard for the economy of time. So Hume's strong and subtle intellect takes up a great many problems about which we are naturally curious, and shows us that they are essentially questions of lunar politics, in their essence incapable of being answered, and therefore not worth the attention of men who have work to do in the world. And he thus ends one of his essays.—

"If we take in hand any volume of Divinity, or school metaphysics, for instance, let us ask, *Does it contain any abstract reasoning concerning quantity or number?* No. *Does it contain any experimental reasoning concerning matter of fact and existence?* No. Commit it then to the flames; for it can contain nothing but sophistry and illusion."

'Permit me to enforce this most wise advice.' (Huxley, 'Physical Basis', pp. 144 f.; the quotation from Hume is the conclusion of *An Enquiry*.)

22. Kant, *Prolegomena*, §52. In *Prolegomena*, the antinomies are these (§51):
'Thesis: the world has, as to time and space, a beginning (limit).
Antithesis: the world is, as to time and space, infinite.
Thesis: everything in the world consists of [elements that are] simple.
A. there is nothing simple, but everything is composite.
T.: there are in the world causes through freedom.
A.: there is no liberty, but all is nature.
T.: in the series of the world-causes there is some necessary being.
A.: there is nothing necessary in the world, but in this series all is incidental.'

23. For a judicious analysis of Kant's conception of teleology, see McFarland.

24. For the strictly Kantian basis of Otto's argument, see particularly *Idea*, 'The Holy as an a Priori Category', pp. 116 ff.

25. See ref. 21, above.
26. See p. 6.
27. Schlick, p. 147.
28. Husserl, *Cartesian Meditations*, p. 5.
29. Id., *Paris Lectures*, p. 9. The point was expressed with equal poignancy by Alan Coren, reflecting on his contributions to *Punch*: 'The final sentence having been nailed to the page, the world goes on pretty much as heretofore, unshaken and unchanged.'
30. *P.L.*, p. 39; *C.M.* pp. 156 f.
31. *C.M.*, p. 31.
32. *P.L.*, p. 5.
33. 'Evidence is, in an *extremely broad sense*, an "experiencing" of something that is, and is thus; it is precisely a mental seeing of something itself . . . For everyday life, with its changing and relative purposes, relative evidences and truths suffice. But science looks for truths that are valid, and remain so, *once for all and for everyone*; accordingly it seeks verifications of a new kind, verifications carried through to the end. Though *de facto*, as science itself must ultimately see, it does not attain actualization of a system of absolute truths, but rather is obliged to modify its 'truths' again and again, it nevertheless follows the idea of absolute or scientifically genuine truth; and accordingly it reconciles itself to an infinite horizon of approximations, tending toward that idea. By them, science believes, it can surpass *in infinitum* not only everyday knowing but also itself . . . According to intention, therefore, the idea of science and philosophy involves an *order of cognition, proceeding from intrinsically earlier to intrinsically later cognitions*; ultimately, then, *a beginning and a line of advance* that are not to be chosen arbitrarily but have their basis "in the nature of things themselves".' *C.M.*, p. 12.
34. *P.L.*, p. 9. Cf. *C.M.*, pp. 23–5.
35. *P.L.*, p. 9.
36. 'This ubiquitous detachment from any point of view regarding the objective world we term the *phenomenological epochē*. It is the methodology through which I come to understand myself as that ego and life of consciousness in which and through which the entire objective world exists for me, and is for me precisely as it is. Everything in the world, all spatio-temporal being, exists for me because I experience it, because I perceive it, because I remember it, think of it in any way, judge it, value it, desire it, etc. It is well known that Descartes designates all this by the term *cogito*. For me the world is nothing other than what I am aware of and what appears valid in such *cogitationes*. *The whole meaning and reality of the world rests exclusively on such cogitationes* . . . I am not the ego of an individual man. I am the ego in whose stream of consciousness the world itself—including myself as an object in it, a man who exists in the world—first acquires meaning and reality.' *P.L.*, p. 8.
37. *P.L.*, p. 13.
38. *C.M.*, p. 35.
39. *P.L.*, p. 15.
40. *P.L.*, p. 14. This was one of the critical points on which Sartre (see bibl. ad loc.) broke away from phenomenology as Husserl conceived it.
41. *P.L.*, p. 15.
42. *P.L.*, p. 12. Cf. *C.M.*, pp. 31–3.
43. For an example, in the case of science, see ref. 33, above.
44. *Logical Investigations*, v. 10 (pp. 555 f.).

45. *P.L.*, pp. 12 f. Cf. *C.M.*, pp. 41-53.

46. *P.L.*, p. 20.

47. *L.I.*, vi. 70 (p. 851); but note that in using this phrase, Husserl was writing, not of statements in general but of those which involve or refer to decision.

48. *P.L.*, p. 18.

49. *P.L.*, p. 25.

50. *P.L.*, p. 38.

51. *P.L.*, p. 23.

52. *P.L.*, p. 26.

53. 'We must now deal with the one thought that is truly disturbing. If I, the meditating "I", reduce myself through an *epoché* to my absolute ego and to that which constitutes itself therein, then, do I not become the *solus ipse?* Did not then this whole philosophy of self-examination turn out to be pure solipsism, even though a transcendental and phenomenological solipsism?' *P.L.*, p. 34. Another way of expressing this 'disturbing thought' occurs in the Preface to *Logical Investigations:* 'The fundamental doubt more and more disturbed me, as to how the objectivity of mathematics, and of all science in general, is consistent with logic having a psychological basis.' Cf. also 'Inaugural Lecture', p. 16.

54. *P.L.*, p. 11.

55. *P.L.*, p. 34.

56. *P.L.*, p. 39.

57. One of the clearest descriptions possible of this Husserlian approach to ontology (or at least of this way of 'returning reality to the world') occurs in (of all surprising places) Ayer's *The Analytic Heritage*:

'How then can we accommodate the causal account of perception? How can we reconcile the objectivity which we are attributing to perceptual space with the fact that, as Russell puts it, "The observer, when he seems to himself to be observing a stone, is really, if physics is to be believed, observing the effects of the stone upon himself?" [*Inquiry*, p. 15.] The answer, I maintain, is that it is possible, without any logical inconsistency, first to identify a physical object with a standardised percept, and then, at the theoretical level, to distinguish the object as it is in itself from the various perceptions that different observers have of it. What happens, as I have tried to show in the last section of my book *The Origins of Pragmatism*, is that having developed the common-sense conception of the physical world as a theoretical system with respect to a basis of sense-qualia, we can interpret into this system the elements upon which it was founded. The physical object which was originally constructed out of percepts acquires, as it were, a life of its own. Since the perceptual qualities with which it is credited in the theory are supposed to be constant, or at least not to change without a physical alteration in the object, they come to be contrasted with the fluctuating impressions which different observers have of them. In other words, the standardised percept comes to be set over against the actual percepts from which it was abstracted, and indeed regarded as causally responsible for them. A primitive distinction having been made between what in *The Origins of Pragmatism* I call the main story, the organisation of those of one's experiences that seem to fit into a regular pattern, and the subsidiary stories to which are relegated the experiences that do not fit in, the identification of other observers, with [i.e. having] the same main story but their own subsidiary stories, permits the distinction to be sophisticated to the point where the main story itself is contrasted with any particular relation of it and all experiences, including those that furnish the main story, are regarded as subsidiary. So all percepts, whether veridical or delusive, come to be thought of as subjective, and as coming at the end of a causal process of which some physical object, itself no more than a standardised percept, is the source. There is a sense, therefore, in which our physical theory denies its starting-point, but it is rather the sense in which a self-made man may repudiate his humble origins. I cannot see that there is any logical incoherence in the process which I have outlined.' (pp. 127 f.)

Nor could Husserl see any logical incoherence in his own version of the same process. This remarkable concurrence needs, I suggest, to be taken very seriously, because it suggests that the gap between the empiricist 'analytic heritage' and phenomenology is, in this respect, nothing like as wide as it seemed in the 1930s.

58. *P.L.*, p. 24.
59. Forest, p. 300.
60. Young, pp. 70 f.
61. Ayer, p. 127.
62. Trollope, p. 134.

IX. CONCLUSION

1. Eliot, 'Prelude' (p. xv).

BIBLIOGRAPHY

AARONSON, B., and OSMOND, H., edd., *Psychedelics: The Uses and Implications of Hallucinogenic Drugs*, New York, 1970.

ALLBERRY, C. R. C., *A Manichaean Psalm-Book*, Stuttgart, 1938.

ANDREWS, G., 'Annihilating Illumination', in edd. Weil, G. M., *et al.*, q.v., pp. 59–61.

ANNANDALE, N., MS. letter to J. G. Frazer, 1 June 1904, Trin. Coll. Cambr., Frazer Letters, 27.

ARMSTRONG, R. P., *The Affecting Presence: An Essay in Humanistic Anthropology*, Urbana, Ill. 1971.

ARNOLD, M., *Poems*, London, 1853.

ASHBY, W. R., *An Introduction to Cybernetics*, London, 1964.

Atti della Cremazione di Alberto Keller, Milan, 1876.

AUBRY, G. J., *Joseph Conrad: Life and Letters*, 2 vols., London, 1927.

AYER, A. J., *Russell and Moore: The Analytical Heritage*, London, 1971.

BAINES, J., *Joseph Conrad: a Critical Biography*, London, 1971.

BAR-HILLEL, Y., ed., *Logic, Methodology and Philosophy of Science*, Amsterdam, 1965.

BARNETT, S. A., ed., *A Century of Darwin*, London, 1962.

BATESON, G., 'Metalogue: What is an Instinct?' in edd. Sebeok, T. A., and Ramsay, A., *Approaches to Animal Communication*, The Hague, 1969.

BECK, L. W., 'The "Natural Science" Ideal in the Social Sciences', in edd. Manners, R. A., and Kaplan, D., q.v., pp. 80–9.

BECKER, D. I., APPEL, J. B., and FREEDMAN, D. X., 'Some Effects of LSD on Visual Discrimination in Pigeons', *Psychopharm.*, xi, 1967, pp. 354–64.

BELL, C., *Art*, London, 1920.

BENTHAM, J., *The Constitutional Code*, in *Collected Works*, Edinburgh, 1843, vol. ix.

—— *Commonplace Book*, in *Works*, x.

—— *Memoirs of Jeremy Bentham*, in *Works*, x.

BERGER, P. L., *The Sacred Canopy: Elements of a Sociological Theory of Religion*, New York, 1967; pub. in England as *The Social Reality of Religion*, London, 1969.

—— *A Rumour of Angels*, London, 1970.

—— and LUCKMAN, T., *The Social Construction of Reality*, London, 1967.

BERLIOZ, H., MS. letter to Carolyne von Sayn-Wittgenstein, 22 July 1862, Hopkinson Berlioz Collection, Edinburgh.

BERNARD, C., *Les Phénomènes de la Vie*, Paris, 1878.

BERREMAN, G. D., 'Cultural Variability and Drift in the Himalayan Hills', *American Anthropologist*, lxii, 1960, pp. 774–94.

BLOUGH, D. S., 'Effect of Lysergic Acid Diethylamide on Absolute Visual Threshold of the Pigeon', *Science*, cxxvi, 1957.

BLUM, R., ed., *Utopiates: The Use and Users of LSD 25*, London, 1964.

BOURNE, L. E., *Human Conceptual Behaviour*, Boston, 1966.

BOWKER, J. W., *The Targums and Rabbinic Literature: An Introduction to Jewish Interpretations of Scripture*, Cambridge, 1969.

—— *Problems of Suffering in Religions of the World*, Cambridge, 1970.

—— 'Can Differences Make a Difference?', *Journal of Theological Studies*, 1973.

BUCKLE, H. T., *History of Civilization in England*, 3 vols., London, 1899.

CANNON, W. B., *The Wisdom of the Body*, London, 1932.

CAVA, R. DELLA, *Miracle at Joaseiro*, New York, 1970.

CHOMSKY, N., 'A Review of B. F. Skinner's *Verbal Behaviour*', *Language*, xxxv, 1959, pp. 26–58.

—— 'The Formal Nature of Language', in Lenneberg, E., q.v., pp. 397–442.

—— 'Linguistic Theory', in ed. Lester, M., q.v., pp. 51–60.

CLARK, W. H., 'The Psychedelics and Religion', in Aaronson and Osmond, q.v., pp. 182–95.

CONRAD, J., *Lord Jim*, Edinburgh, 1900; ed. cit., London, 1971.

CONYBEARE, F. C., MS. letter to J. G. Frazer, 26 Oct. 1899, Trin. Coll. Cambr. Frazer Letters, 221.

Cremation Considered in Reference to the Resurrection, London, 1874.

DAHL, J. S., 'The Ideal Crematorium', in *Cremation in Great Britain*, London, 1945.

DALLY, P., *Chemotherapy of Psychiatric Disorders*, London, 1967.

DATTA, L. E., 'Family Religious Background and Early Scientific Creativity', *American Sociological Review*, xxxii, 1967, pp. 626–35.

DAVIS, M., and HERSH, R., 'Nonstandard Analysis', *Scientific American*, ccvi, 1972, pp. 78–86.

DISRAELI, B., *Coningsby, a Tale*, London, 1844; ed. cit., New York, 1962.

DOBZHANSKY, T., *Mankind Evolving: The Evolution of the Human Species*, New York, 1970.

DOWNING, J. J., and WYGANT, W., 'Psychedelic Experience and Religious Belief', in Blum, q.v. pp. 187–98.

DURKHEIM, E., *Suicide: A Study in Sociology* (1897), trs. cit., London, 1952.

DURKHEIM, E., *The Elementary Forms of the Religious Life: A Study in Religious Sociology* (1912), London, 1915.

—— Review of Labriola, *Essais sur la conception matérialiste de l'histoire*, in *Revue Philosophique*, xliv, 1897, pp. 645–51.

ECKHART, J., *Talks of Instruction*, in trs. R. B. Blakney, *Meister Eckhart: A Modern Translation*, New York, 1941.

EDGCUMBE, R. P., *The Works of A. C. Hilton*, Cambridge, 1904.

ELIOT, G., *Middlemarch*, Edinburgh, 1871; ed. cit., Oxford, 1947.

ELIOT, T. S., *On Poetry and Poets*, London, 1957.

ELLIS, H. R., *The Road to Hell: A Study of the Conception of the Dead in Old Norse Literature*, Cambridge, 1943.

EMBREE, L. E., ed., *Life-World and Consciousness: Essays for Aron Gurwitsch*, Evanston, Ill., 1972.

EMERSON, R. W., Journal, 14 Sept. 1839, in Whicker, S. E., ed., *Selections from R. W. Emerson*, Boston, 1960.

FAIRBAIRN, W. R. D., *An Object Relations Theory of the Personality*, New York, 1954.

FANN, K. T., *Wittgenstein, The Man and His Philosophy*, New York, 1967.

FARBER, S. M., and WILSON, R. H. L., edd., *Control of the Mind*, New York, 1961.

FARRELL, B. A., 'The Scientific Testing of Psychoanalytic Findings and Theory', *British Journal of Medical Psychology*, xxiv, 1951, pp. 35–51.

—— 'Can Psychoanalysis be Refuted?', *Inquiry*, iv, 1961, pp. 16–36.

—— 'The Status of Psychoanalytic Theory', *Inquiry*, vii, 1964, pp. 104–22.

Final Catalogue, Newmarket December Sales, 1967.

First Supplement to the Historical Register of 1900, Oxford, 1921.

FIRTH, R., *Elements of Social Organization*, London, 1951.

—— 'Problem and Assumption in an Anthropological Study of Religion', *Journal of the Royal Anthropological Institute*, lxxxix, 1959, pp. 129–48.

FISHMAN, S., *The Interpretation of Art*, Berkeley, Calif. 1963.

FLEW, A., and MACINTYRE, A., edd., *New Essays in Philosophical Theology*, London, 1955.

FOREST, A., 'St. Anselm's Argument in Reflexive Philosophy', in edd. Hick, J., and McGill, A., q.v., pp. 275–300.

FRAZER, J. G., MS. letter to W. Robertson Smith, 22 July 1889, Cambr. U.L. Add. MS. 7449(c) D237.

—— *Aftermath*, London, 1936.

FREEMAN, A. C., in *Cremation in Great Britain*, London, 1931.

FREUD, S., *Totem and Taboo*, New York, 1918.

222   BIBLIOGRAPHY

FREUD, S., *Group Psychology and the Analysis of Ego*, London, 1922.
—— *Introductory Lectures on Psychoanalysis*, London, 1922 (*Gesammelte Werke*, xi, London, 1940).
—— *The Future of an Illusion*, London, 1928, 1962.
—— *The Problem of Anxiety*, New York, 1936.
—— *Moses and Monotheism*, London, 1939.
—— *An Outline of Psychoanalysis*, London, 1949.
—— 'Project for a Scientific Psychology', in *The Origins of Psychoanalysis: Letters to Wilhelm Fliess, Drafts and Notes, 1887–1902*, New York, 1954.
—— *Collected Papers*, 5 vols., London, 1924–50.
—— *Letters*, London, 1961.
FRISCH, O. R., *The Nature of Matter*, London, 1972.
FÜRER-HAIMENDORF, C. von, *The Apa Tanis and Their Neighbours: A Primitive Civilization of the Eastern Himalayas*, London, 1962.
FURST, P. T., ed., *Flesh of the Gods: The Ritual Use of Hallucinogens*, London, 1972.
FUTTON, R., ed., *Death and Identity*, New York, 1965.
GAIDOZ, H., 'Comme quoi M. Max Muller n'a jamais existé: étude de mythologie comparée', *Mélusine*, ii, 1884, pp. 73–90.
GASTWIRTH, P., 'Concepts of God', *Religious Studies*, viii, 1972, pp. 147–52.
GIEDION, S., *The Eternal Present: A Contribution on Constancy and Change*, II: *The Beginnings of Architecture*, Oxford, 1964.
GOIN, C. J. and GOIN, O. B., *Man and the Natural World: an Introduction to Life Science*, New York, 1970.
GOODE, W. J., *Religion Among the Primitives*, New York, 1951.
GÖRRES, J. J. von, *Mythengeschichte der asiatischen Welt*, Heidelberg, 1810.
GRAHAM, A., *Conversations: Christian and Buddhist*, London, 1969.
GUILFORD, J. P., *The Nature of Human Intelligence*, New York, 1967.
GUNTRIP, H., *Psychoanalytic Theory, Therapy, and the Self*, London, 1971.
HACKER, P. M. S., *Insight and Illusion: Wittgenstein on Philosophy and the Metaphysics of Experience*, Oxford, 1972.
HAMMERTON, M., 'Freud: The Status of an Illusion', *Listener*, 1968, pp. 264 f.
HARARY, F., NORMAN, R. Z., and CARTWRIGHT, D., *Structural Models: An Introduction to the Theory of Directed Graphs*, New York, 1965.
HARRÉ, R., and SECORD, P. F., *The Explanation of Social Behaviour*, Oxford, 1972.
HEBB, D. O., 'Drives and the C.N.S. (Conceptual Nervous System)', *Psychological Review*, lxii, 1955, pp. 243–54.

HEINE, H., 'Einleitung zu "Kahldorf über den Adel" ', in *Werke und Briefe*, Berlin, 1961, iv, pp. 275 89.
—— *Zur Geschichte der Relation und Philosophie in Deutschland*, ibid., v, pp. 167–308.
HEMPEL, C. G., *Fundamentals of Concept Formation in Empirical Science*, Chicago, 1952.
HICK, J., *Faith and Knowledge*, London, 1967.
—— and McGILL, A., edd., *The Many-Faced Argument*, London, 1968.
HIMWICH, H. E., 'Anatomy and Physiology of the Emotions and Their Relation to Psychoactive Drugs', in edd. Marks and Pare, q.v., pp. 3–24.
HOCKETT, C. F., and ASCHER, R., 'The Human Revolution' in ed. Montagu, M. F. A., q.v., pp. 20–101.
HOLLAND, J. G., and SKINNER, B. F., *The Analysis of Behaviour*, New York, 1961.
HOLST, I., *The Music of Gustav Holst*, Oxford, 1951.
—— *Gustav Holst: A Biography*, Oxford, 1969.
HUDSON, L., *Contrary Imaginations*, London, 1966.
HUME, D., *A Treatise of Human Nature*, ed. cit., London, 1969.
—— *An Enquiry Concerning the Human Understanding*, ed. cit., Oxford, 1894.
HUSSERL, E., *The Paris Lectures*, trs. cit., The Hague, 1967.
—— *Cartesian Meditations: An Introduction to Phenomenology*, trs. cit. The Hague, 1970.
—— *Logical Investigations*, trs. cit. London, 1970.
—— 'Inaugural Lecture at Freiburg im Breisgau, 1917' in ed. Embree, q.v., pp. 3–18.
HUXLEY, T. H., 'On the Physical Basis of Life', in *Lay Sermons, Addresses, and Reviews*, London, 1871, pp. 120–46.
JAMES, E. O., *The Concept of Deity*, London, 1950.
JARVIK, M., 'Drugs, Hallucinations and Memory', in ed. Keup, W., q.v., pp. 277–301.
JEFFERS, R., 'Cremation', in *Beginning and the End and Other Poems*, New York, 1963.
JEFFRESS, L. A., ed., *Cerebral Mechanisms in Behaviour*, New York, 1951.
JEPSEN, G. L., 'Terrible Lizards Revisited', *Princeton Alumni Weekly*, lxix, 1963, p. 7; in Goin, q.v.
JONES, E., 'Mother-Right and Sexual Ignorance of Savages', in *Essays in Applied Psychoanalysis*, London, 1951, ii, pp. 145–73.
—— *Sigmund Freud: Life and Work*, 3 vols., London, 1953–7.
KANT, I., *Prolegomena to Any Future Metaphysics* (1783), trs. cit., New York, 1969.

224   BIBLIOGRAPHY

KELLY, G. A., *The Psychology of Personal Constructs*, New York, 1955.
KELLY, W. H., 'Cocopa Attitudes and Practices with Respect to Death and Mourning', *Southwestern Journal of Anthropology*, v, 1949, pp. 151–64.
KETY, S. S., 'Chemical Boundaries of Psychopharmacology', in edd. Farber and Wilson, q.v., pp. 79–91.
KEUP, W., ed., *Origin and Mechanism of Hallucinations*, New York, 1970, pp. 345–76.
—— 'Structure-Activity Relationship among Hallucinogenic Agents', ibid., pp. 345–76.
KHINCHIN, A. Y., *Mathematical Foundations of Information Theory*, New York, 1957.
KITZINGER, U., 'An Anatomy of Rebellion', *New Society*, 4 May 1972, pp. 231–3.
KLINE, P., *Fact and Fantasy in Freudian Theory*, London, 1972.
KRISTEVA, J., ed., *Approaches to Semiotics*, The Hague, 1969.
KÜHNEMANN, E., *Schiller*, 2 vols., Boston, 1912.
—— *Kants und Schillers Begründung der Aesthetik*, Munich, 1895.
LA BARRE, W., 'Hallucinogens and the Shamanic Origins of Religion', in ed. Furst, P. T., q.v., pp. 261–78.
—— *The Ghost Dance: The Origins of Religion*, London, 1972.
LANDIS, C., and CLAUSEN, J., 'Certain Effects of Mescaline and Lysergic Acid on Psychological Functions', *Journal of Psychology*, xxxviii, 1954, p. 211.
LANG, A., *The Making of Religion*, London, 1898.
—— MS. Letters in Cambr. U.L., Add. MS. 7449, D.384, 388, 389.
LASHLEY, K. S., 'The Problem of Serial Order in Behaviour', in ed. Jeffress, L. A., q.v., pp. 112–36.
LEACH, E., ed., *The Structural Study of Myth and Totemism*, London, 1967.
—— *Lévi-Strauss*, London, 1970.
LEAR, E., 'The Courtship of the Yonghy-Bonghy-Bò'.
LEARY, T., 'The Religious Experience. Its Production and Interpretation', in Weil, *et al.*, q.v., pp. 191–213.
—— ALPERT, R., and METZNER, R., 'Rationale of the Mexican Psychedelic Training Centre', in Blum, q.v., pp. 178–86.
LEE, S. G. M., and HERBERT, M., edd., *Freud and Psychology*, London, 1970.
LEHRMAN, R. L., *Race, Evolution, and Mankind*, New York, 1966.
LEIDERMAN, P. H., and SHAPIRO, D., edd., *Psychobiological Approaches to Social Behaviour*, London, 1965.
LEIGH, J., *What Can You Do?*, London, 1968.
LENNEBERG, E., *Biological Foundations of Language*, New York, 1967.

LESTER, M., ed., *Reading in Applied Transformational Grammar*, New York, 1970.

LÉVI-STRAUSS, C., 'The Structural Study of Myth', *Journal of American Folklore*, lxviii, 1955, pp. 428–44.

—— *The Savage Mind*, trs. cit., London, 1972.

—— *Structural Anthropology*, trs. cit., New York, 1963.

—— *Totemism*, trs. cit., London, 1969.

LIENHARDT, R. G., 'Religion', in ed. Shapiro, H. L., q.v., pp. 310–29.

LIGHTFOOT, R. H., *History and Interpretation in the Gospels*, London, 1935.

LIGHTSTONE, A. H., 'Infinitesimals', *American Mathematical Monthly*, lxxix, 1972, pp. 242–51.

LINDSLEY, D. B., 'Emotion', in Stevens, S. S., ed., *Handbook of Experimental Psychology*, New York, 1961.

LOCKE, J., *An Essay Concerning Human Understanding* (1690), ed. cit., Oxford, 1924.

MCFARLAND, J. D., *Kant's Concept of Teleology*, Edinburgh, 1970.

MACKAY, D. M., 'In Search of Basic Symbols', in Förster, H. von, ed.. *Proceedings of the Eighth Conference on Cybernetics*, New York, 1952.

MACKINNON, D. W., 'The Personality Correlates of Creativity: A Study of American Architects', in *Proceedings of the Fourteenth Congress on Applied Psychology*, ii, 1962, pp. 11–39.

MACRAE, D. G., 'Darwinism and the Social Sciences', in ed. Barnett, S. A., q.v., pp. 296–312.

MALINOWSKI, B., 'Psychoanalysis and Anthropology', *Psyche*, iv, 1923, pp. 293–322.

MANDELBAUM, D., 'Social Uses of Funeral Rites', in ed. Futton, R., q.v., pp. 338–60.

MANNERS, R. A., KAPLAN, D., edd., *Theory in Anthropology*, London, 1969.

MARANDA, P., *Mythology: Selected Readings*, London, 1972.

—— and MARANDA, E. K., *Structural Models in Folklore and Transformational Essays*, The Hague, 1971.

MARKS, J., and PARE, C. M. B., edd., *The Scientific Basis of Drug Therapy in Psychiatry*, Oxford, 1965.

MARSHALL, A., 'The Old Generation of Economics and the New', *Quarterly Journal of Economics*, xi, 1897, pp. 115–35.

MARSHALL, F. G., 'Memorial Work in Relation to Crematoria', in *Cremation in Great Britain*, London, 1945, pp. 146–8.

MARX, K., 'Contribution to the Critique of Hegel's Philosophy of Right' (1844), trs. cit., London, 1962.

—— and ENGELS, F., *The German Ideology* (1846), trs. cit., London, 1938.

MAYS, W., and BROWN, S. C., *Linguistic Analysis and Phenomenology*, London, 1972.

MEAKIN, A. M. B., *Goethe and Schiller, 1785–1805*, 3 vols., London, 1932.

MEREDITH, G., *The Poetical Works*, London, 1912.

MICHAEL, J., and MEYERSON, L., 'A Behavioural Approach to Human Control', in edd. Ulrich, R., *et al.*, q.v., pp. 23–31.

MILL, J. S., *A System of Logic*, (1843), ed. cit., London, 1875.

MILNE, A. A., 'Explained', in *Now We Are Six*, London, 1927.

MONTAGU, M. F. A., ed., *Culture: Man's Adaptive Dimension*, Oxford, 1968.

MÜLLER, M., *Lectures on the Science of Language*, New York, 1870.

—— 'Comparative Mythology' in *Chips From a German Workshop*, New York, 1881.

MURRAY, J., *Genetic Diversity and Natural Selection*, Edinburgh, 1972.

NADEL, S. F., 'Two Nuba Religions: an Essay in Comparison', *American Anthropologist*, lvii, 1955, pp. 661–79.

NAUTA, D., *The Meaning of Information*, The Hague, 1972.

NEURATH, O., 'Protokollsätze', in *Erkenntnis*, iii, 1932.

NIELSEN, K., *Contemporary Critiques of Religion*, London, 1971.

OTTO, R., *The Idea of the Holy* (1917), trs. cit., Oxford, 1926.

PAHNKE, W. N., 'Drugs and Mysticism: An Analysis of the Relationship Between Psychedelic Drugs and the Mystical Consciousness', Harvard thesis, 1963.

—— 'Drugs and Mysticism', in Aaronson and Osmond, q.v., pp. 145–65.

PARSONS, A., *Belief, Magic and Anomie: Essays in Psychological Anthropology*, New York, 1969.

PARSONS, T., and BALES, R. F., edd. *Family: Socialization and Interaction Process*, London, 1956.

PASSMORE, J., 'Modern European Philosophy', in edd. Chisholm, R. M., *et al.*, *Philosophy*, Princeton, 1964.

PENFIELD, W., 'The Physiological Basis of Mind', in edd. Farber, S. M., and Wilson, R. H. L., q.v., pp. 3–17.

PETERKIEWICZ, J., *The Other Side of Silence: The Poet at the Limits of Language*, Oxford, 1970.

PHILLIPS, D. Z., *Religion and Understanding*, Oxford, 1967.

PIAGET, J., *Structuralism*, London, 1971.

POLANYI, M., *Knowing and Being*, London, 1969.

POLLARD, J. C., UHR, L., and STERN, E., *Drugs and Phantasy: The Effects of LSD, Psilocybin, and Sernyl on College Students*, Boston, 1965.

PREUSS, K. T., 'Der Ursprung der Religion und Kunst', *Globus*, lxxxvi, 1904.

—— 'Die Astralreligion in Mexico . . .', in *Transactions of the Third International Congress for the History of Religions*, Oxford, 1908, i, pp. 36–41.

PRIBRAM, K. H., 'The Foundation of Psychoanalytic Theory: Freud's Neuropsychological Model, in ed. id., *Brain and Behaviour: Adaptation*, London, pp. 395–432.

—— 'The New Neurology and the Biology of Emotion: A Structural Approach', in op. cit., pp. 452–66.

—— 'Proposal for a Structural Pragmatism: Some Neuropsychological Considerations of Problems in Philosophy', in op. cit., pp. 494–505; also in ed. Wolman, B., q.v.

Proceedings of the Royal Society of London, lv, 1894; Ser. A, xlvi, 1920.

PURVIS, J. S., *Tudor Parish Documents of the Diocese of York*, Cambridge, 1948.

QUINE, W. V. O., *From A Logical Point of View*, New York, 1961.

—— *Ontological Relativity and Other Essays*, New York, 1969.

RABEL, G., *Goethe und Kant*. Vienna, 1927.

ROBINSON, A., *Non-Standard Analysis*, New York, 1966.

—— 'Formalism 64' in ed. Bar-Hillel, Y., q.v., pp. 228–46.

ROGERS, C. R., ed., *The Therapeutic Relationship and its Impact: A Study of Psychotherapy with Schizophrenics*, Madison, Wis. 1967.

ROHEIM, G., *Psychoanalysis and Anthropology*, New York, 1950.

ROKEACH, M., *The Three Christs of Ypsilanti: A Psychological Study*, London, 1964.

ROMER, A. S., *The Vertebrate Story*, Chicago, 1959.

ROSENBERG, M., 'The Dissonant Religious Context and Emotional Disturbance', *American Journal of Sociology*, lxviii, 1962, pp. 1–10.

RUFER, J., *The Works of Arnold Schoenberg*, London, 1962.

RUNCIMAN, W. G., 'The Sociological Explanation of "Religious" Beliefs', in *Sociology in its Place*, Cambridge, 1970.

RUSSELL, B., *An Inquiry Into Meaning and Truth*, London, 1940.

SACKVILLE, M., 'Everyman', in ed. Wollman, M., *Poems of Twenty Years: An Anthology, 1918–1938*, London, 1938.

SADE, D.-A.-F. de, *A Dialogue Between a Priest and a Dying Man*, trs. cit. New York, 1966, pp. 165–75.

SARGANT, W., *Battle for the Mind*, London, 1957.

SARTRE, J.-P., *The Transcendence of the Ego*, trs. cit., New York, 1957.

ŠAUMJAN, S. K., *Principles of Structural Linguistics*, The Hague, 1971.

SCHACHTER, S., 'The Interaction of Cognitive and Physiological Determinants of Emotional State', in edd. Leiderman, P. H., and Shapiro, D., q.v., pp. 138–73.

SCHACHTER, S., and SINGER, J., 'Cognitive, Social and Physiological Determinants of Emotional State', *Psychological Review*, lxix, 1962, pp. 379–99.

—— and WHEELER, L., 'Epinephrine, Chorpromazine, and Amusement', *Journal of Abnormal Social Psychology*, lxv, 1962, pp. 121–8.

SCHEIBEL, M. E., and SCHEIBEL, A. B., 'Transactional Paths in the Reticular Activating System', in Keup, q.v., pp. 59–69.

SCHLICK, M., 'A New Philosophy of Experience', in *Gesammelte Aufsätze*, Vienna, 1938, pp. 136–49.

SCHMIDT, P. F., *Religious Knowledge*, New York, 1961.

SCHMIDT, W., *Der Ursprung der Gottesidee*, Münster, 12 vols., 1926–55.

SCHMITT, R., 'Transcendental Phenomenology: Muddle or Mystery?' in Solomon, q.v., pp. 127–44.

SCHOENBERG, A., see Rufer.

SEBEOK, T. A., and RAMSAY, A., *Approaches to Animal Communication*, The Hague, 1969.

SEGAL, S. J., 'Imagery and Reality: Can They Be Distinguished?' in Keup, q.v., pp. 103–13.

SHANDS, H. C., *Semiotic Approaches to Psychiatry*, The Hague, 1970.

SHANNON, C. E., and WEAVER, W., *The Mathematical Theory of Communication*, Urbana, Ill., 1949.

SHAPIRO, H. L., ed., *Man, Culture, and Society*, Oxford, 1956.

SHERRY, P., 'Truth and the "Religious Language-Game" ', *Philosophy*, xlvii, 1972, pp. 18–37.

SIMKINS, L. D., *The Basis of Psychology as a Behavioural Science*, Waltham, Mass. 1969.

SKINNER, B. F., *Science and Human Behaviour*, New York, 1953.

—— *Verbal Behaviour*, New York, 1957. See also Holland, J. G.

SLONIMSKY, N., *Lexicon of Musical Invective*, Seattle, Wash. 1965.

SMILES, S., *Self-Help: With Illustrations of Character and Conduct*, London, 1863.

SOLECKI, R. S., 'Shanidar Cave: A Palaeolithic Site in Northern Iraq', *Smithsonian Annual Review*, 1954, pp. 389–425.

—— 'Three Adult Neanderthal Skeletons from Shanidar Cave', ibid., 1959, pp. 603–35.

SOLOMON, R. C., ed., *Phenomenology and Existentialism*, New York, 1972.

STAATS, A. W., and STAATS, C. K., *Complex Human Behaviour: a Systematic Extension of Learning Principles*, New York, 1963.

STAFFORD, P. G., and GOLIGHTLY, B. H., *LSD: The Problem-Solving Psychedelic*, New York, 1967.

STEWART, T. D., 'Restoration and Study of the Shanidar I Neanderthal Skeleton in Bagdad, Iraq', *Year Book of the American Philosophical Society*, 1958, pp. 274–8.

SWANSON, G. E., *The Birth of the Gods: The Origin of Primitive Beliefs*, Ann Arbor, Mich., 1960.

TALMON, Y., 'Pursuit of the Millennium: the Relation Between Religious and Social Change', *Archives Européennes de Sociologie*, iii, 1962, pp. 125–48.

TAYLOR, N., *Narcotics: Nature's Dangerous Gifts*, New York, 1963.

TENNYSON, H., *Alfred, Lord Tennyson, A Memoir*, 2 vols., London, 1897.

THAYER, A. E., *The Life of Ludvig von Beethoven*, 3 vols., New York, 1921.

THOMAS, K., *Religion and the Decline of Magic*, London, 1971.

THOMSON, G. P., *The Foreseeable Future*, Cambridge, 1955.

Transactions of the Cremation Society of Great Britain, iv, 1891.

TROLLOPE, A., *The Eustace Diamonds* (1873), ed. cit., Oxford, 1968.

TURNER, W. J., *Beethoven: The Search for Reality*, London, 1927.

TYLOR, E. B., *Primitive Culture*, London, 1871; 4th edn., 1903.

—— MS. Letter to F. J. H. Jenkinson, 12 Nov. 1903, Cambr. U.L. Add. MS. 6463. 5515.

ULRICH, R., *et al.*, edd., *Control of Human Behaviour*, Glenview, Ill., 1966.

VAIHINGER, H., *Die Philosophie des Als-Ob*, Berlin, 1911; trs. London, 1924.

VERNON, J. A., *Inside the Black Room: Studies of Sensory Deprivation*, London, 1966.

VOLTAIRE, *Zadig*, trs. J. Butt, London, 1964.

—— *Philosophical Dictionary* (1764), trs. cit., London, 1971.

VORLÄNDER, K., *Kant, Schiller, Goethe: Gesammelte Aufsätze*, Leipzig, 1923.

WALLACH, M. A., and KOGAN, N., *Modes of Thinking in Young Children: A Study of the Creativity-Intelligence Distinction*, New York, 1965.

—— 'A New Look at the Creativity-Intelligence Distinction', *Journal of Personality*, xxxiii, 1965, pp. 348–69.

WEBSTER, D. L., 'Electricity', in *Ency. Brit.*, Chicago, 1970, viii.

WEIL, G. M., *et al.*, edd., *The Psychedelic Reader*, New York, 1965.

WEST, L. J., *Hallucinations*, New York, 1962.

WINNICOTT, D. W., *The Family and Individual Development*, New York, 1965.

WITTGENSTEIN, L., *Philosophical Investigations*, trs. cit., Oxford, 1953.

—— *Tractatus Logico-Philosophicus*, London, 1961.

WOLCOT, J., *The Works of Peter Pindar, Esq.*, 4 vols., London, 1797.

WOLMAN, B., ed., *Scientific Psychology*, New York, 1965.

YOUNG, A., *Out of the World and Back*, London, 1961.

ZELDITCH, M., 'Role Differentiation in the Nuclear Family: a Comparative Study', in edd. Parsons, T., and Bales, R. F., q.v., pp. 307–51.

INDEX